W9-BBI-497

Conversations with Joseph Heller

Literary Conversations Series

Peggy Whitman Prenshaw
General Editor

Susan M. Hogue

Conversations
with Joseph Heller

Edited by
Adam J. Sorkin

University Press of Mississippi
Jackson

Books by Joseph Heller

Catch-22. New York: Simon and Schuster, 1961.
We Bombed in New Haven. New York: Alfred A. Knopf, 1968.
Catch-22: A Dramatization. New York: Samuel R. French, 1971. [Trade edition—New York: Delacorte Press, 1973]
Clevinger's Trial. New York: Samuel R. French, 1973.
Something Happened. New York: Alfred A. Knopf, 1974.
Good as Gold. New York: Simon and Schuster, 1979.
God Knows. New York: Alfred A. Knopf, 1984.
No Laughing Matter. Written with Speed Vogel. New York: G.P. Putnam's Sons, 1986.
Picture This. New York: G.P. Putnam's Sons, 1988.

Copyright © 1993 by the University Press of Mississippi
All rights reserved
Manufactured in the United States of America
96 95 94 93   4 3 2 1
The paper in this book meets the guidelines for permanence and durability
of the Committee on Production Guidelines for Book Longevity of the Council
on Library Resources.

Library of Congress Cataloging-in-Publication Data

Heller, Joseph.
    Conversations with Joseph Heller / edited by Adam J. Sorkin.
      p. cm. — (Literary conversations series)
    Includes index.
    ISBN 0-87805-634-3 (cloth). — ISBN 0-87805-635-1 (paper)
    1. Heller, Joseph—Interviews. 2. Novelists, American—20th
century—Interviews. I. Sorkin, Adam J. II. Title. III. Series.
PS3558.E476Z462   1992
813'.54—dc20   92-44967
                                                 CIP

British Library Cataloging-in-Publication data available

Contents

Introduction

It was roughly a year after the initial publication of *Catch-22* at the start of the fall book season in 1961 that the first interviews with Joseph Heller began to appear in print. *Catch-22* had recently come out in a Dell paperback and was on its way to becoming one of the publishing success stories of the decade—and beyond. The novel, still selling steadily today in the Dell mass-market edition, made Joseph Heller close to a household word. It won him widespread popularity and established his reputation among academics and those in the literary establishment, an eminence its author maintains largely because of his achievement in presenting *the* absurdist antihero, Yossarian, at the center of a world defined and granted vitality by his own bitter-sweet, comic-satiric sensibility. *Catch-22* was also one of the most influential countercultural phenomena of the Vietnam War period—although Heller, according to what he said to Brother Alexis Gonzales a decade later, believes that books don't "influence" but "confirm." Shaping force or expressive self-confirmation, the novel emerged throughout the 1960s and early '70s from bookbags, knapsacks, and the frequently embroidered back pockets of well-worn blue jeans, maybe scuffy and tattered in its pages but, to its readers, still clear, politically pertinent, and undiminishingly funny in its message, a nonconformist token all the while bearing on its cover an advertising proclamation of the ever-rising total of copies in print.

At the time these early interviews were printed in 1962, however, much of the acclaim awaited the novelist, and Heller was a kind of coterie figure, the bohemian fringe's enthusiasm, the cognoscenti's fad. Thus *Newsweek,* in the first conversation published, interviewed the author with the slant of presenting the success-story celebrity behind the hottest topic of the cocktail-party set. On the other hand, with similar journalistic timeliness, Paul Krassner, editor of *The Realist,* the important ancestor of the alternative press movement and a model of its underground seriousness and anti-establishment irreverence, talked with Heller as a kindred spirit of a different sort, paying homage to his ironist's sardonic vision, his impolite cultural critique, and his conjoined political idealism and sharply focused cynicism. And the third early '60s piece, which came out in the Manchester *Guardian,* treated the novelist's work as a sign of major change in the attitudes of American society, a new willingness to laugh at itself and publicly criticize the officially sacrosanct—although Heller himself, both in this interview with W.J. Weatherby and more insistently on many other occasions, has pointed out not only predecessors and influences from the period but also works by contemporary writers that date the beginnings of this change at least to the period when he himself conceived and began working on *Catch-22,* the early and mid-1950s.

What is interesting, if one looks at these three early interviews together, is that they establish most of the essential threads that weave their way through the many conversations that succeeded them. This is not altogether surprising when one remembers that, unlike the freedom riders, anti-Vietnam War student left, hippies, yippies, and, later, young yuppies who formed the basis of his readership and kept his popularity escalating, Heller was thirty-eight when *Catch-22* was published and almost forty when his first novel began to receive the attention it deserved. His personality, attitudes, tastes, and literary predilections were well formed—which is not to imply that the interviews that comprise this book will seem dull or merely repetitive. Repetitions there are, of course, since it is unavoidable in a series such as the Literary Conversations that some of the selected pieces will overlap. But the reiterated material itself can have its own fascination, as in the instance of Heller's changing opinions about whether he would rewrite and clarify the intentionally confusing beginning of *Catch-22* or make more obvious at the end that Yossarian will not make it to Sweden until, in the late '80s, he avows he would not change a thing if he had the chance.

Not only is Heller relatively consistent in many of his primary interests and concerns, he is also, most often, more than just willing to respond to questions about his biography and the varying circumstances of his own life, about the makeup of his characters and the shape, intentions, and effects of the works they take form in, and the relation of these works to one another and to other writings, his own and others'. In all of this, moreover, the liveliness of Heller's mind, both its seriousness and its playfulness, as well as its retentiveness, along with

the writer's self-confidence and his readiness to reflect seriously and
thoughtfully, provide considerable interest even to a reader who might
choose to read straight through this book. Interviews can be daunting,
uncontrolled, haphazard occasions for anyone in the public eye. More
than many, Joseph Heller makes these his own.

Among the interesting characteristics of Joseph Heller as protagonist
of these literary dialogues is the development of some of the fundamental concerns that are an integral part of the works, such as his
political and social observations. From his early opinions about the
hypocrisy of governments and the incompetence, mendacity, self-
ishness, and mediocrity of American presidents, generals, and business
executives to his criticisms of the Persian Gulf War in the most recent
interview almost three decades later, Heller seems little changed in his
views, even if increasingly detached from political processes and
institutions. Similarly, he appears little changed in his admiration for the
civil rights activists or the Vietnam War-period draft resisters or, more
abstractly, Socrates in some of his most recent conversations, or in his
spirited mockery of McCarthyism and his raillery at select political
figures, notably Richard Nixon, Nelson Rockefeller, Henry Kissinger,
and most recently, George Bush, with the scorching political passion
that underlies the Juvenalian side of *Good as Gold*. In reverse, it might
be said that it is the much more overtly cynical novelist whose sensibility and manipulations govern *Picture This* who seems to have
changed and to have narrowed his aesthetic distance from the human
being. The authorial voice in the novel sounds eerily like the Heller who
in 1988 speaks to Bill Moyers, among others, so bitterly and pessi-
mistically about American democracy and imperialism (and almost so
gleefully in his grim news about Athenian democracy and imperialism)
as well as about their pretensions—sounding also rather like the aging
and sarcastic Mark Twain about American pretensions and imperialism
some one hundred years ago. Like Twain, Heller characteristically
resists and excoriates regimentation and hypocrisy, recurrently speaking
for independence of mind and freedom of the spirit. And like Twain,
too, a stage presence on the lecture circuit (as Heller has been from time
to time) and a writer who cultivated this kind of role much more
assiduously, Heller increasingly assumes a posture of public spokesman
as his reputation becomes established. Perhaps this stance is partially a
response to the kinds of questions directed at him, but perhaps it goes

along with the increasing directness and lack of dissembling in the
tension between dramatization and thematics of his works.

   The early interviews likewise present Heller as a highly self-aware
and self-analytical novelist. The Phi Beta Kappa undergraduate, Ivy
League graduate student, and Fulbright scholar in English is perceptive
and astute in discussion of his own works, cogent, technically sophisticated, and detailed in his handling of interpretation and its textual
support. Although he is never deeply private or emotional in these conversations, it is nonetheless the literary critic side of Heller that most
of all merits George Plimpton's description in the *Paris Review* interview of the novelist's speaking "with the detachment of someone talking
about a third person." Repeatedly, Heller demonstrates almost disinterested appreciation for the readings of critics, reviewers, and scholars
as well as a subjective tolerance for various misreadings or wayward
notions. From his extensive comments on *Catch-22* to Krassner in the
Realist interview to his detailed discussions of *Something Happened*
in quite a few mid-1970s interviews to his almost professorial explica-
tions of *Good as Gold, God Knows,* and *Picture This* talking with, for
instance, Charlie Reilly, Chet Flippo, and David L. Middleton, re-
spectively, Heller could be said to be one of his own best critical
interpreters. One can even imagine sometimes a not unjustified pride in
his capacities as textual analyst. Unlike some writers, Heller certainly
shows no reluctance to explore the components of his characters and
their relation to their creator, go into thematic ideas and interconnec-
tions, and dissect and elucidate the workings of his plots, no aversion
to commenting on his own strengths (such as, obviously, comedy) and
limitations (among the latter, his not being good at description), no
unwillingness to reveal his tastes and antipathies in his own reading (as
in the Dale Gold interview, among others), no hesitation to define
generic distinctions such as the realistic novel versus more fantastic and
distorted expression. Likewise, he demonstrates no disinclination to
point out other writers whose works specifically influenced the style or
texture or narrative distance he developed in his own novels in his own
transformations. His discussions of his feelings about his characters
while he writes, and the process by which he is moved to sympathy with
even the most vile and repugnant of them, are fascinating on many
levels. Heller's comments on the quality and strength of American novel
writing from the mid-'50s, especially his admiration for the writers he

calls "the crazies" to Mel Brooks, show a parallel openness about the context of his literary career. Finally, it is likely that, consciously or unconsciously, part of him also wants to have a voice in shaping the understanding developed within the interpretive community to which ultimate evaluation of his career achievement must be turned over.

I suggest that it is a similar impulse that leads the novelist-turned-playwright to explain to Elenore Lester of the *New York Times* during the rehearsals for *We Bombed in New Haven* that "I don't want Joseph Heller distorted" and to go on, only half-joking, that "I want the director to know what's in my mind and . . . do what I want him to do without my trying to dominate him."

Heller also is more than willing to discuss his working methods, both the conception and planning of his novels and the day-to-day routine of the writing professional, as well as the slowness of his work, which he admits again and again. The repeated pattern Heller notes of the genesis of his novels as ideas which, it may be said, seem to come to him rather like sudden intrusions of otherworldly grace or the ministrations of some modern muse, to some extent disguises his readiness and mental preparation, hints of which the interviews provide. In a larger instance, the attitudes about Athenian government that form the thematic analogy underlying his most recent novel, *Picture This,* are articulated almost a decade earlier in the 1979 interview with *U.S. News and World Report* written up as a kind of pastiche-article. If nothing else, then, between books, when the novelist worries about getting his next idea, his creative facilities must be mysteriously at work as it were even without him. He confesses to Plimpton about his imaginative process that he feels "very much at its mercy." I do not mean to suggest that in the interviews Heller, like Henry James in his prefaces, is posing as a magician who pulls intricate novels like aesthetic rabbits out of ex-perience's hat, although Heller's descriptions of the way *Something Happened* came to him, as he describes it in the *Paris Review* interview, and also elsewhere, might justify the friend's quip Heller recounts to Charles T. Powers: "Heller didn't write that book, he has a medium." At times, however, the medium must have provided only incomplete transmission of the spirit matter, for in the course of these conversations Heller mentions a number of projects that never materialized, such as the Dunbar novel or the book about the '30s, *Peddler's Cry.* Of note in relation to all this is Heller's insistence on his having to have an entire book planned out, beginning and end as well as most of the middle, with actions, characters, the tone, and key lines, before he can write at all. In contrast to Philip Roth's practices, which Heller reports in his exchange with Curt Suplee of the *Washington Post,* Heller remarks on his horror at the possibility of scrapping a story after a substantial beginning because of "*not* know[ing] where I'm going." The key lines he jots down often years in advance may get shifted or rejected—like the original opening and closing of *Something Happened*—but they provide for his imagination a necessary framework of productive resistance. When he says that he's only had a few ideas for a book, this is what he seems to mean: ideas for novels have to be integral and comprehensive, fully imagined and fully developed in their outline, before they are ideas to him. On the other hand, when the ideas are fruitful, the novels seem to grow recursively and organically, and Heller freely gives accounts of the process of expansion passages undergo as well as the later cutting he does, in final stages with the aid of his editor.

Heller's much talked-about working routines underscore the writer's careful control of his final product. The daily grind of relatively short periods of work (beginning with his composing *Catch-22* in the evenings after his advertising promotion work during the '50s) is a continuum throughout the conversations. So, too, are his copious notes, lines, phrases, jokes, etc., arranged into files during a sometimes lengthy period of gestation after a story is conceived, and his descriptions of working from longhand draft to extensive hand-written revision, then to his own typescript, itself a process of rewriting, cutting, and moving material, or later to a computer version, and finally, after further rewriting, to a typist's manuscript that can go to his agent or editor. The painstakingness of Heller the craftsman comes through most strongly in these descriptions of the hard work he puts into his novels. And even when he discusses how slowly he works (seven years for his first book, thirteen until his second), the point is frequently the concentrated effort during these limited but intense work sessions. These individual working methods, in fact, comprise what seems his favorite illustration of one of the main subject matters he talks of communicating to students in his teaching positions and campus visits: the need for imaginative preparation, for writing and rewriting, for technique at the service of intricate and thorough planning. This is the Heller whose deceptive stylistic naturalness—in Martin Amis's phrase, prose that "doesn't sniff of the lamp"—is, as he informs many an interviewer in different ways, achieved through discipline and cold calculation, a process which he likens to his experience writing advertising copy. Although he tells Moyers that "a novel by nature is an adversarial form of expression," paradoxically he insists more strongly on its artistic autonomy, saying typically to Krassner in 1962 that he was producing not a treatise but "a work of fiction—of literary art." His stress is always on fully conscious achievement, the "craft" which can be taught while (in phrases he uses to Plimpton) "the aesthetic quality of the sensibility of the writer," or talent, cannot. "Form *is* content," Powers quotes Heller citing Beckett to U.S.C. students.

Also apparent in these early interviews is that Heller is openly pleased by his own success—his success in moving people to laughter or to tears, and his success, especially after the best-selling *Something Happened,* in getting them to buy his books and thus in winning the financial independence largely to live on his writing income after the mid-1970s, without the advertising and promotion jobs he worked at full-time until *Catch-22* came out, or the later professional positions and his filmscript and TV script work. Heller's self-satisfaction in this is understandable (though it might have been less so to his loyal '60s following—Susan Braudy reports student dismay after a talk at Yale that Heller "comes on like a real Madison Avenue fat cat," not a novelist, an image that from Heller's photographs shows change within half a decade). But his self-satisfaction comes across to the reader as less affecting than his enthusiasm for the responses he received from ordinary readers of *Catch-22* (as he tells Krassner and others) and later in his career, as in the case of *Something Happened,* from both average readers or student audiences and more eminent readers such as Mike Nichols or Bruno Bettelheim. And there is a charm to his self-esteem and his sense of accomplishment, central to which, one feels, is the writer's avowal of his delight in being "a show-off." He tells the *Paris Review,* "When I write I want other people to notice me and that I'm doing something different from other people." He notes with approval an anecdote about Arthur Miller's exhilaration at people's weeping during the previews of *Death of a Salesman,* and he is himself gratified by the pathos produced during his readings on campuses of Snowden's death scene in *Catch-22.* This is not smugness or cynicism on Heller's part but further manifestation of a craftsman's standards and highly

developed critical faculties. On the other hand, in not the only contradiction in these conversations (no dull, foolish consistency for Heller's
playful mind), Heller the manipulative author at other moments does
stress Heller the idealist's values, the moral core of his vision. In a
sense, in the combination of these, he seems to get the best of Yossarian's "despicable deal" in chapter 40 of *Catch-22,* achieving reputation
and success while remaining free to tell everybody grim and unwanted
truths. And like Yossarian, the writer as self-pleased technician still can
savor his little tricks, as when he discusses the inside jokes in *Catch-22*
or the one-liners he's had on note cards that he finally gets to use in just
the right place in *God Knows.*

Additionally, in the early interviews, there is the expected persona of
the author of *Catch-22*: Heller the comedian, the deadpan ironist, the
aficionado of the absurd, the connoisseur of the blackest of wit, the
acerbic bard of *non sequitur* and spinning paradox, the wise-guy asker
of good questions (again, like his Yossarian), his humor often delivered
in such a dry manner that not infrequently it is hard to tell how serious
he is. This side of Heller helped make good press, to be sure, and was
the most immediate factor in establishing the "cult" (as *Newsweek* called
it) that brought him to prominence. In fact, later on, Heller speaks of
being a happy man who writes depressing books, and there is a kind of
optimism and energy in his outlook, the "joy" that Weatherby empha-
sized. The role of *eiron* seems natural to him, and he looks at much of
the public world as "a spectator sport," a phrase he uses to Moyers
about politics. Barbara Gelb, in her *New York Times Magazine* profile,
reports Heller's long-time crony Mel Brooks as saying, "Joe plays the
best verbal Ping-Pong of anyone I know." This Heller appears inter-
mittently in the interviews, although generally he retreats into the
background, as if the novelist has decided fairly early in his career that
it would be too easy to play standup comic to the media. Again and
again, in different ways, the master of aphoristic wit and zany hilarity
expresses reservations at being too funny in his books. Occasionally the
comic persona becomes preeminent, as in two dialogues with close
friends. Talking with his childhood friend George Mandel in a 1970
article done for *Penthouse,* the comic sparring and repartee dominate,
along with farcical lying and conscious braggadocio. In the *Washington
Post* conversation (or anti-conversation) almost a decade later, "Mel
Brooks Meets Joseph Heller," one can see both sides of the novelist,

from the opening evocation of juvenile humor to the one-of-the-guys parrying of Brooks to what can almost be described as a kind of strategic feint into seriousness, with mock annoyance playing straight man against Brooks' burlesque put-ons. In other interviews, as with the little-known talks with student editors the year *Something Happened* was published, Heller comes across as mainly frank, straightforward, and generous with his time, despite moments of joke cracking. He enjoys being a novelist and relishes discussing these literary works, even if they are his own. Such qualities appear in almost all the longer interviews, and are part of the appeal of the novelist. Gelb's affectionate portrait notes that even his friends can find him hard to get along with— she writes of his "pose of tempered bellicosity (sometimes not so tempered)"; and Speed Vogel, no doubt exaggerating but from a basis of truth, in his first section in *No Laughing Matter* describes Heller before his illness in a catalogue of unpleasant behaviors that might be summed up as combining Bob Slocum with the worst of Heller's satiric butts. This side of Heller, however, rarely appears in his public interviews, although it may well be a factor behind some of the less informative interviews not collected in this volume. In any event, Vogel disingenuously admits that Heller's friends still "liked him ... but we were extremely hard put to explain why" (13). For a reader Heller's winning qualities are what shine through in the incisive and entertaining aspects of his narrative presence and the pleasure given by his works, easier-to-explain attributes that can be seen also in the interviews.

Heller's status of cult celebrity soon grew into his more imposing stature of major author as his first novel very quickly became accepted into the canon of American literature as a classic, but Heller repeatedly notes the acclaim never became "an inhibiting factor," a phrase he uses in 1984 to Suplee: indeed it gave him "tremendous encouragement" that however much he might tax his reviewers' and readers' patience in his books, they would treat him seriously. Heller's patience with interviewers must have taxed *him* many times, yet he continued to go over and over, and apparently find pleasure in discussing, *Catch-22* as well as his succeeding works. One result of his general prominence, however, might well have been his almost studied avoidance of discussing his private life very closely. This can be seen throughout the entire span of interviews, and it is not without accuracy that the subhead of Chet

Flippo's *Rolling Stone* interview termed him "the reluctant hero of three
generations." Heller is not stand-offish, and he does mention his wife,
his children, his divorce, his illness and its symptoms, his feelings about
his characters and about his war experiences. But there is finally a veil
of reticence about intimate things. This is very much part of his
character; he jokes to *Playboy* about getting questioned on his sex life,
but after reading the interviews, one cannot imagine the creator of Bob
Slocum ever wallowing in the subjective as revealingly as that intensely
inward character. Similarly the kind of jokes Mandel and he make about
his marital relationship—typically, they distance rather than approach
the subject—are as close to that subject as he ever gets, even at the
time of, and after, his separation and divorce. When the issue of
autobiographical content in *Something Happened* is broached, Heller
takes great pains more than once to hold himself, and particularly his
wife and family, separate from the personages in the novel, insisting on
the distinction between facets of a writer's life going into a book as
components of its material and that book's being a self-exposure of
personal attitudes and actual feelings or a representation of the writer's
biographical situation. Indeed he observes, in regard to the use of
personal-historical material, that *Catch-22* is the more autobiographical
work. In relation to a book's exposing inward actuality, he stresses
instead the achievement of the first-person soliloquy that is *Something
Happened* as an imitation, "the *manner* of self-revelation," as he puts it
to fellow novelist Amis. At times, art seems in Heller's words not so
much the extension as the disguise of the self. "He masks his feelings
with mockery and laughter," writes Gelb, and Heller comes closest to
intimate comment with his friend, who, observing Heller's buried
fragility, his fears, and his need for control, quotes her subject tellingly
in the *Times*: "I can let myself feel for people and I can let myself stop
feeling for them. . . . It's easy, it's a skill—like an ability to draw."

Another side of Heller's prominence as a figure of public attention is
the constraint of expectations brought to his works by readers and
reviewers. Throughout his career reviewers seem to be disappointed in
his later works, fine as they are, for not being the exemplary comic
novel his first book was. Heller, however, takes considerable pride in
achieving different artistic goals, working with new challenges in
narrative mode and convention, and varying subject matter with each
successive work. And it should be no small consolation, even to the

sometimes privately self-doubting Heller, that *Catch-22* is ultimately the kind of book which, after a quarter century and more, an exacting critic like Joseph Heller himself can come back to and admire. The novelist remarks his continued satisfaction with this first work throughout the late 1980s interviews around and after the time of the twenty-fifth anniversary of its initial publication, when he also speaks of working with the character Yossarian once more in a sequel. From the first interviews to the most recent, these literary conversations chart the career of an author whose importance in a sense has been reconfirmed by others' initial disappointment in each new work, but whose sureness in his own judgment is, in this reader's view, more likely to stand the test of time.

Like many writers' interviews, Heller's tend to cluster about significant events in his career: after *Catch-22*, the 1967 and 1968 New Haven and New York productions of his play, *We Bombed in New Haven*; the release of the 1970 Mike Nichols movie of *Catch-22*, which brought attention (as well as a surge of paperback sales) to the author and to his long-in-progress next novel; the 1974 publication of *Something Happened*, a best-seller, and his promotion tours, which produced the largest concentration of interviews, focusing not only on the new novel but on its differences from the already canonized first work; and then a similar pattern with the release of each subsequent book, although eliciting fewer interviews, possibly because of less exhausting promotion. The flow of material was largely interrupted only once, from late 1981 to 1984, a hiatus caused by Heller's paralysis from Guillain-Barré syndrome, his slow recovery, and the limitations on his activity, as well as, one suspects, the events in his private life that independently paralleled the illness: his separation and divorce from the former Shirley Held, whom he had married in 1945, and then his new relationship with Valerie Humphries, whom he met in 1982 while he was a patient in Mt. Sinai Hospital.

Of these many interviews in print and other media—ninety plus, with the total still growing—I have selected as essential about a third to represent Heller. All are reprinted largely uncut and unedited, save primarily for silent correction of obvious small errors and typos. In one case—the most ambitious early interview, the Krassner dialogue I mention often—I have collated slightly different versions with material added from its reprinting in a *Realist* anthology. Included are all but one of the long, more substantial and wide-ranging interviews, the notable exception being Charles Ruas's interesting talk with Heller done the year before the publication of *God Knows,* which can easily be found in Ruas's 1985 Knopf book, *Conversations with American Authors.* I have also tried to include a balance of articles from the realm of popular print journalism, both magazines and newspapers, from academic and intellectual periodicals, and from nonprint media. One dialogue appears for the first time, David L. Middleton's never before published report of Heller's remarks in San Antonio in 1986. I am pleased also to include three largely unknown interviews that came out in university newspapers and magazines, the Yale *New Journal,* the *Harvard Crimson,* and the *Chicago Maroon.* I'm likewise glad to find room for two zany but not frivolous, or *not only* frivolous, conversations with close friends and fellow Gourmet Club gourmands, Mel Brooks and George Mandel, the latter of which had been entered into early Heller bibliographies with the wrong year and disappeared from later listings. Two other interviews by friends include the Robert Alan Aurthur *Esquire* piece and the Barbara Gelb profile-interview from the Sunday *Times Magazine,* which, in the course of quoting Heller significantly if not substantially, presents the most comprehensive and insightful view of the man behind the books and in its accuracy supersedes all previous biographical reports. Martin Amis's exchange with Heller is a trenchant example of a writer taking a fellow writer seriously. Every interview in this book contains something not quite available in any other conversation or dialogue.

In acknowledgment of essential help in my task as editor, I have many people to thank. First of all, I want to express gratitude to Joseph Heller for his expressions of support for this project and, especially, for his cooperation in carefully going over and revising the chronology in order to rectify what in a letter he advised me from the beginning were a variety of errors about him that had crept into print and proliferated. In the same 1991 letter, Heller warns me about writers' interviews, "Don't believe we always mean what we say," but I take it that this doesn't apply to his own changes of my original chronology. Any mistakes that remain are my own. Next, gratitude is due those whose permission was so freely given to use their work in this collection. I thank them and their publishers, and I also thank the many interviewers whose good articles there just wasn't room for. Unnamed but essential are all the reference librarians, interlibrary loan professionals, and archive specialists who had a hand in providing specific pieces of material. Grateful acknowledgment is due the Penn State University Libraries Interlibrary Loan Department in Pattee Library, University Park Campus, and locally, even more so to the unflappable Jean Sphar, the Penn State Delaware County Campus interlibrary loan clerk, for coping good-humoredly with my deluge of requests, so many needed right away, or sooner. Susan Ware, reference librarian at the Delaware County Campus, is due special mention for providing prompt, tireless, skilled, inventive professional research assistance that went far beyond the call of duty both in coming up with big things and following up on the little ones. My editor, Seetha A-Srinivasan, is due thanks for her advice, aid, and persistence. Last but not least, I also want to acknowledge my wife, Nancy, for putting up with a maniac at work as I got near the end, and also for being understanding about the many times my papers and files were spread out all over the living room, keeping her from spreading out her own papers and working comfortably herself: thanks for being there even when there was no room to be there!

AJS
September 1992

Chronology

1923   Joseph Heller born 1 May in the Coney Island section of Brooklyn, New York. Father, Isaac Heller, a Russian immigrant who arrived in the U.S. in 1913, a bakery delivery-truck driver; mother, Lena Heller, also a Russian immigrant who spoke little English, married Isaac about 1919. Brother, Lee, 14, born in Russia, and sister, Sylvia, 7, both born to Isaac's first wife, who died 1916.

1927   Isaac Heller dies from a botched ulcer operation.

1941   Graduates from New York City's Abraham Lincoln High School (Flatbush section of Brooklyn); file-room clerk at casualty insurance company.

1942   Blacksmith's helper, Norfolk Navy Yard; enlists in Army Air Corps.

1944   Completes training as bombardier

1944–45   Flies combat missions over Italy and France as a B-25 wing bombardier in the 488th Squadron, 340th Bombardment Group, 12th Air Force, based on Corsica. On his 37th mission, over Avignon, JH believes his plane has been hit and is going down; fellow crew member is wounded severely in the thigh.

1945   Rotated home upon completion of tour of duty with 60 missions. After serving for a short time as public relations officer in Texas, discharged as First Lieutenant with an Air Medal with 5 Oak Leaf Clusters and a Presidential Unit Citation. Marries Shirley Held. First published fiction, a short story in Whit Burnett's *Story* magazine. Under G.I. Bill, begins college at University of Southern California.

1946   Transfers to New York University

1948   Baccalaureate degree from N.Y.U., elected to Phi Beta Kappa; publishes two short stories in *Esquire,* where a nonfictional piece had appeared the year before, and two in *Atlantic Monthly.*

1949   M.A. from Columbia University with a thesis on "The Pulitzer Prize Plays: 1917–1935"; studies on Fulbright scholarship at Oxford University (St. Catherine's College). "Castle of Snow" (*Atlantic Monthly, 1948*), chosen for *The Best American Short Stories 1949.*

1950–52   Instructor of English composition at Pennsylvania State University

1952   Daughter Erica born

1952–55   Works in New York City as advertising copywriter at Remington Rand and another small ad agency

1955   Publishes "The Texan" in *New World Writing,* first chapter of novel then called "Catch-18," for which he began making notes in 1953.

1955–58   Advertising-promotion copywriter, *Time* magazine, New York

1956   Son Theodore born

1957   Contract with Simon and Schuster for his novel-in-progress after young editor, Robert Gottlieb, reads about 250 pages of manuscript

1958–59   Advertising-promotion writer, *Look* magazine, New York

1959–62   Copywriter and advertising and promotion manager,
McCall's magazine, New York

1961   *Catch-22*—his first novel's title having been changed at
Gottlieb's suggestion to avoid confusion with Leon Uris's
soon-to-be issued novel, *Mila 18*—published by Simon and
Schuster in October; though never on *New York Times* best-
seller list, sells over 32,000 in first year. Conceives of book
that will become his second novel.

1962   Movie rights to *Catch-22* sold to Columbia Pictures; leaves
McCall's; works on second novel; writes a pilot script for
McHale's Navy TV series. Dell paperback edition of
Catch-22 comes out in October and is immediately popular,
selling over 2,000,000 copies in one year and 8,000,000 by
1971.

1963   National Institute of Arts and Letters grant in literature

1964   In Hollywood to rewrite filmscript for *Sex and the Single
Girl* (Warner Brothers), credited with David R. Schwarz,
whom he never met

1966   *Esquire* publishes "Something Happened," the first section
of novel in progress, in September issue.

1967   Commuting from New York City, teaches creative writing
for one semester both at the University of Pennsylvania
(fiction), and at Yale, where he is Playwright-in-Residence.
We Bombed in New Haven produced 4 December by Yale
School of Drama Repertory Theater, directed by Larry
Arrick, starring Stacy Keach. Works for two weeks as script
doctor on fifth James Bond film, *Casino Royale,* doing
scenes that were never read or used (Columbia Pictures,
uncredited).

1968   *We Bombed in New Haven* opens in New York on 16
October at the Ambassador Theater, directed by John

Hirsch, starring Jason Robards, Jr.; runs eleven weeks. Play published by Knopf.

1970   Release of film version of *Catch-22* (Paramount Pictures), directed by Mike Nichols, script by Buck Henry, starring Alan Arkin. Sales of *Catch-22* flourish, though film is critical and financial failure. Rewrite of screenplay for *Dirty Dingus Magee* (Metro-Goldwyn-Mayer, credited with script authors Tom Waldman and Frank Waldman).

1971   Completes *Catch-22: A Dramatization*; play opens in East Hampton's John Drew Theater on 23 July, directed by Larry Arrick. Acting edition published by Samuel R. French (trade edition, Delacorte, 1973). Appointed Distinguished Visiting Professor, City College of the City University of New York; reappointed through 1974.

1973   Samuel R. French publishes *Clevinger's Trial,* a one-act play originally begun as part of *Catch-22: A Dramatization.*

1974   Second novel *Something Happened* completed and published by Alfred A. Knopf in October; immediate best-seller. "Catch-22" as a common noun made an entry in new edition of *Webster's New World Dictionary of the American Language* (2nd College Edition), first formal recognition of the currency gained by the novel's title.

1975   Gives up teaching appointment at City College to devote full time to writing; starts to write a novel on Jewish-American experience.

1979   Simon and Schuster publishes *Good as Gold.*

1980   Begins work on King David novel

1981   Separates from wife Shirley. Comes down with Guillain-Barré syndrome in December, at a point when 325 type-script pages of *God Knows* have been completed. On 13

December, begins 5-month hospital stay (44 days in Mt. Sinai Hospital in New York City, 108 more days in N.Y.U.'s Rusk Institute of Rehabilitation Medicine), and continues 8 months of physical therapy at home. In Mt. Sinai, meets Valerie Humphries, a private-duty nurse.

1982 Discharged in May, moves to his East Hampton, Long Island, house.

1984 Alfred A. Knopf publishes *God Knows* in October. Divorce from Shirley Held finalized.

1985 Is recovered sufficiently for an around-the-world promotional tour in the fall; accompanied by Valerie Humphries. Starts new novel focusing on Rembrandt's painting, "Aristotle Contemplating the Bust of Homer," and Aristotle's Athens, first called "Poetics," later published as *Picture This*.

1986 G.P. Putnam's Sons publishes *No Laughing Matter* in February, written jointly in alternating sections with Speed Vogel.

1987 Marries Valerie Humphries

1988 Publishes *Picture This* in September with G.P. Putnam's Sons

1989 Begins work on a new satiric novel, working title "Closing Time," resurrecting Yossarian and other characters from *Catch-22* and also depicting George Bush as well as various members of his administration

1991 Christensen Fellow at St. Catherine's College, Oxford University, to confer with students engaged in fiction writing

1993 Returns to Oxford as Christensen Fellow

Conversations with Joseph Heller

The Heller Cult

Newsweek/1962

From *Newsweek* 1 October 1962, AJS: 82–83. Copyright © 1962, Newsweek, Inc. All rights reserved. Reprinted by permission.

"It's not a book you like a little," says . . . Joseph Heller about his wild, exuberant first novel, *Catch-22,* and that may go down as the understatement of the publishing year. Not since *The Catcher in the Rye* and *Lord of the Flies* has a novel been taken up by such a fervid and heterogeneous claque of admirers.

Lawyers like it, and so do cartoonists. Poet John Ciardi stayed awake all night to finish Heller's comic extravaganza about a war run by lunatics and a young bombardier whose only target is to keep himself alive. The director of public relations for CARE, Sam Kaufman, was so taken with *Catch* he considered attaching a flyer to all CARE publicity, advising "Send CARE packages to the hungry overseas. They need it. And don't fail to read *Catch-22.* You need it."

Heller has fans at the Rand Corp., the Behavioral Sciences Center at Stanford University, and the Kansas City *Star.* Producer David Merrick likes the zany, unclassifiable novel so much he wants to do a Broadway version. Columbia Pictures has paid $150,000 for the movie rights and hired Heller to write the screenplay. Anthony Quinn, Jack Lemmon, Ben Gazzara, Paul Newman, and Eli Wallach all want to play the hero, the bombardier Yossarian.

The book obviously inspires an evangelical fervor in those who admire it. Newscaster John Chancellor is so eager to spread the word that he printed up stickers reading "Yossarian Lives" and "Better Yossarian than Rotarian." Father Charles E. Sheedy, dean of the College of Arts and Letters at Notre Dame, was so caught up by *Catch* that he raved about it after a lecture on ethics at the U.S. Air Force Academy, and convinced some less enthusiastic airmen to take another look at the book, which is, of course, about their arm of the service.

Philip Toynbee liked it so much he called it "the greatest satirical work in English since *Erewhon,*" and the English liked it so much that within a week of its publication this summer, *Catch-22* became London's No. 1 best seller.

Although the novel has sold 40,000 copies in the U.S., it has never made the best-seller lists here, because these are national surveys, and most of the book's sales were in New York. Last week, the novel came out in paperback, making it a virtual certainty that *Catch* will spread throughout the U.S. It has already swept the cocktail-party circuit where *Catch-22* is the hottest topic going and Joe Heller himself is the hottest catch, although he usually declines invitations.

But he is no recluse like J.D. Salinger. "I like Salinger," Heller said last week. "I think he's unique. I love him as a person—because it's impossible to see him. But being alone is appealing only when you're not alone. I need outside disturbances. I draw inspiration from daily embarrassments. If I were in New Hampshire, now, far away from anyone close to me, I would be frightened. I'd go there only if I could be next door to Salinger, but if I were next door, he would immediately move to Wyoming."

Heller's personality pattern, what his friends call his "wacky-looking sanity," was set sometime during the Depression when he was growing up in Coney Island. At 19 he went off to World War II and was stationed on the island of Corsica, as a bombardier like Yossarian.

"I am one of those who benefited from war," said Heller. "If I had not gone to war, I would not have gone to college, and if I had not gone to college, I would not have been a writer. I don't know what would have become of me." As things turned out, he studied at NYU and Oxford, taught English composition for two years at Penn State, then became a full-time advertising copy writer.

The discovery of Louis-Ferdinand Céline and Vladimir Nabokov "literally in the same week" inspired him to start *Catch-22*. "What I got from Céline," he said, "is the slangy use of prose and the continuity that is relaxed and vague rather than precise and motivated; from Nabokov's *Laughter in the Dark*, the flippant approach to situations which were filled with anguish and grief and tragedy. *Catch-22* is really a juxtaposition of life and death. Laughter and loving are life and war is death."

The first chapter came quickly and was dispatched to *New World Writing*, which published it under its original title, *Catch-18*. (Later the title was changed to avoid confusion with Leon Uris' forgettable *Mila 18*. Heller says: "I was heartsick. I thought eighteen was the only number.") For two hours almost every night, five nights a week, for seven years, Heller wrote his novel. Once, for two weeks, he quit in disgust, turned to television and other pastimes, finally bored himself stiff. "What do people who are not writing novels do with their evenings?" he asked his wife, and then returned to novel-writing.

What kind of book is it? "A moral book," says the author, "dealing with man's moral dilemma. People can't distinguish between rational and irrational behavior, between the moral and the immoral." Can Joe Heller? "I can really, but it's not easy. It's insane when I think this is a world in which the keepers are as nutty as the inmates. . . ."

This past summer on Fire Island, Heller began making notes for his new novel "about a married man who is working for a large company and who wants to work himself up to the point where he makes a speech at the company's annual convention in Bermuda." Pressed for details, Heller confessed, "It has implications."

He also found time to answer some of his voluminous mail, which includes such letters as the following from one of the eight countries where *Catch-22* is coming out in other languages: "I am translating your novel *Catch-22* into Finnish. Would you please explain me one thing: What means Catch-22? I didn't find it in any vocabulary. Even the assistant air attaché of the U.S.A. here in Helsinki could not explain exactly."

Joe Heller, who knows there is a catch to everything, comments dryly: "I think in Finland the book will lose a great deal in translation."

An Impolite Interview with Joseph Heller

Paul Krassner/1962

From *The Realist,* November 1962, 18–31. Reprinted, with some changes and new material, in *Best of the Realist.* Philadelphia: Running Press, 1984, 75–81. The version below adds the new closing material from the latter version to the 1962 text. Reprinted by permission of the author.

Q. *Has* Catch-22 *been banned anywhere?*

A. No.

Q. *Are you disappointed?*

A. Not anymore. I'm really delighted because it seems to have offended nobody on the grounds of morality or ideology. Those people it has offended, it has offended on the basis of literary value. But I'm almost surprised to find that the acceptance of the book covers such a broad political spectrum and sociological spectrum as well.

This pleases me first because it pleases my ego, but next because I put an optimistic interpretation on it: I think there is close to a common reservoir of discontent among people who might disagree with each other and not realize that their basic disagreements might stem from the same recognition of a need for correction in certain areas.

I learned from Murray Kempton's column also—and this to my surprise—that it's quite an orthodox book in terms of its morality. He referred to its being almost medieval in its moral orthodoxy, which had not occurred to me. But of course as soon as I read his column, I realized he was correct. I suppose just about everybody accepts certain principles of morality. The differences appear in testing certain institutions against those basic principles.

There is a tradition of taboo against submitting to examination many of our ideological beliefs, religious beliefs; many things that become a matter of traditional behavior, or habit, acquire status where they seem to be exempt from examination. Or even to suggest that they do be examined becomes a form of heresy.

Now the book might be surprising in that respect, but—with the exception of a certain appreciation for lechery, which you wouldn't find

6

among the basic virtues; you might find it among the deac
don't think there's any principle of morality advocated in t
which most intelligent—even *in*decent—people will disag

Q. *Well, when I was reading it, I first did a double take
Yossarian is censoring the letters, and my sympathy immediately fell to
the people who were getting these letters.*

A. Really? Well, that hadn't occurred to me. They probably have the
same status as the victims during a Shakespeare play. When critics deal
in terms of classical tragedy—when they interpret Shakespearean
tragedy—they see this as an examination of crime, the tragic flaw, and
the retribution as representing a certain system of justice; but they
ignore, let's say in *Macbeth,* all those children of—was it Macduff or
Malcolm?—his wife is killed, his children are killed, and Banquo is
slaughtered. All the peripheral characters seem to be exempt from the
working-out of this moral principle.

I suppose it had not occurred to me that these people getting these
letters would be perplexed by them. I'm not particularly disturbed by
that.

Q. *Maybe I'm hypersensitive. . . . Getting back to what you said
about people not being offended, isn't this type of satire by its very
nature subversive—in the James Thurber sense of the word—to the
establishment?*

A. Oh, I think anything *critical* is subversive by nature in the sense
that it does seek to change or reform something that exists by attacking
it. I think the impetus toward progress of any kind has always been a
sort of discontent with what existed, and an effort to undermine what is
existing, whether it's barbaric or not barbaric.

So, in the sense that the book is aware of certain faults or short-
comings—as much, I think, in the make-up of the individuals' characters as in the make-up of a society—in that sense, it is a very critical
book, certainly. But it doesn't necessarily follow from that, that people
would take exception to it.

Q. *What about the people who are criticized?*

A. I've met nobody yet who did not identify with my sympathetic
characters. And among the people who did identify were a few of the
prototypes of some of the more reprehensible characters in the book. I
think anybody today feels, for example, that he is at the mercy of
superiors—who don't know his job as well as he does, who don't know

their own jobs as well as *he* knows their jobs and who, he feels, hamstring him or limit him in the execution of his duty.

Q. *And this includes superiors?*

A. Oh, yes—this includes his superiors as well. It occurred to me at a certain point that even General Walker, at the height of his troubles, could very easily have identified with one of my sympathetic officers, because he himself was being the victim of the Pentagon and the politicians in Washington who were jeopardizing everything, say, good—and preventing *him* from existing and performing work at the height of his capabilities.

Q. *Have you gotten any unofficial reactions to the book from Air Force personnel?*

A. I have gotten no official reaction. I've gotten fan letters from people in the service—at least two, I believe, from officers, one of whom is with the Air Force Academy, but he was writing to express his approval of the book as literature rather than expressing any sympathy with the ideas.

I think another reason I have not heard any objections is that most people *are* treating it as a *novel* and judging it in those terms, as a work of fiction rather than as an essay or as a propaganda tract. It's not *intended* to be a sociological treatise on anything, although it—the substance of the fiction—is almost an encyclopedia of the current mental atmosphere.

It is certainly a novel of *comment;* there are comments about the loyalty oath, about the free enterprise system, about civil rights, about bureaucracy, about patriotism—but these are the ingredients out of which to create a fictional narrative.

In writing the book I was more concerned with producing a *novel* that would be as contemporary as possible. I don't mean contemporaneous with World War II; it is contemporary with the period I was writing in. I was more concerned with producing a work of fiction—of literary art, if you will—than of converting anybody or arousing controversy. I'm really afraid of getting involved in controversy.

Q. *Are you serious?*

A. Oh, yes—I'm a terrible coward. I'm just like Yossarian, you know. It's the easiest thing to fight—I learned that in the war—it *takes* a certain amount of courage to go to war, but not very much, not as much as to refuse to go to war. I think that's the danger that the world

faces today; war might be the easiest solution to problem:
country or the other might rely on war as a solution, not b
dictated, but simply because it's a way out of frustration.

Q. *I can't accept your implication, a minute ago, that i
controversy is necessarily a barometer of bravery—because I love
controversy, but I'm a coward, too.*

A. No. I didn't mean that. I don't love controversy—I don't like
personal controversy.

Q. *No, no, I don't mean personal controversy, I mean controversy of
ideas—*

A. Oh, yes, that's fine—but when I have a complaint against a
department store, I try to avoid making it in person, I try to avoid using
the phone—I'd much rather put it on paper and avoid all danger of any
personal combat.

Q. *Your book received some fanatically favorable reviews, but there
was one stern critic who said: "If* Catch-22 *were intended as a commentary novel, [the] sideswiping of character and action might be taken
care of by thematic control. It fails here because half its incidents are
farcical and fantastic. The book is an emotional hodge-podge; no mood
is sustained long enough to register for more than a chapter." Now I
don't want to put you in the silly position of saying, "But I don't
sideswipe character and action" —*

A. Well, I *do* sideswipe character and action. I think that's one of the
approaches to the book that gives it what effect it has. I tried to avoid,
first of all, the conventional structure of the novel; I tried to give it a
structure that would reflect and complement the content of the book
itself, and the content of the book really derives from our present
atmosphere, which is one of chaos, of disorganization, of absurdity, of
cruelty, of brutality, of insensitivity, but at the same time one in which
people, even the worst people, I think are basically good, are motivated
by humane impulses.

And I tried to emphasize this by the structure, much the same way
that many of your modern artists have resorted to a type of painting as
being most suitable to the emotions they want to express, to the visions
they have; and your very good contemporary composers are using
dissonances and irregular tempos and harmonics to get this same
feeling.

I did consciously try to use a form of what might be called dramatic counterpoint, so that certain characters suffer tragedies, and they're dismissed almost flippantly—a line or two might describe something terrible happening to a character, whereas whole pages might be concentrated on something of *subordinate* dramatic value.

And by doing that, I tried to do two things. One was to emphasize the sense of loss, or the sense of sorrow, connected with it; and also to capture this thing in experience which permits us to survive the loss of people who are dear to us, so that nobody's suffering lingers with us very long.

People die and are forgotten. People are abused and are forgotten. People suffer, people are exploited, *right now;* we don't dwell upon them 24 hours a day. Somehow they get lost in the swirl of things of much less importance to us and to them and to the human condition.

So in that case I don't quarrel with the review; there was a definite technique, at the beginning of the book particularly, of treating people and incidents almost in terms of glimpses, and then showing as we progress that these things do have a meaning and they do come together.

Q. *That same reviewer also said: "As satire* Catch-22 *makes too many formal concessions to the standard novels of our day"* —

A. I don't know what he means. I don't know whether his standards of satire should be accepted. There are formal concessions to the standard novel, certainly. You can't write a novel on piano. So as soon as you begin using words, then you begin making concessions to the form.

Catch-22 is not to my mind a far-out novel; it is not to my mind a formless novel. If anything, it was constructed almost meticulously, and with a meticulous concern to give the appearance of a formless novel. Now that's much different, in much the same way as with Joyce's *Ulysses,* which is possibly one of the most confusing novels when you first approach it, and yet there's a structure and tension in virtually every word.

Incidentally, it's turning out to be a very easy novel to read, because among the letters I get are *many* from people in high school and freshmen in college. I have a collection of letters that could be called love letters—from people of all three sexes, probably, and of all ages, and they're just rhapsodic in their enthusiasm.

I've yet to receive one letter that criticizes, but that may be that when people don't like a book they just don't write letters about it. What I do get is a kind of "God bless you" approach, or maybe a "This might save the world" feeling.

One thing I'm certain of, all these letters—and there must be about three or four hundred by now—I'm sure that the writers of each of these letters would like each other enormously if they met. People that I have met as a result of these letters—if they're in New York and I have seen them—there's almost an instantaneous rapport.

I think that comes from the fact that I express so much of my own views in the novel, and my own personality, with the result that anybody who responds to the book is going to respond to me. We meet, and almost immediately we're conversing like old friends.

Q. *I was talking to Ralph J. Gleason, and he was wondering how you feel about certain other writers' approaches to the insanity of our time. I'll name them one at a time. Louis-Ferdinand Céline?*

A. Céline's book, *Journey to the End of the Night,* was one of those which gave me a direct inspiration for the form and tone of *Catch-22.*

Q. *Nelson Algren?*

A. *The Man with the Golden Arm,* which I had read earlier, became an almost unconscious influence in the form of this type of open hero.

Q. *Ken Kesey?*

A. I haven't read *One Flew Over the Cuckoo's Nest* yet—his book came out after mine—but I bought it a few weeks ago.

Q. *Terry Southern?*

A. I read *The Magic Christian* very quickly, and there were parts of it I liked enormously, and parts that just eluded me. I'm not a very good reader. I had not read his book before I wrote *Catch-22,* but I think those people Southern influenced through his book might very well have influenced me.

Q. *Richard Condon?*

A. I read *The Manchurian Candidate* and I read *The Oldest Confession.* When I read the review of *The Manchurian Candidate,* I was in about the middle of *Catch-22,* and I had a feeling, well, here's a guy who's writing the same book *I* am; I'd better read this quickly because he might have already written it.

And then I read it, and I think there's a great deal of similarity, first of all in the concern, or the use of political and social materials—or products of the political and social conflicts—as the basis for his book, and there's a great similarity in the attitude toward them, so that they are at once serious and at the same time it's almost like watching a kind of burlesque and also a kind of Everyman show on stage.

There's a definite feeling of kinship with him, but I don't think they're the same kind of novel. Mine is, I suppose, an optimistic novel with a great deal of pessimism in it—there's a very heavy sense of the tragic—particularly toward the end, where I almost consciously sought to re-create the feeling of Dostoevsky's dark passages, and I have one or two allusions to chapters in Dostoevsky.

Q. *In relation to the humorous aspect of the book, I want to ask you about the use of exaggeration as a vehicle for satire; do you think you may have exaggerated too much beyond the possibilities of reality?*

A. Well, I *tried* to exaggerate in almost every case, gradually, to a point beyond reality—that was a deliberate intention, to do it so gradually that the *un*reality becomes *more* credible than the realistic, normal, day-to-day behavior of these characters.

Certainly, there are things in there which could not—well, there's one thing that could not . . . well, everything could *possibly* happen; nothing in there is supernatural—but it defies probability. But so much of what we *do*—without even thinking about it—so much of what is *done* in our day-to-day existence defies probability if we stop to examine it.

And this is the effect I wanted to achieve. Now, I was hoping to do this, and with many people I succeeded, to make these characters seem more real in terms of their eccentricities carried to absurdity.

Q. *You started to say that there was one thing in particular in the book that defies probability.*

A. That's a scene which to many people is the high spot of the book and to other people it's the point at which their credulity was strained. And that is the incident—incident is an incongruous word for it—in which Milo bombs his own squadron and escapes without punishment.

I would say that more critics who praised the book singled this out as a triumph, with special appreciation, than any other single incident. On the other hand, most people in conversation, in discussing it, say that this was the one thing that they found hard to believe.

Now, I sincerely think that this is an impossibility; this is the one thing that could not happen—literally. I don't think that in time of war a man could get up and actually drop bombs deliberately on his own people and then escape without punishment, even in our society.

I think people in every country commit *actions* which would cause infinitely more *damage* to the national strength, to the national survival, to their fellow citizens; even commit actions which result in more deaths, physical deaths, as well—and be *lionized* for it; be made into heroes for it. But I don't think the actual *act* of killing would be allowed to escape punishment with everybody's approval.

Q. *There are other things which I think go beyond the area of possibility. The soldier in white, for example, who is nourished by continuously being fed his own waste products intravenously—*

A. No, he's not—well, yes he is, I suppose—that had not occurred to me. Of course, if you assume that there's a human being inside the bandages, then he could not be kept alive by his own waste products; that's a scientific impossibility. But if you begin to question, as I do, whether there *is* a human being inside, then it becomes a matter of economy just to keep using the same fluid to put back inside him.

But he is handled almost always as a kind of gruesome symbol of many things. In one instance, he is discussed as a middle-man. If you look at man—remove the conscience, remove the sensibility—well, if you look at his position in the nature of things, in one sense he can be no more than a middle-man: he takes matter, he absorbs it, he excretes it or uses it up, and this is a natural process in which he is just one tiny phase of the whole cycle.

As an animal, man is a vegetable. And that was the point of using the soldier in white that way.

No, he could not happen, I suppose, unless there *was* some gigantic conspiracy—it's almost supernatural—in which the reasons defy explanation; they decide to put this form swathed in bandages in the hospital and put nothing inside.

Q. *Did you ever read* Johnny Got His Gun—*which was about a basket case—by Dalton Trumbo?*

A. Oh, sure. The thing that I liked best about *Johnny Got His Gun* was that the *Daily News* wrote an editorial recommending it and praising it. It came out when the *News* was in its isolationist phase; anti-Roosevelt phase.

Q. *I understand* The Daily Worker *was serializing it at the time, and they suddenly stopped right in the middle without a word of explanation when the peace pact between Stalin and Hitler was signed. . . . There were a couple of other areas in your book of probability versus possibility. Like eating chocolate-covered cotton—*

A. Oh, it's not impossible that a man would try to market cotton covered with chocolate. It is impossible, I suppose, that they can eat it. And nobody does eat it in the book. In fact, when Milo gives it to Yossarian, Yossarian tastes it, then spits it out and says, "You can't give it to people, they'll get sick." So this is not done; in the book people do *not* eat chocolate-covered cotton, but there is a man trying to *market* it. Now, I think the corollaries of *that*. . . .

Q. *What about the loyalty oath scene, where they have to pledge allegiance hundreds of times and sing* "The Star-Spangled Banner" *all over the place—*

A. Again, that is not a physical impossibility. You know, in the first outline of this book, when it was first conceived—in my mind; it was never down on paper—there were going to be a number of deliberate anachronisms, very *conspicuous* anachronisms—there are anachronisms in now that are deliberate—there were going to be a number of super-natural things taking place, without any explanation for them, so that the impossible—the physically impossible—would be worked in with the possible, and be recognizable.

And then, I forget the motive, I decided nothing in this book would be something that's physically impossible.

Consequently, even in the latter half of the book, where you have this whore with the knife coming up in all kinds of disguises, the effect I give is that she's moving from place to place with the speed of light, because the scale there is changed to give you fast action; but it's always two hours or three hours that go by, so that he pushes the girl out of the plane in Rome, then flies back to the airfield, and you get the impression that she's waiting there, she's beat him there, and she stabs him, but if you look, he spends a few hours running to find Hungry Joe, the pilot, to fly him back.

So the explanation would be: in that time, she could've hopped a plane somehow and gotten there. In the first writing, she was going to pop up with a speed that would've been impossible. And then I decided, let's keep consistent about this.

Now there are, I suppose, things which don't even occur to me, like the soldier in white. But it's not physically impossible that somebody, for reasons of their own, would take this zombie—which is what he's supposed to be: a zombie, really, or nothing; and I don't know if there's much difference, let's say, between the human animal that lacks sensi-bility, and nothing but matter—but it is not physically impossible, it's *improbable,* that an organization would exist to perpetrate this kind of trick.

If any government wanted to, for reasons of their own, get some kind of wire-structured *papier maché* and cover it with bandages and pass it off as a man who's been seriously wounded in the war—I'm saying they *could* do it; that's what I mean by its not being physically impossible.

Q. *All right, what about the family visiting the hospital and failing to recognize that Yossarian isn't their son.*

A. Well, the only one who accepts him as the son almost instantly is the mother.

Q. *Of all people. . . .*

A. Well, it's easier for mothers to accept strangers—I've noticed that about women and men—women seem to be much fonder of other people's children than of their own, and men don't care; the only children men care for are their own.

In that scene, it makes no difference to the mother; she says, "What difference does that make?" The sailor says, "He's not Giuseppe, he's Yossarian." And I forget what the father does. In that unforgettable chapter, I forget what happens.

Again, it is improbable—certainly, it is improbable—but, again, it is not *impossible* that this conversation should take place. It's an unusual reaction, but not an impossible one.

Q. *In retrospect, are there any important changes you would make in the book?*

A. I can't think of any. I would not change Milo bombing his squadron because, on one level, this book is an allegory—not on a level, but there are *passages* where it becomes allegoric; there are other passages where it becomes realism—and I think that, allegorically, that is a consistent action and a most logical action.

It's no more improbable than other things Milo has done out of the goodness of his heart. What is improbable is not that a man should *do* this and find a *rationale* for doing it—Milo is very good at finding that—but what's improbable is that any society would permit it to go unpunished.

Q. *Some of the stuff that does go unpunished in real life makes it seem almost possible after all—*

A. Well, it is possible, for example, in this country, and in Russia, in

England—it is possible for individuals to be murdered, put to death, without any legal sanction for it, and for the people who did it to be known and to escape punishment. That is conceivable. In fact, it's almost a daily occurrence here.

But Milo's action transcends this. It's a time of war, and he bombs indiscriminately, and it's an act of *physical* violence. It is conceivable to me that somebody might manufacture a food product or a drug product that would *poison* people, and the punishment for this would be slight; there would be extenuations if not justifications.

I don't think it's probable that this same person could indiscriminately run through New York, let's say, firing a machine gun, and escape without punishment.

It depends to a large extent, *always,* on whom your victims *are.* Or who *you* are. And in this case it was just an attack on his own society; it's the society, or the members of it, that are being attacked almost without discrimination. That couldn't—it's just inconceivable that it *would*—go unpunished.

I suppose if I re-read the book—each time I do read it, I find I'm angling for something; I'll read a chapter and I'll say, "Maybe I can make this into a recording," or "Maybe this would go well at Upstairs at the Downstairs," and the next thing you know, I'm scheming commercially—but I think one thing I would probably do would be to cut.

And what I would cut would probably be language rather than incident. I did cut enormously. Bob Gottlieb, my editor, and a very tactful man as well, made only two suggestions, really. Let me say also that at the time I handed this book in, it was 800 typewritten pages, and his first reaction was that it's the most upsetting book he's ever read, and it's a splendid, splendid book, and he would publish it just as is.

I said to him, "Well, if you have any suggestions. . . ."And he said, "Well, of course, we'll talk about it. . . ." It was down to about 600-625 typewritten pages when it was finally submitted. And that's an enormous amount of cutting. He never said *cut,* but on the basis of his suggestions, I went back and made my own corrections.

With this suggestion in mind, I cut something like a third of the first 200 pages—about 60 pages—without cutting a single incident; it was all in terms of language or dialogue.

Even in its final version, one of the general criticisms against the book is that it's too long and that it does tend to be repetitious. Other people take this repetitious quality—they don't use that word—if they *don't* like the book, it's repetitious; if they *like* it, it has a recurring and cyclical structure, like the theme in a Beethoven symphony.

Q. *Now—this being quite unusual—your sympathetic central character is an atheist; was there any reaction to this, say by members of the clergy?*

A. None whatsoever. One of the nicest and earliest letters I got was from a member of the clergy on the faculty of Notre Dame. This flabbergasted me. I remember I was in the office at *McCall's* when I got the envelope from Notre Dame, and it was addressed to me at Simon & Schuster, which meant it was in reference to the book. A chill went through me—the same kind of chill I got when I received this letter from the Air Force Academy—you know: *here it comes . . .* until I knew what was inside . . . and then I was amazed and delighted.

Then I realized that my amazement comes from my own naïveté about other people. I've been very naïve about the Republican mind, because a few friends I have who are Republicans embraced this book immediately; I thought it was a liberal book, and they said "No, it's not a liberal book, it's anti-everything."

And I was very naïve about the mind of the intellectual Catholic or the intellectual religious leader—a friend who was educated at Marquette told me about the Jesuit Catholic as opposed to many of the superstitions and practices and narrowmindedness of other Catholics. The book got a good review in *Jubilee,* which is a Catholic publication, and a fairly good review in the University of Scranton, which, I think, reads for the Index and classifies books.

But Yossarian is the kind of atheist—I'm not sure he's an atheist—

Q. *Well, I'm taking his word for it—*

A. Does he say he's an atheist?

Q. *Sure.*

A. When?

Q. *When he's talking to Scheisskopf's wife on Thanksgiving.*

A. Oh, he had that argument over God. He says to her, "I thought you didn't believe in God." And she says, "I don't believe in God as much as you don't, but the God I don't believe in is a humane God." So I suppose that is a giveaway, . . . but I don't conceive of Yossarian as an atheist any more than I conceive of the chaplain as necessarily believing in God.

I see Yossarian as having no positive attitude on the subject, and I see the chaplain as having no definite attitude on the subject. I would prefer to think of Yossarian as an atheist when pushed for an answer, but also as someone who regards any discussion of it as having no relation to the problems of the moment.

I don't think he's un-Christian in his feelings if we take the term Christian to mean what it ought to mean.

Q. *Why did you have an Assyrian as the central character?*

A. Because I was looking for two things. I got the idea, frankly, from James Joyce's placing Bloom in Dublin. I wanted somebody who would seem to be *out*side the culture in every way—ethnically as well as others.

Now, because America is a melting pot, there are huge concentrations of just about every other kind of nationality. I didn't want to give him a Jewish name, I didn't want to give him an Irish name, I didn't want to symbolize the white Protestant—but somebody who was almost a *new* man, and I made him Assyrian (but what I was ignorant of, for one thing, his name is not Assyrian; I've since been told it's Armenian).

But I wanted to get an extinct culture, somebody who could not be identified either geographically, or culturally, or sociologically— somebody as a person who has a capability of ultimately divorcing himself completely from all emotional and psychological ties.

Q. *There was some speculation by a couple of my friends that you got the idea from William Saroyan's "Twenty Thousand Assyrians."*

A. It was from that story that I first learned the Assyrians were extinct, or almost extinct. But my purpose in doing so was to get an outsider, a man who was *intrinsically* an outsider, who had the capability of being a complete outsider. It's very hard for a person really to shake off all his roots.

I like to think that I am not Jewish, but certain tastes for foods, certain odors, associations. . . .

Q. *If you like Chinese food, too, that doesn't make you Chinese.*

A. No, not the same way. I don't like Chinese food. And I don't like *Jewish* food. I think Jewish food is worse than Chinese food. But there's a consciousness. Even if *I* could forget it, other people won't let me forget it completely. And I imagine this is true of everybody. I have certain friends from the South who are always self-conscious.

That's the big myth about this country, by the way—the melting pot.

It isn't. They never melted. I think everybody in this country has a minority complex. Even the majority—they're guilty about being the majority.

Yossarian will be able even to be outside his own family tradition. You know, his family is never mentioned—I *think* it's never mentioned—brothers, sisters, father, mother. I forget now whether I refer to his grandmother and aunt, or other children's on the block. But he has no family. I'm not sure where he came from.

His background—you don't know whether he went to college or not—you assume he did because he gets in certain discussions and conversations which would presuppose a degree of education. I wanted to be vague in those areas, but the name would be the same, without making it one of these Restoration names, where the name itself suggests a word.

Q. *My biggest shock in the book was to find out that Yossarian's first name was John.*

A. I thought that was funny to mention just once. That it should be a name like John. There were certain instances in there where I just could not avoid putting something in because it made me laugh. I think, too, that he should have a first name, so that he doesn't become completely a symbol. I wanted to give him some orientation.

You know, he's not a perfect hero. There are certain things he does of which I don't approve. He has certain flaws in relationship to women, for example. Now, to an extent, it's joyous and robust, but it's not *nice*—it's not really gracious on his part—never to think of this girl by her name, but always as Nately's whore.

And there are other instances, in which he reacts—well, when he punches Nately in the nose, I think, is an indication of the extreme emotional state he's in, that he'd do this, but he himself is contrite immediately afterward.

I certainly didn't want him to become the ideal hero. He's human, and the temptation to sell out when he's offered and he agrees to it—is another indication of that. And I think *John* just puts him right back where he belongs.

If he were English, I probably would have called him Charlie, because the word Charlie in England has certain associations; it's a synonym for *chump*. A John is the name that call girls use to identify customers, so it's so typically *nebbish,* you know?

Q. *Just for the benefit of people not in the know, what's the translation of Lieutenant Scheisskopf's name?*

A. Shithead.

Q. *Thank you.*

A. Yeah, but who's not in the know?

Q. *I wasn't in the know; somebody had to tell me.*

A. *I* didn't know; I had to ask my secretary. When I got to him, and I had to give him a name, I decided I'd want to call him the German translation of shithead, and my secretary's roommate then was a Fulbright scholar from Germany, so I wrote down, "Find out. . . ."

But there again, that let me use an inside joke which pleased me very much, and possibly which other people didn't notice. At one point in dialogue, someone says, "I wonder what that Shithead is up to"—with a capital S there. I have a number of things like that which I like to think are only mine; it gives me an edge on the world. But one by one, I give them away.

Q. *All right, how about the background of the chaplain being an Anabaptist?*

A. There again, the explanation is similar to the one that accounts for Yossarian's name. I am not that well informed about religion, but I assume that Anabaptists are either extinct or not very militant. I was looking, again, for a religion that would sound familiar and yet would not have associations with any of our established religions.

So, the chaplain, by virtue of being associated with this kind of faith, could then be capable of certain acts, certain thoughts, and sympathies. They'd be a little more plausible, rather than anybody associated with a religion with which we're familiar, because people who think in stereotypes—well, people *are* stereotypes to begin with—and you don't want a rabbi or a Baptist minister, or a Catholic priest acting too far outside the stereotype or the circumference of behavior which *other* people think limits his action. They may not exist, but people have conceptions of how other people's professions act.

This gives the chaplain a certain amount of latitude of reaction and response in actions. Also, I didn't want him to be either sympathetic or non-sympathetic to any of these groups. He's really a religious man, but he's a nondenominational minister.

Q. *Jacques in* Candide *was an Anabaptist—*

A. I didn't know that. I've never read *Candide*.

Q. *That's funny, because some people I know have thought all along that this was one of your private jokes.*

A. I'll tell you, I got this letter from an English instructor who wanted to do a paper on *Catch-22,* and he asked me a whole load of questions, with a certain intent to know the symbolic value, and I replied as honestly as I could. He was right, I had not thought of it, that one of the prevailing ideas was one of withdrawal. It had not occurred to me. I know I have characters disappear, and I have characters who disappear by dying, and I have Yossarian disappear at the end. I had not seen this pattern that extensively. So I learned something from him.

But then he got to miracle ingredient Z-247, which is mentioned at the beginning as Yossarian is boasting, "I'm Pepsodent, I'm Tarzan, I'm miracle ingredient Z-247. . . ." He looked that up and found it's an element called Einsteinium, named after Einstein.

And then, toward the end, in that chapter, "The Eternal City," Einstein becomes the universal hero when Yossarian, just brooding, subtracted all the people who were suffering and all the people afflicted, and you might be left with Albert Einstein and an old violinist somewhere.

Now he had linked these two up!

Q. *You mean the secret ingredient and this reference to Einstein?*

A. Yes. He said he can't believe that's just accidental. That I picked this ingredient Einsteinium because of Albert Einstein.

Q. *And it was pure coincidence?*

A. Yes, I didn't know this. I just picked Z-247 right out of the blue.

Q. *In the process of writing* Catch-22, *did you ever change your mind about how you were going to end it?*

A. No. The ending was written long before the middle was written. I suppose right after I sold the book, I was riding on the subway one day, and I actually wrote the words to the ending—this was perhaps four years before the book was finished—and I didn't change it once.

I couldn't see any alternative ending. It had a certain amount of integrity, not merely with the action of the book—that could've permitted anything—but with the moral viewpoint of the book; the heavy suffusion of moral content which is in there, it seemed to me, required a resolution of *choice* rather than of accident.

Q. *But you know what people will say—and this is one of the things I meant before when I asked about people who might've found the book* *objectionable—Yossarian deserts at the end. Now this is what people always say about pacifists and conscientious objectors: If this is the moral, then everybody should desert, and we would've lost the war.*

A. I thought I had gone beyond that point by a discussion preceding his act of running. The last chapter or two is almost in the nature of disputation, in which all the possibilities are discussed and resolved. The answer to that one—that if everybody deserts—then he would be a damn fool *not* to.

When he says, "I'm tired, I have to think of myself, my country is safe now," he's told, "Well, suppose everyone felt that way," and he says, "Well, I'd be a damn fool to feel differently."

I also tried to make it very evident that the war was just about over.

Q. *Would it have made any difference if the war weren't over?*

A. Oh, certainly. I mean if this book had been set two or three years earlier, before the beachhead, then it would be a completely different book.

Q. *Suppose he had flown that many missions, and it was still the middle of the war?*

A. Well, if the book were written then—if he had that many missions and the other conditions were the same, that he were being asked to fly more purely to help a superior officer achieve a promotion—then I would've had him desert, because the replacements are waiting there, as they are at the end of the book; there are replacements ready. So there would not have been any great loss as far as the military effort were concerned.

But if you postulate *this* situation: It's right after Pearl Harbor, and we *don't* have enough planes, and we *don't* have enough men, and Hitler *is* in a dominant and threatening position, then it would be a completely different situation.

I regard this essentially as a peacetime book. What distresses me very much is that the ethic that is often dictated by a wartime emergency has a certain justification when the wartime emergency *exists*, but when this thing is carried *over* into areas of peace—when the military, for example, retains its enormous influence on affairs in a peacetime situation, and where the same demands are made upon the individual in the cause of national interest; the line that I like very much is when Milo tells Yossarian that he's jeopardizing his traditional freedoms by exercising them—when this wartime emergency ideology is transplanted to peacetime, then you have this kind of lag which leads not only to absurd situations, but to very tragic situations.

I worked over certain lines very carefully. On that loyalty oath crusade, I don't remember the actual words, but a sentence is used to the effect that the combat men soon found themselves at the mercy of the administrators appointed to serve *them*. You have this inversion.

Now this is the kind of thing that happens very easily. There's no question that policemen are public servants, but they're *not* in a position of servitude in relation to the people that they're supposed to serve.

There's a kind of blindness which did carry over to peacetime. I recognize the difference that if a house is on fire you grab something and run out and you leave the door open; if the house is not on fire then it should be locked up.

The stimulus for certain action justifies an action. If the stimulus is not there and the action exists anyway, then you've got a right to examine why you're doing it.

Q. *In the end, Yossarian deserts in order to find sanity in Sweden—*

A. But he's not going to get there, he knows that.

Q. *He's not?*

A. Oh, no. I mean he's told, "You'll never get there." And he says, "I know, but I'll try."

Q. *People aren't sure of this, just as they're not sure whether Franny is pregnant or not—*

A. They're not sure because they're hopeful he'll get there, I suppose. For one thing, he's choosing the wrong way. You could get there by rowing the way Orr did, but he's going to Rome, and he's told two or three times, "You'll never make it." Or, "You can't get there from here." But he says, "Well, at least I'll try."

There's also implicit—well, it's not implicit if people miss it—that this is an act of opposition or an act of protest. It's the only way left that he *can* protest without cutting his own head off. And he doesn't choose to do that; he's not a martyr. But the very act of *doing* what he does will stir up things, will stir up a certain amount of talk and dissension, will embarrass his superior officers. I don't think Sweden is paradise.

Q. *That's what my question was going to be. Whether or not Yossarian gets there, do you think Sweden doesn't have Catch-22?*

A. Oh, I don't know. Sweden was important to me as a *goal*, or an objective, a kind of Nirvana. It's important, if you're in a situation which is imperfect to an extent where it's uncomfortable or painful, that you have some *objective* to move toward in order to change that situation.

Now, in Yossarian's situation—his environment, his society, the world; and it's not just America, it's the world itself—the monolithic society closes off every conventional area of protest or corrective action, and the only choice that's left to him is one of ignoble acceptance in which he can profit and live very comfortably—but nevertheless ignoble—or *flight,* a renunciation of that condition, of that society, that set of circumstances.

The only way he can renounce it without going to jail is by deserting it, trying to keep going until they capture him. I like to think of him as a kind of spirit on the loose. You know, he is the only hope left at the end of the book. Had he accepted that choice. . . .

Q. *Is he the only hope? What about the chaplain and Major Danby?*

A. Well, until Yossarian makes that decision, he is the only hope. Major Danby and the chaplain are sort of inspired by him. But, remember, a consequence of his accepting the compromise that's offered him—the rest of the men will then continue to fly more missions without protesting.

Now all the way through, there is this theme about the bulk of the men either being *indifferent* to what's happening to them, or not *knowing* what's happening to them. It occurs in their acceptance of Milo. Even in Yossarian's acceptance of Milo. Yossarian is actually fond of Milo, and I am too, as an individual. There's a certain purity of purpose about him. Even about his hypocrisy. It's not nearly as malignant as other characters in the book. Although he does the most damage.

There's that situation when Yossarian is kidding Milo about the time the mess sergeant poisoned the men: put laundry soap in the sweet potatoes to prove that the men don't know what's good for them. They all came down with this epidemic of diarrhea. And Milo said, "I guess that showed him how wrong he was." And Yossarian said, "No, on the contrary, it showed him how right he was. The men lapped it up and clamored for more." They *knew* they'd been poisoned, though they didn't know how, or why, and they really didn't care.

Now Yossarian doesn't care—this does not motivate him—this business of selling out the other people. At this point he has become estranged from them, as individuals. But one of the consequences of his accepting the medal would be that everybody *else* would continue to fly more missions without protest.

And yet there is also this hint of dissatisfaction, because while he's ostracized in the daytime, at night different people keep popping up and asking him the same question, "How are you doing?" But in the daytime they won't associate themselves with him. Even Appleby, who has been the perfect model of a very good combat man, begins to have misgivings toward the end and pops up out of the darkness to tell him that they're going to offer you this deal, and he's beginning to become disillusioned with the concept of following orders because they're orders.

Q. *Let me just read this little clipping to you—it sounds as if it's right out of your book:*

STOCKHOLM, NOV. 6 [AP]—Security arrangements within the Swedish armed forces are under scrutiny following the recent disappearance of 24,000 secret documents from the offices of the Comptroller General of the Armed Forces, it was disclosed today.

The documents were gone for nine days before a civilian truck driver returned them, saying he had picked them by mistake.

The documents contained full information on Swedish amunition supplies, estimated ammunition needs in case of mobilization and locations of Swedish munition dumps.

Security police said the truck driver, employed by an electronic firm, had orders to pick up eight boxes of electronics equipment at the Comptroller General's office.

A. It's not out of *Catch-22*; I like to think that *Catch-22* is right out of circumstances like *that*. Things like this are inevitable. I think if you want to start clipping paragraphs from newspapers, you'll find that organization today, any organized effort, must contain the germ of continuing disorganization.

The most effective business enterprise, I should think, is a single proprietorship, where one man goes into business for himself and has to hire nobody. The next best possibly is two men as partners; they work harder—there must be some kind of mathematical ratio, particularly when it involves government, I think, because government is so *huge*.

And that includes the Army, for example. You're dealing with millions of people, and there are certain personality- or mental-types that are attracted to that kind of work, either because they can't get a job anywhere else, or because they like doing that.

I cannot imagine anybody who's really ambitious, anybody with any real talent, anybody of any real intelligence, choosing to place himself within a large organization, where he functions in relationship to dozens or hundreds of other people, because every contact is an impairment of his efficiency.

And the kind of person who would stamp documents or classify documents is a kind of person that would not normally be expected to excel in the matter of efficiency or in the matter of making astute judgments, value-judgments.

Q. *But you know that intelligent people do go into large organizations; the trend is more and more toward that—*

A. I'm speaking mainly of government. I would say no, that there are certain types of intelligence that do well in business; I think that to succeed in business—and this is based on limited observations, but personal observations—to really get to the higher echelon of a large company requires at least one special kind of intelligence, and requires a great deal of energy and hard work and ambition.

At the same time, the company, the organization that these people manage, is *incredible*. I mean, nothing in my book—nothing in the wildest satire—goes beyond it. The inter-office rivalries; the mistakes in communications; the difficulties of finding people to promote who can do a job well—the amount of waste in the life of any corporation, at the least the ones I've been with, is just extraordinary.

Now, on the other hand, it's hard to find anybody you'd classify as an intellectual as being associated with a business. To me, and I think to most people who have a high degree of intelligence, creative intelligence, business is boring after a certain point. There really are no new challenges.

The kind of choice becomes between showing the gross profit 4 million dollars one year, how do we boost it to 4½ million the next year, how do we keep it from slipping back—and after a while you really don't give a damn.

And I begin to wonder whether the people involved *really care* about it as a profit thing. I think they care about it in terms of (1) their own security and (2) their own ego-fulfillment. It becomes a personal challenge rather than distributing more gaskets.

I don't think they really care about the stockholders—the widow who is dependent on increased dividends—it's just even like a beaver building a dam. A beaver builds a dam—I don't know why a beaver wants a dam, by the way, but I have a feeling that it may not even *need* the dam—it builds a dam because it's a *beaver*. And a person trained to one occupation, even when he gets to the top, he continues doing accountancy because he's an *accountant*.

Q. *I have a few real-life items in mind which, I think, say more about what Catch-22 is than any definition possibly could, and I'd like to get whatever reactions they evoke in you. Item: The Department of Welfare has finally revised a long-standing rule so that now, when a public assistance case is closed because of the death of the person who had been receiving the public assistance, it's no longer necessary that the deceased person be notified by mail that he won't get any further public assistance.*

A. It does not surprise me at all. That's like that educational session in the beginning of the book, with the rule Colonel Korn employs: to cut off these embarrassing questions, the only ones who would be allowed to ask questions were those who never did.

But it does not surprise me. There is a law of life: People in need of help have the least chance of getting it. Here again, we can almost establish a mathematical relationship. The chance of a person getting help is in inverse proportion to the extent of his need.

And this is true of mental cases; this is true in social work; it's certainly true in business; it's true of people who want credit; it's true of friendship.

Now, that happens with Major Major too. I hate to keep referring to my book—I *love* to keep referring to my book—there's a line about Major Major: Because he needed a friend so desperately he never found one.

I think it's certainly true of mental cases. A person who's in out-and-out need, who's on the verge of suicide, who *is* paranoic on the strength of it, is going to get no help from anybody; a mild neurotic will be encouraged to see a psychiatrist, his friends will want to help him and indulge him, but when the need becomes critical, then—if I might quote an old philosopher—goodbye, Charlie.

Q. *Do you think that, in the film version of* Catch-22, *Major Major should be played by Henry Fonda or by an actor who looks like Henry Fonda?*

A. Assuming that that's left in the movie version, then I would say an actor who either *looks* a little like Henry Fonda or who looks nothing at *all* like Henry Fonda.

But, you know, I must have 40 to 60 characters in this book; there's so much, just physically, that won't be able to go into a picture. And you start thinking, what are those things that are most valuable, which you want to keep? One of the first things you have to put in the non-priority category are those things which are funny and nothing else.

And what are most valuable? Well, the things of continuity, the theme of insanity accepted without any eye-blinking, the feeling of frustration—of impotence, actually—a succession of scenes where the characters just can't *do* anything, physical or mental.

This chapter that comes earlier, that people don't talk about as much as I thought they would, which impresses me enormously every time I think of it—it's a scene in the nose of the plane, where Yossarian is there with Aarfy, the navigator, and he tries to tell him to go out to the back of the plane, and Aarfy smiles—because he's not afraid of the flak, and he does not hear what Yossarian is saying.

And Yossarian—mounting frustration—between guiding the pilot out, turning around and being poked in the ribs by Aarfy, and hitting the ceiling because he thinks he's dying, and then finally he's slamming Aarfy with all his might, and Aarfy keeps *smiling*—it's like hitting a sofa pillow. And he bursts into tears in utter frustration; the whole thing has become so unreal to him. Well, there's a sense of inability to get across something so simple in a time of danger.

The truth is so simple and so evident. Later on, he's bleeding, he's wounded, and Aarfy is there again. And you have almost the same scene repeated. He thinks he's been hit in the testicles—he hollers, "I lost my balls!"—he's sitting in a puddle of blood, and Aarfy doesn't hear him, and doesn't understand. And Yossarian says, "I'm dying and nobody knows."

The truth—the dangers—are so obvious and so simple, yet he can't make himself understood. That is something I'd want to keep in the picture version. I want to keep this sense of injustice—the element of the tribe—the judges waiting to judge, having this tremendous amount of power of force behind them.

Q. *Would you care to say a few words about the art of protest?*

A. I think the only people left that I'm capable of admiring are those people who *do* protest, and at grave risk to themselves. The colored people, CORE, the sit-ins, the students evoke a feeling of admiration I can't recall ever having for anybody else. They are the heroes of the time.

And there's also a natural sympathy for the underdogs, and when the underdog is on the side of a principle that is so patently just . . . the photographs you see every fall of children going to school, little colored girls in their pretty dresses, and then you have these raving lunatics with this *phenomenal* ugliness of hatred on their faces—the contrast leads me to believe that the white race could profit a great deal if intermarriage became more prevalent; it's something I think that the Southern white might do everything to encourage for his *own* good. The real difficulty we find today is that there are at *least* two sides to many questions. It's terrible when people can't see the other person's point of view; it's even worse when you *can* see both points of view, because then you're almost incapable of taking action with any degree of conviction.

Q. *Now, do you think that the work of a sanitation man, pragmatically, may be more important than yours? We can do without your book, but we can't do without the sanitation man—yet you get more respect than the sanitation man. Do you think you should?*

A. I *get* it. I get it for reasons that other people get respect. There is nothing dignified and noble about labor. As far as I can see, there's never been anything noble or dignified about labor.

The people that a society glorifies and exalts—and this is true even in a workers' paradise—are the people who get their rewards by not working as hard. You're dealing with the factor of status. As long as we live, the man at the bottom is not going to be treated as well as the man at the top. The man who chlorinates the water we drink is an essential person, but he's easily *replaced,* I suppose. Fifteen million people could do whatever he does.

I think eventually that's what's going to happen to our astronauts. Millions of people, I suppose, would volunteer to be astronauts. If they called for volunteers to be the first man to the moon, and the odds were against getting back, there'd be no shortage of people.

The ultimate contribution there is not the guy in the capsule, but the guy at M.I.T.—it's a scientific achievement. The human element might be necessary, but the rare skills are what produced it. It's a hard thing to invent the engine which drives a sanitation truck. We've always had a man with a shovel to throw the garbage in.

The Joy Catcher

W. J. Weatherby/1962

From *The Guardian*, 20 November 1962, 7.

It has taken us a long time to see the funny side of the Second World
War. I don't mean the safe jokes that ignore the horror; we have had
more than enough of those. But it is only recently that we seem to have
been able to face up to the funny side of the horror itself. Understandably enough, when literature was first demobbed from propaganda
service in 1945, writers concentrated on describing what the censor had
forbidden—the naked horror of the dead. Then came the Cold War, the
Korean War, the nuclear threat, and for a long time it was these added
horrors that obsessed the writers and their public, one presumably
influencing the other, though we cannot be sure which one it was.
Nothing much has changed, the Cold War is still with us, and yet
recently we have started to look satirically as well as realistically at
what went on in the Second World War—at what goes on in all wars.

The first sign of the change I remember was when a prominent satirist
on the American night-club circuit told me he was getting away with
"*real* war jokes" without being accused of sick humour. But the real
breakthrough for most people was probably the best-seller, *Catch-22*, in
which the author, Joseph Heller, makes good fun of the wartime defini-
tions of Courage and Cowardice and reveals the hypocrisy behind so
much of any war effort. It is hard to imagine his book being a best-seller
even five years ago, and we can only conjecture as to why it has proved
so much in keeping with the general mood now when the Cold War is
still with us. It may be that the only way we can live indefinitely in this
state of tension, with this kind of reality, is to be coldly, even cynically,
realistic about it. Just as the poor man must face reality every day
whereas the rich man need not, so perhaps now we must face the reality
of war, whereas before the nuclear threat we could be fooled by the
romance of it.

Mr. Heller—a round, realistic New Yorker of 39—generously
brooded over this theory at a meeting at O. Henry's Steak House at

West Fourth Street and Sixth Avenue in Greenwich Village, which is on
the site of the old "Hell Hole" where the young Eugene O'Neill tried to
drink himself to death. "I think people are more realistic now. I think
we've got to be to live with the world the way it is," he said sitting with
his back to the world of Sixth Avenue. "There's more cant and more
hypocrisy and more hollow rationalisation being directed at humanity
than ever before and it becomes so obvious that fewer and fewer people
are taken in by it. Yet it persists, so that Americans can still talk of this
as the land of liberty, the land of freedom and democracy, while at the
same time they are trying to cope with many widespread problems
arising from the exhaustion of opportunities and the severely limited
freedom of each other and the liberties of large groups, without being
aware of any inconsistency and not being troubled by it." Mr. Heller
shook his head wonderingly over Man's inconsistencies, just as O'Neill
may have done on the same spot 50 years ago. "We have situations in
which those business organisations which campaign most vociferously
against increasing taxes are the same ones which form illegal agree-
ments with other organisations so that they can sell goods to the Government at artificial prices."

"Even in war-time?"

"Of course."

"And you mean people are more aware of this cynicism, they are less
willing now to be kidded?"

"I think so. It's a crazy world. Don't forget war now touches everybody—even in peacetime. Pretty well every young man in this country
has a period of military service to look forward to which most of them
will enjoy tremendously. They will have no responsibility and more
freedom than they will probably ever have again after they marry and
settle down."

"What do you think *Catch-22*'s reception would have been if it had
been published, say, ten years ago?"

Mr. Heller grinned. "I can't speak for the readers, only for myself.
I couldn't have written it ten years ago. Let me go back a bit. I was
born in Brooklyn, I went to college on the GI Bill of Rights after the
war, I wrote a few short stories which were published, then I did some
teaching in Pennsylvania, but I wasn't happy away from New York so
I came back and became a copywriter in an advertising agency. In
Pennsylvania I had had a period when I virtually stopped writing. It was

only when I returned to the more competitive world of New York I
began again. I had wanted to write a war novel but those I read were not
very interesting to me. There was a terrible sameness about books being
published and I almost stopped reading as well as writing. I didn't want
just to write the kind of book I had stopped reading. Then Evelyn
Waugh got through to me, and then Nabokov and Céline. They all did
something unique in organising the novel and they showed me the
possibilities still inherent in it."

An O. Henry waiter came to review our situation, looked glumly at
our glasses still half full, and wandered off again. "Then there were two
conversations with two friends which influenced me," said Mr. Heller.
"Each of them had been wounded in the war, one of them very seriously
and the other less so. The first one told some very funny stories about
his war experiences, but the second one was unable to understand how
any humour could be associated with the horror of war. They didn't
know each other and I tried to explain the first one's point of view to the
second. He recognised that traditionally there had been lots of graveyard
humour, but he could not reconcile it with what he had seen of war. It
was after that discussion that the opening of *Catch-22* and many incidents in it came to me."

The waiter hovered nearby, looking longingly at our glasses, so we
dutifully emptied them for him and he brought two more replacements.
"Nabokov in *Laughter in the Dark* takes an extremely flippant approach
to situations deeply tragic and pathetic, and I began to try for a similar
blending of the comic and the tragic so that everything that takes place
seems to be grotesque yet plausible. I was thirty when I began to write
and it took me nearly eight years though a publisher bought it when it
was only about a third done and four years away from completion."

The film rights have already been sold and Mr. Heller would be very
pleased if Orson Welles were the man to make the film, though no
decision has yet been made. He is also at work on a musical comedy,
on a film script and on plans for a new novel. Another *Catch-22*? Mr.
Heller brooded. "It will be like it in approach but otherwise completely
different." And how would he describe the "approach"? He brooded
again. "One of cynicism, seasoned with bitterness and mingled with
pessimism." Was it as grim as that? "Well," he added as we emerged
on to Sixth Avenue, "it should also satisfy my appetite for joy."

A Few of the Jokes, Maybe Yes, But Not the Whole Book

Susan Braudy/1967

From *The New Journal* 26 November 1967, 7, 9–10. Reprinted by permission of the author.

> *"I believe that Joseph Heller is one of the most extraordinary talents now among us."* —Robert Brustein, 1961
>
> *"I like a lecture that mentions* Catch-22.*"*
> —Yale Freshman, 1967

"I had lunch today with Joseph Heller. You know what he talked about during lunch. Lunch. He talked about lunch," said a graduate student. "Orange drink at Yale. Either that guy is wearing a mask or else he didn't write that book."

"Joseph Heller, an easy-laughing man," was the way *Vogue* magazine saw Heller a year after *Catch-22* was published. *Vogue* held a manicured finger to the fashion winds and called Heller a new trend in fashion, along with the high-waisted dress and the overblouse.

But Heller doesn't laugh easily and he did write *Catch-22*. When Heller, the master of tragi-comic farce, laughs, he sounds only obliging. It's as though he were reading, hahahaha, from a script of the conversation.

When he writes, Heller uses humor to lure his audience into unexpected confrontations with a tragic truth. Suddenly the immediacy of your laughter brings you face to face with man's vulnerability. But in real life Heller uses his humor to keep people from looking too closely at him and, more important, to defend himself from the truths he too easily sees.

"Of course he's masked," says a close friend of Heller's. "He'd be an open wound otherwise. There's nothing arty about Joe's mask, either. He's often mysterious because he's so plain."

"Today's Rosh Hashanah, a religious holiday, right? No classes on Rosh Hashanah. So what're you doing here?"

Heller greets the playwriting students waiting for him in the gloomy hall of the Drama School annex. He sees he is the only one enjoying his joke. He laughs loudly and shifts his gum massage stick from the side to the front of his mouth.

"All right, you convinced me. We'll have our class."

This semester Heller is teaching a graduate playwriting seminar and an undergraduate creative writing class at Yale, while the Drama School is producing his new play, *We Bombed in New Haven,* which opens December 4.

Heller is a thick and handsome 44. He looks like he might have made a lot of money publishing popular art books in New York. His face is large and fleshed out, but not fat. His large brown eyes seem to stare directly inward as well as outward. He looks prosperous.

Despite the expensive navy or green blazer, the striped shirt and tie, Heller looks tough. Maybe it's the Stim-u-dent toothpick that hangs out of the side of his mouth. Maybe it's his graying curly hair long in the back and in the sideburns, but slicked back from a widow's peak. It could be his broad shoulders or the slight swagger in his walk. The effect is exotic for Yale, but not for the Drama School.

Twenty years ago *Esquire* printed a Heller short story along with a picture of Heller, 24 years old, a junior Phi Beta Kappa at NYU, married, and the owner of a good conduct medal from the war.

In *Esquire'*s picture, his large nose and eyes sit uneasily on a dark, skinny face. He looks scared and underfed. Like most pictures, if you stare at it long enough, the eyes seem to stare directly outward and directly inward at the same time.

"Listen, you're crazy," a tired Heller rubs the back of his neck in the New Haven railroad station. "You've over-researched this article. What do you want to work so hard for? Next time you write an article, take my advice, hand the guy 20 questions and a tape recorder, and that'll be your article."

Heller had agreed to let me interview him on the train back to New York after his Thursday classes. I started to leave him to buy my ticket. "Better take your notes with you," he said, "or I may burn them. Who would be interested in all that junk about me anyway?"

Heller has a thing about money. He enjoys talking about it. A few years ago Heller and Edward Albee were both guests at a small dinner party. Albee wanted to talk Art. But he never got the chance. Heller spent all evening talking about taxes.

"My generation was oriented to the Depression," Heller once said. "When I was in school, we all wanted to get out and make a good living. Today most students do not know what they want to do. They only know what they *don't* want to do—go to war."

In the dining car of the train, Heller begins, "I'm probably going to fall asleep before I can answer any of your questions. Tell me again why you're writing this article. Somebody must be paying you a lot of money to ride into New York with me. You're probably crazy."

He leans across the table and whispers, "If you sit here in the dining car, sometimes you can get a free ride."

Interviewer: "What did you hope to accomplish by writing *We Bombed in New Haven,* Mr. Heller?"

Heller (rolls his handsome head and sighs to the ceiling before he puts a fresh Stim-u-dent in his mouth. He talks like the guy eating at the delicatessen after Saturday morning golf.): "What else, I wanted to make a million dollars."

Interviewer: "No, really."

Heller: "All right. Right now I want to make every woman cry and every man feel guilty when he has to go home and face his sons. What can fathers do about Viet Nam? (Heller pauses and says with emphasis) "You ask what did I mean to accomplish. I meant to write a very good play."

The Resistance has bought tickets for the play to aid the movement against the war. Heller predicts that, if things continue as they are now, in six or eight months 100,000 Americans will be under indictment for breaking laws in draft protests. "This could end the war. They can't put everybody in jail."

Heller believes this war is different from World War II. World War II, he believes, had to be fought.

A little over a year ago, *Holiday* sent Heller (and his wife and two children) back to the air base in Corsica where most of his war, World War II, took place. From there, Heller had flown missions as a wing bombardier.

But Corsica was no longer the place his war had been. His war was over and gone, and he saw that even his travel-weary, ten-year-old son realized it.

"What the grouchy kid didn't realize though was that his own military service was still ahead; and I could have clasped him in my arms to protect him as he stood there, half hanging out of the car with his sour look of irritation."

In *We Bombed in New Haven,* Captain Starkey must personally induct his son into the army. Starkey always does what he is told. He fits into the system, and the system destroys him.

Heller never read Pirandello, but Pirandello's spirit is in the play. The characters are both actors and soldiers at the same time. Their parts and their lives as soldiers are controlled by an existing script that they have read and by a metaphysical script to which only the Major has access.

When another character refuses to die, as the script dictates, the Major is not surprised. Because he has the ultimate script, the Major knows how this man must ultimately die.

One of Heller's playwriting students remarked on the relevance of the play metaphor. "Most guys think they'll go in, play the role of the soldier for two years, and then come back and pick up where they left off. They don't think: go in, play soldier, and be killed. If they knew what Heller's characters know about their own deaths, they wouldn't take it so lightly."

The Drama School publicity people asked Heller if they could advertise the play as a comedy. Heller said no. Even though, he says, if you call it a comedy, more people will probably buy tickets to see it. But Heller uses comedy and satire for other ends. There are many jokes in the first act of the play. But early in the second act, a soldier says, "There'll be no more laughing tonight," and the play moves swiftly to its tragic conclusion.

   Heller (showing no signs of falling asleep as he eats his chicken dinner in the dining coach of the New York train): "I know what you can write about. I'll give you the anecdote about how I happened to write the play."

Heller was born in Coney Island in 1923. In *Show* magazine, he wrote: "Coney Island is beautiful to children and ugly to adults, and, in this respect, it is often typical of life itself."

After graduating from Abraham Lincoln High School in 1941, Heller went to work as a blacksmith's helper in the Norfolk Navy Yard, though at the time he was too skinny to lift a sledge hammer.

He enlisted in the Army Air Corps in 1942, a few months before he would have been drafted. Like Yossarian, Heller figured that the war would be over before he got into it.

"What incredible optimism we had in those days. We believed that any country that tried to take on the US would be knocked off in a week."

First Heller went to armorers' school. Then he transferred to cadet school when rumors began to circulate that armorers became gunners. Gunners didn't last long in combat.

Heller went into combat as a wing bombardier in 1944, two years after he enlisted. He remembers that at first he was disappointed because his missions were milk runs, that is, nobody shot back at his plane.

"I was a jackass. I thought war would be a lot of fun, but I wasn't the only one who was naïve."

Heller listened quietly as a playwriting student told him about Jack Valenti's recent talk in the Law School. Valenti, who is of Italian descent, claimed to have killed 10,000 Italians by bombing during World War II, and used patriotism to explain conscience away.

"If he said that," said Heller quietly, "then he's a schmuck. First, I would suspect he's a liar because no one can keep such accurate count, especially from the air, of how many people are killed when a bomb explodes. Second, if he had indeed killed that many people, he's really something for boasting about it."

Heller says people can fight wars because they don't understand the seriousness of what they are doing. It was not until Heller's 37th mission, his second over Avignon, when a gunner in his own plane was wounded, that Heller came to a startling realization. "Good God, they're trying to kill me, too," he thought. After that it wasn't very much fun.

Yossarian, the main character of *Catch-22*, had his moment of truth about the nature of war in a flight over Avignon:

Yossarian ripped open the snaps of Snowden's flak suit and heard himself scream wildly as Snowden's insides slithered down to the floor in a soggy pile and just kept dripping out. . . . Here was God's plenty, all right, he thought bitterly as he stared—liver, lungs, kidneys, ribs,

l bits of the stewed tomatoes Snowden had eaten that day for
Man was matter, that was Snowden's secret. Drop him out a
he'll fall. Set fire to him and he'll burn. Bury him and he'll
rot like other kinds of garbage. The spirit gone, man is garbage. . . .
   "I'm cold," Snowden said. "I'm cold."
   "I am not Yossarian," Heller once said. "He is who I might like to have been, had I the knowledge then that I now have."

When the war ended, Joseph Heller married, spent one year at USC, got his BA from NYU and his MA from Columbia, and won a Fulbright to Oxford.

   He also published two pieces in *Esquire* (one on horse racing) and two in the *Atlantic*.

   Heller's first story appeared in the *Atlantic* in March 1948 with the following *Atlantic* introduction:

   "A veteran, now in his twenty-fifth year, who is thinking and writing in terms of peace, JOSEPH HELLER is a *junior* at New York University, where he is majoring in English and producing short stories which in our judgment give very real promise."

   Heller's second story appeared in the *Atlantic* five months later with the following *Atlantic* introduction:

   "A veteran, now in his twenty-fifth year, who is thinking and writing in terms of peace, JOSEPH HELLER is a *senior* at New York University, where he is majoring in English and producing short stories which in our judgment give very real promise."

   It was while Heller was at NYU that he decided that if he couldn't make it as a writer, he would teach. Then from 1950 to 1952, he taught English at Penn State and didn't like it. So, in 1952, the Hellers moved back to *the city* (the way all New Yorkers refer to New York, no matter where they are) to work for 10 years in the advertising departments of *Time, Look,* and finally *McCall's* magazines.

   While he was on his way to success in the advertising world, Heller wrote *Catch-22*, the novel about the horrors inflicted on people by both war and peacetime bureaucracies. At night, sitting at his kitchen table, Heller wrote a book attacking the kind of bureaucracy he helped perpetuate during the day.

   Friends who summered with the Hellers on Long Beach, Long Island, remember that Joe and Shirley always left parties very early. "The novel, you know," people would say significantly after they'd gone.

During these years, Heller professed to love the advertising game. But he also enjoyed changing jobs. Every time he was given a raise or a promotion, he began looking for a new job. He also kept working steadily on the novel. He did not want to write just any novel. He wanted to write a masterpiece.

Even today, Heller still insists that working in advertising was a great life. People in the advertising departments of magazines like *Time* and *McCall's* were more intelligent and better to be with, he says, than any group he's found since, not excepting any in academic communities.

But when he's pushed, Heller admits that although he enjoyed doing advertising in his 20's and his 30's, he always knew he would get out. He knew he would not have a salaried job his whole life. Still, long lunches, no time clocks, and lots of parties also helped make his work in advertising very desirable to Heller when he had to work.

Heller joined *McCall's* in 1958 as a presentation writer, when Herbert Mayes took over the editorial side of the magazine, during a *McCall's* top management shake-up. In two years, *McCall's* surged from fourth to first place in the women's magazine field.

After *Catch-22* came out, Herbert Mayes complained, "Heller's a hell of a good publicist. Sorry we lost him. What I'd like to know, though, is how he got the time on my time to write that book."

At *McCall's,* Heller prepared slide and film shows, flip charts, and direct mailing to be presented to salesmen selling magazine space and to advertisers buying.

He wrote scripts for "dog and pony shows" which were presentations shown throughout the country to big advertising agencies and prospective clients. It was a million-dollar business. Salaries were high. One travelling show might cost as much as 90 thousand dollars in non-personnel expenses alone.

Heller also organized the yearly sales convention for *McCall's* space salesmen in Nassau in 1961. Heller's slide show "The Pages That Sell" was the main attraction for salesmen at this convention.

But pages of another sort were preoccupying Heller at this point. He took a boat rather than a plane to Nassau, so he could read the galley sheets of *Catch-22*.

While other conventioneers spent night and day boozing it up at the bar, Heller spent his free time out on the beach reading those galleys.

His former associates remember Heller as a great advertising writer with a fantastic sense of the trends of the times and what was important to the people buying.

But they also remember days when Heller would come to the office and announce he was just going to brood and not work. Not everything was parties, long lunches, and trips to Nassau.

"I think Joe escaped from the bureaucracy and all it stood for by writing his novel," says someone who used to work with him. "Just like Orr, the guy who always had horse chestnuts and crab apples in his mouth when it came time to answer important questions, but who managed to row from the Mediterranean all the way to freedom and Sweden."

"Don't forget," he added, "Joe worked on his own escape, that novel, for over eight years."

When rave reviews started coming in, Heller took to carrying them around at work. He became so excited about Brustein's review in the *New Republic* that he told friends Brustein probably wrote better than he did. Heller signed countless books for *McCall's* people, but he never gave anyone free copies. He chided people who brought their copies discounted from Korvette's. But he treated friends to lunch if they promised to check how the book was selling at nearby book stores.

His business friends found it difficult to believe he had actually written *Catch-22*. "C'mon Joe," they would say to him. "A few of the jokes, maybe yes, but not the whole book. You don't have that kind of tragic sense."

In November, 1961, two weeks after publication date, Brustein and Heller met for the first time at the home of the *Village Voice* art critic. Heller was so thrilled about going to parties and meeting famous people during this time that it took him months to catch on that parties had been thrown so that people could meet him. He was the guest of honor.

That night, Heller talked about things he'd been through in the army. He talked about being so high in the clouds that when you hit a bridge, you couldn't tell if there were people on it or not.

Heller took a leave of absence from *McCall's* a few months after *Catch-22* was published, and he never returned. During the next five years he wrote critical and autobiographical articles for national magazines, went to Hollywood to write the "polish" (the final script) for *Sex and the Single Girl,* worked on his next novel which he predicts will be finished in the next two to twelve years, and toured college campuses speaking and reading from *Catch-22.*

Catch-22 was translated into 12 languages, became a best seller in countries like England and Czechoslovakia, and sold more than 3,500,000 copies. Heller sold an option until 1969 on the production rights to Columbia Pictures for a reported $150,000.

Heller is not interested, he says, in whether the book is ever made into a movie. Filming may begin this summer. Mike Nichols was slated some time ago to direct the movie. Alan Arkin was chosen as the movie's star.

It was while Heller was doing reading and speaking tours on *Catch-22* that he conceived of having four actors and an actress do readings from *Catch-22* plus source readings from Shakespeare from which a surprising number of *Catch-22* passages derive.

"Sort of readings and misreadings from Shakespeare," was the way Heller described his plan to a Filmways executive who had bought production rights from Columbia.

But after Heller began to look for a device to give his play more form, he decided to drop *Catch-22,* which was becoming a burden, and to write an original play. His first draft contained Falstaff's speech on honor among other Shakespearean passages, most of which have been cut from the final draft.

At this point, late last fall, Heller came to Yale to give a talk at Calhoun College, during which he described himself as "a born promotion man."

"He's incredible," was the reaction of one Yale student after Heller's speech. "He comes on like a real Madison Avenue fat cat with that born promotion man business. If I were the author of *Catch-22,* I'd bill myself as a born American author."

The next night, Heller had dinner with the Brusteins at their home. During dinner he discussed his idea for the play. Brustein was very excited and encouraged Heller to get to work on it.

The first draft of the first half of the first act appeared in Brustein's mail along with an outline of the rest of the play about a month later. As soon as he read it, Brustein realized that Heller had obviously thought much more deeply about the play than he had let on when they had talked about it.

After four more months of hard work, Heller sent Brustein the second draft of the whole play. Brustein read it and became so excited by the last act that he read it first to his wife, and was still so excited that he called Philip Roth long distance and read it to him.

Brustein then invited Heller to be Playwright-in-Residence for this semester and contracted for Yale Drama School to produce the first production of *We Bombed in* _____. (The title changes each time the play is produced in a different city.) Thus the play would be known first as *We Bombed in New Haven*.

The first public reading of the play in late October was a smash hit. The actors read it before the entire drama school. At the play's end, Heller himself was among those moved to tears.

One student said he didn't see how the play could ever be better. Many agreed they had never heard a first reading so good. The actors sounded so natural that people kept referring back to their scripts to make sure they weren't improvising.

After the reading, Larry Arrick, the director, fresh from the off-Broadway production of *Fragments* by Murray Schisgal, asked students to go and come quietly from rehearsals without disturbing the cast. He also asked them not to sit back and snipe and criticize.

Then Heller, joking in his best *Catch-22* style, told students they could make as much noise as they wanted at rehearsals, and for God's sake, if they had any criticism, please speak up.

That day, Heller remembered all the reasons he had decided to open his play in New Haven. Without Brustein's encouragement, first of all, there might not have been a play at all. Also he viewed his first play as an educational experience. He had felt that at Yale he would have the most creative freedom to develop and change his script.

"The pressure here at Yale," he told his playwriting class while he loosened his tie and unbuttoned the top two buttons on his shirt, "would never be as bad as New York where every jerk you meet wants to change your script."

We Bombed in New Haven went into rehearsal October 30, inside the dark, deserted, and often chilly, old WNHC building on Chapel Street.

After one rehearsal Heller was a nervous wreck. He told his play-writing students about a night of fitful sleeping at the Midtown Motor Inn, tossing and turning in anguish over what he had seen at rehearsal. All night long, maniacs on either side of his room banged walls and played radios. At 5 a.m. a distraught Heller discovered that, in fact, the radio built into his own night table had been on all night.

Heller was now having trouble remembering the reasons he had brought his play to Yale. He had just been told that the actors would not be able to rehearse on stage with props and correct spacing until four days before opening night, because the stage was being used by undergraduates and the San Francisco Mime Troupe. And Stacy Keach, the star of *We Bombed in New Haven,* would not be able to attend the first week and a half of rehearsals.

"They've been rehearsing a different play all this week," Heller said, "It's called *Waiting for Stacy.*"

Heller was also shattered after the first rehearsal to find his stage directions ignored, verbal emphases changed, jokes lost, and continuity continually disrupted.

Lines were dragging that Heller had envisioned as fast repartee. If an actor would say a line as Heller had envisioned it, he would heave a sigh and think, great he's got it. But ten minutes later in another run-through of the same scene, the actor would say the line completely differently.

"I can't understand it," Heller told his playwriting students. "Maybe I just better stay away from rehearsals for my own peace of mind, my own sanity."

The young playwrights had almost all been through bad moments like these. They told Heller that the best thing he could do would be to stop going to rehearsals, until right before the play opened. They assured him that things always spring into shape during final rehearsals with or without the then-broken figure of the playwright.

Heller agreed and seemed to cheer up. But he decided to go to one more rehearsal.

After rehearsal number two, he told his students, huddled in a dark corner watching the play through a glass window, that Anthony Holland and Ron Leibman were adding new comic levels and texture to the characters they played.

"I'm learning. I'm learning," said Heller later that day on the train, "that I wrote a script not a production. In novels, the writer defines and limits his characters, but not in plays. If an actor has any talent and is working with a good director, he will fill out bare words in the script."

But the play was still making Heller very nervous. He decided to stay away for two weeks, cross his fingers, and hope everything would come out all right.

"Otherwise," he said weakly, "I think there will have to be some unpleasantness."

But Heller couldn't stay away for two weeks. He was back one week later for Stacy Keach's first rehearsal. After the rehearsal, he was joking, but he was still very upset.

"Listen, who's nervous," he said, "I'm a veteran of the theater now. After two weeks experience I've learned a lot. I've learned to suffer excruciating torture without making a sound while they blow my play."

But Heller was feeling better. He allowed as how he was beginning to like the theater. He was even beginnng to take actors seriously after a long evening with Ron Leibman.

But Heller had a new worry. In the week that he was gone, the Major had developed a southern accent. Heller said, "I don't like the Major with a southern accent. I don't want the audience to think he's supposed to be Johnson. By projection the play is about the Viet Nam war. Specifically, it's about a very unspecific war."

"The Major is supposed to be as sinister and mysterious as fate or destiny or God. I don't want him to be turned into a southern jingoist."

What will you do after this play, asks a student.

"I don't have a work compulsion, I don't have to write plays or novels. What're you laughing about, Allan? I had one when I was your age, but I don't have one anymore. I just want to write a good novel or a play once in a while. I can make enough money to live doing movie polishes. I can get a certain amount of satisfaction from doing that. I don't always have to be doing great art."

One can understand. *Catch-22* and *We Bombed in New Haven* are both about war, but beyond that they're about the fragility and vulnerability of people, about the wars that people wage against other people and against themselves. When you see and feel this evil, as Heller did over Avignon, you will never forget it, but you can't take the pain of constantly facing it.

    Interviewer: "Isn't it a funny feeling that so many people you don't even know were so moved by your book and will also be moved by your play?"

    Heller: "Not a funny feeling. It's a good feeling. See that guy over there. (He points to a man across the aisle eating soup and engrossed in a paperback.) When my book first came out in paper, I'd get into the subway or train and look at the books people were reading. If the paperback had blue edges, it was Dell. My book is in Dell, so then I'd have to try to see the cover. If the guy was reading my book, it was a good feeling."

Playwright-in-Anguish

Elenore Lester/1967

From *New York Times* 3 December 1967, II, 1, 19. Copyright 1967
by The New York Times Company. Reprinted by permission.

A sharp November blue sky blazed like a pennant above Harkness tower
and the Yale campus was a dazzle of noontime sun. But Joseph Heller,
the playwright-in-anguish, emerging from the Drama School, was at
odds with the picture postcard setting. Heavy-set, dark and brooding,
looking un-chic and un-Ivy League in his spanking new sheepskin
jacket, he lumbered along, weighed down on one side by an overloaded
briefcase.

Rehearsals for Heller's play, *We Bombed in New Haven,* which opens
tomorrow night at the Yale Repertory Theater, had just passed the
halfway mark, and the playwright, author of the long-term-best-selling
novel, *Catch-22,* was feeling a little frayed around the edges as a result
of his first excursion into the theater. He had just gotten word that Mike
Nichols, Barbara Harris, Paul Newman and Walter Kerr were planning
to attend the opening and he wasn't entirely overjoyed.

"I thought we were going to have a good time putting on a play at
Yale, but this way . . ." he shrugged. "You have all the stresses of a
Broadway opening without its actually being Broadway."

He sighed heavily as we set out for an off-campus restaurant. "So it's
like I was telling my psychiatrist," he said in the down-to-earth, sour-
cream-and-pot-cheese Brooklyn accent carefully nurtured by many New
York sophisticates successful in the arts, "It's not that I'm trying to
dominate the director; it's just that I want the director to know what's in
my mind and have the same thing in his mind so that he'll do what I
want him to do without my trying to dominate him."

Having summed up for all time the problem of playwright-director
relations and having done it in terms reminiscent of *Catch-22,* where
simple logic always collides with an absurdly structured universe, Heller
seemed to feel a little better and was able to muster a smile. "You want
to know the real truth?" he asked. "The real truth is that things have

been going beautifully. Larry Arrick, the director, and the actors have
been a revelation to me—the way they've gotten hold of this thing.
After the first week they understood the play better than I did. They've
seen things in it, psychological meanings, I never thought of. Now I see
that actors are real creative artists. They've brought so much imagination and enthusiasm. They're really wonderful, only . . ." he paused
and nose-dived back into his Dostoevskian mood. "The only thing is
I'm not happy."

So what's wrong?

Two things, Heller indicated, carefully, lovingly hanging up his
sheepskin ("it's not really very expensive and I hear they last forever")
and sliding into a booth.

"It's my nature to be suspicious. I just don't trust people. I know it's
not right, but that's the way I am. I'm trying to be flexible and I think I
have been so far. I don't mind making changes—as long as they're on
minor matters. But I'm concerned about my literary personality. I don't
want Joseph Heller distorted. I don't want anything on stage I wouldn't
like to see as a member of the audience, and up to this point we've had
no serious problems. Only—well, I am the way I am, and I'm biting
my nails. And the second thing is I just don't like the theater."

YOU DON'T LIKE THE THEATER ! ! !

"No. And I'm not kidding." He shook his head sadly. "I think it's a
very limited medium. I hardly ever go. Even the few times you see
something good it's never really *that* good. Drama critics are too
generous. They over-praise things."

But how come this play?

"Boredom. What's there to do in the evening if you don't go to the
theater?" he offered reasonably. "You certainly can't watch TV. I had
been working on my new novel—it's about a middle-aged man caught
in a sterile, monotonous, regimented existence, very different in style
and content from *Catch-22,* and I found I had a few hours for meditation every evening, so I started to play around with the idea of dramatiz-
ing *Catch-22.* After a while I found myself with a new set of characters
and new ideas and I started getting really excited about it."

The play, which resembles *Catch-22* insofar as it concerns a group of
men who go on bombing missions, is somewhat abstract. Its setting is
any theater and city in which the play is given. The time is always the
present. The stage illusion is constantly broken by the characters' efforts

to break out of their roles. ("They told me it was something like Pirandello's *Six Characters in Search of an Author*," said Heller. "But I had
never seen or read the play. I finally read it and I don't think much of
it.") The Yale Drama School publicity office describes the play as a
"surreal comedy of war"—a description that raises Heller's hackles.

"War is no comedy; it's a tragedy. The play is a drama with a tragic
ending. And by the way, I don't like the cuteness and archness in the
title. It just happens that it's an accurate one. The men really do bomb
in New Haven. I realize I'm considered a humorous fellow, but the truth
is I wouldn't bother writing comedy," he said. "People find things to
laugh at in *Catch-22* and probably they will in the play, but that's just
because laughter is part of life. The things I write are funny only up to
a point. Actually I am a very morbid, melancholy person. I'm preoccupied with death, disease and misfortune." He cast a long look of un-
utterable pain over his hot roast beef sandwich.

"No, don't classify me as a writer of black comedy either," he continued. "I don't want to be grouped with *those* writers." The writers
he really loves, Heller explained, are Shakespeare and T. S. Eliot. And
if the Heller humor is to be compared with anyone else's, he'd like it to
be Nathanael West, or Nabokov, or maybe Aristophanes. The modern
dramatist he most enjoys is Beckett, "but I'd rather read him than see
him staged."

Heller doubts whether he'll do much more serious writing for the
theater although he thinks he might like to try a musical. He has interrupted work on the novel to handle a few Hollywood "polish" jobs,
among them *Sex and the Single Girl*, and to write *We Bombed in New
Haven*, which took him four or five months. And now the 44-year-old
author is involved in a teaching schedule that takes him to the University of Pennsylvania one day a week and to Yale another day for courses
in fiction and dramatic writing.

In the past seven years Heller's reputation as a novelist has assumed
the legendary proportions that Salinger once claimed on campus.
Heller's regular-guy manner and apparently offhand teaching technique
have reinforced his popularity among Yale students.

"We can't go on with our regular discussion today," he announced to
his students as I entered the dramatic writing class with him. "You
know, about whether _____ _____ is really a fairy. The *New York
Times* is here." Then he slumped in his seat and asked for the latest

gossip about the progress of his play (Drama School students may observe all rehearsals). They chatted and Heller mentioned that he had asked to have a bit of stage business taken out. "I found it offensive," he said. "You see, I'm a Puritan." The students looked a little shocked, but they relaxed and smiled indulgently when he continued, "I don't like to see things on stage that seem to expose an actor or actress to any indignity." (He later amplified this and told me he doesn't like any character in fiction, even contemptible ones, treated with contempt. "I always come to sympathize deeply with my villains.") Finally Professor Heller was ready to deal with the subject of the day—Aristotle's *Poetics*.

In the classroom the playwright and students discussed Aristotle's theories of drama and in a nearby rehearsal hall the *We Bombed in New Haven* company wrestled with the problems of bringing a play to life. Director Larry Arrick, formerly associated with the Second City company and most recently director of Murray Schisgal's *Fragments*, took a break and slipped into a luncheonette for a bowl of pea soup. He had the intense look of a man in the throes of creation and clearly would have preferred to be left alone with his pea soup, but was willing to talk between sips.

"This is the best company I've ever worked with anywhere," said Arrick. (It includes students and professionals, among the latter Anthony Holland and Ron Leibman, both Second City alumni, and Stacy Keach, who created the title role in Barbara Garson's *MacBird*.) "And the play is marvelous—its subject is war, but its theme is not. War is a metaphor here for a game these people are playing. We are all playing a kind of game in this country today, you know. We go to the theater or we look at Picasso's Guernica in the Museum of Modern Art and we say, 'Yes, war is terrible' and then we go and have some coffee. We aren't changed at all. We go to be moved, yet we aren't changed. This is a self-serving thing that gets us nowhere. It's easy to write an anti-war play today. The characters in this play are caught up in this game and trying to break out of their roles, but they can't."

Arrick felt he couldn't compare Heller's play with that of any other playwright. "He's really closer to the Jewish sensibility of novelists like Mailer, Roth, Bellow and Malamud who have a kind of self-loathing that is in itself a form of purification—their work comes out of a certain sense of pain and—God!" he said taking a horrified glance at his interviewer's notebook. "What does all that sound like?" He grabbed his jacket. "You can watch the rehearsal if you insist," he said. "But how would you like me to hang over your shoulder while you write your article?" I took the hint.

While Arrick was going through the torments of a mother in labor and Heller was agonizedly pacing the floor like an expectant father and students buzzed around like nurses and interns in various stages of training, Robert Brustein, now in his second year as dean of the Drama School, presided over all with the professionally expansive air of an obstetrician who is satisifed that everything is going normally. He was ready to discuss such side issues as the difficulties he has encountered in trying to build a more or less permanent acting company, which would include professionals and students. "Actors don't want to miss out on TV and Broadway opportunities," he said sadly. "The problem is to get together actors dedicated to their own development as artists and to certain actor-teacher ethical ideals that would enable them to bypass some personal advantages." As for *We Bombed in New Haven,* he felt that there was an extraordinary meeting of minds between actors and playwright. "Heller's script offers a perfect skeleton for using the improvisational and *commedia dell' arte* techniques we are interested in."

Dean Brustein smiled benignly. No reason for him to tense up. The patient would be in labor for another two and a half weeks. In the meantime the students would be learning—and that was what counted.

A week later, playwright Heller, who had stayed away from rehearsals during the interim, was delighted with the play. He said, "At first I was afraid the actors weren't good enough and the director wasn't good enough, but now I am just afraid the script isn't good enough. And I do think I'll write another play."

Did Heller Bomb on Broadway?

Israel Shenker/1968

From *New York Times* 29 December 1968, sec. 2, 1D, 3D. Copyright 1968 by The New York Times Company. Reprinted by permission.

Q. *Have you seen any good plays lately?*
A. Only my own.
Q. *Have you seen any bad plays lately?*
A. Only by other people.

Who else but Joseph Heller could be answering those questions—Joseph Heller, author of *Catch-22,* which has sold almost four million copies, and of *We Bombed in New Haven,* which is closing on Broadway this afternoon after a run of only 11 weeks?

"My play is not a failure," he says. "It's a success by every standard but one, and I don't even know if that standard—the fact that it's not going to run through a whole season—is relevant. The nature of the play, the cost of running it, made it extremely unlikely that it would run as long as it did. Joe Stein said, 'Don't expect to see lines like *Fiddler,* even after the first day's reviews came out.' They were almost uniformly raves. When I said I was going to run down to the box office and watch the lines, he said, 'Don't; they may not be there; it's not that kind of play.'

"It's not like *Rosencrantz and Guildenstern,* or *Marat/Sade,* which made their reputations in London and then came over. It's an original play for Broadway, highly individualistic and very strong in its effect on the audience.

"In the first four or five weeks more people saw my play on Broadway than bought *Catch-22* in the first year. I have a mass audience. The only trouble is it's not massed in New York. It has to come rushing in every weekend from Wisconsin and Phoenix and Berkeley, and that's asking too much even for a play of mine. So I'll bring it to them. The play will go on tour next year, and it will be produced at the Royal Court in London in April. There will probably also be a movie sale."

51

Q. *Why did you choose Pirandello as a model for your play?*
A. I didn't choose Pirandello, I find him trivial and irrelevant.
Q. *Maybe you prefer the Greeks?*
A. The model of the play is Greek tragedy and Greek comedy.

"In Greek plays the endings were inevitable, not necessarily because of any theory on the part of Greek playwrights, but because the audience knew the story—which came right out of Greek myths. Oedipus had to find out he was married to his mother or the audience would have torn the theater apart. In my play the audience gets to realize that in the script the major carried around everything is written down so that the question is: Do the actors have free will? Can they break away from the script?

"Inevitably the people in the play get around to bombing themselves. They raise no more questions about why they must bomb Minnesota than they do about bombing Constantinople. And as everybody knows, Constantinople doesn't even exist any more. It's Istanbul."

Q. *Why did you pick Minnesota?*
A. Because Humphrey wasn't born in Texas.
Q. *What's he done that Johnson didn't do?*
A. He told lies and believed they were true.

"Humphrey was going around defending the Vietnam war with the most bombastic and pompous and fanatic lies and deceits. More than other people. More than Rusk and more transparently, because he grinned, he smiled. Rusk is an automated fossil, but Humphrey has gusto and enthusiasm in describing what he regrets. I can't forgive any of them. I have a spiteful animosity for Johnson and Humphrey because we're not dealing with something insignificant like the Teapot Dome scandal. We are dealing with mass, organized murder.

"Everything else is dwarfed by the monumental atrocity of Vietnam. Any President could have stumbled into the same kind of situation, because Presidents are Presidents. We know where they come from, we know how they're made. But I think that neither Truman nor Kennedy nor Eisenhower would have been capable of the deceits, the shams, the dishonesty.

"Where are Johnson's accomplishments? He may have done something in terms of statutes, but the state of the country is infinitely worse today than when he came in. Any society that puts Cassius Clay and

Benjamin Spock in jail and makes McGeorge Bundy head of the Ford Foundation is not one to which allegiance should be given lightly.

"There are very few groups who feel a sense of allegiance to the ideals that were once effective in molding us into some kind of unified people. Blacks are blacks and whites are whites, and the division between rich and poor is more acute than it ever was before. There's a feeling now that the government is at war with its own people, and I'm one of the people. Reconciliation is not going to come from the Pope or Billy Graham or J. Edgar Hoover or even from Lewis Hershey. If it weren't for my basic optimism, I'd be packing up to leave the country. But I don't like packing.

"I don't know what kind of President Nixon will make. Mediocre people have made effective Presidents. I think he's calculating, cautious, and politic. He won't do anything out of virtue alone—which is the essence of any fanatic action, whether of right or left. Both kinds of fanatics believe their motives are good."

Q. *Then you're happy Nixon was elected?*
A. Are you serious?
Q. *Would you have preferred Humphrey?*
A. Are you kidding?

"Nixon will have to realize that large elements of this country—not just a radical fringe group—are dissatisfied with the distribution of wealth, with the application of force through police and military, with the distribution of authority.

"And I'm worried about Nixon's choice as Attorney General. He's an expert on municipal bonds. That's a complicated field, more complicated than running a government department. Anybody who's become an expert in municipal bonds may not have had time to learn much about anything else.

"But there is one change for the better. Finally we'll be rid of all those Arthurs and Deans and Bundys. And I respect Nixon's refusal to follow the demagogic formula of including a Jew, a Negro, or a woman in the Cabinet. Once they take office, they turn into white Protestants the first time they put on a tuxedo. But maybe he doesn't know any Jews or Negroes or women."

Q. *He didn't know Agnew either and he appointed him Vice President.*
A. He knew Strom Thurmond.

Q. *Who's he?*
A. A friend of Agnew's.

"My view of Agnew is the common one. I didn't like what he was, I didn't like what he said. That's the nature of democracy. Anybody can achieve high office, and anybody usually does. Democracy is not a particularly efficient instrument for selecting our chief executives. The Plantagenets had a better line of rulers than we've been able to collect.

"I don't want civil war, but if the country fragments so that we are at the barricades, despite my middle-class position I could not line up with the army, the police force, the Chamber of Commerce, or B'nai B'rith. I would have to fight on the side of the blacks, the poor, and S.D.S., even though they would not want me. If it came to violence I would not side with the Establishment, though my friendliest banker is there.

"It's not an equal struggle. The cops are on horseback, they've got guns, they've got clubs, they can arrest whoever they want, spectators or otherwise, and escape punishment completely. Whoever they arrest might be declared innocent three days later, but meanwhile he's had his arm twisted, his head smashed, he's had to post bail, he's had his life interrupted."

Q. *What else is new?*
A. I'm preparing another script for the play, to make it economically feasible, deleting two or three of the idiots.
Q. *Idiots?*
A. They're not really idiots.They're no different from you or me, which is why they're idiots.

"And I have a novel I want to finish. It was half or two-thirds finished when this frivolous idea of writing a play came along. The novel is called *Something Happened,* and it's about a man whose ambition is to be allowed to make a three-minute speech at the next company convention in Bermuda. In between he can't stand his life, he can't stand his marriage, he can't stand his job, he's about my age, everything's going to pot around him, including his daughter who is smoking pot. Finally he makes the speech, but it's dismissed in a phrase, so that what seemed the major goal of the book is suddenly handled as a subordinate clause. And his problems aren't settled—not more than yours or mine.

"The book is not about war. I'm not that interested in the subject of war. I wasn't interested in the war in *Catch-22.* I was interested in personal relationships to bureaucratic authority. It distressed me to see *We Bombed in New Haven* described as an anti-war play.

"Of course my attitude is against war. But in my play the crucial things were the aspirations of the people, the absence of any feeling of responsibility toward each other, the very pettiness of their ambitions. They quarrel over toys, they quarrel over lines, they steal each other's lines, ready to fight over them as though their homeland were being destroyed. Ultimately they realize that what they thought was a game was indeed happening. A war is really happening. People are really being killed.

"My motive was to create a new form of literature, or at least a new combination of traditional forms. In the play, whatever thoughts emerge are molded through esthetic concepts rather than in mere polemic.

"There's no remission at the end of my play. I felt the audience didn't deserve any consolation. The poor are suffering, the colored are suffering, the people with sons of 18 and 19 and 20 are suffering. I'm convinced that, if we remain accomplices of evil, we are not only guilty but deserve to be victims as well. That's the theme of the play. But it's not really about that, either. It's a play, a show, a charade, a light comedy full of innocent laughs in which everyone you love gets killed. I wanted to move the heart of every woman and the conscience of every man."

Portrait of a Man Reading

Dale Gold/1969

From *Washington Post Book World* 20 July 1969, 2. Copyright ©
1969 The Washington Post. Reprinted by permission.

*Your kind of humor—black humor, so-called—derives from a long
tradition. Did you ever read Swift or Voltaire, for instance?*

First of all, I don't like the term "black humor." I like to think of it as
sour sarcasm or ugly satire. I don't like comedy for the sake of comedy.

I haven't read Swift since elementary school and I never read Voltaire. On the other hand, I'm influenced by them from secondary
sources—people who write about them, writers who were influenced by
them. This is true of many authors I've not read or not read very
thoroughly and yet whose work I know through having read about them.
I have probably read more scholarly criticism about works of drama,
poetry and fiction than I've read the works themselves, and I like to feel
I have a very thorough and masterly knowledge of authors whom I've
not read.

Can you recall some of those secondary sources?

I'm a highly educated person, perhaps over-educated, and there was
a period in my life—about six or seven years when I was going to college, doing graduate work and getting Fulbright grants—when I was
pretty much immersed in literature almost as an historical phenomenon,
a kind of archaeological approach to it.

I've read a massive amount of Shakespeare criticism from Samuel
Johnson to Jan Kott, and it's impossible to read that much about Shakespeare without reading a great deal about drama and about all important
writers. A work I've reread recently, for example, is *Tragedy: Serious
Drama in Relation to Aristotle's Poetics* by F. L. Lucas. In reading that
book you get exposure to his views on dozens of authors, playwrights
and critics.

I have an impression that neither Swift nor Voltaire requires extensive
study in order to get a pretty good idea of what they were like. Aristophanes, on the other hand, does require familiarity. Even if you get an

accurate impression of Aristophanes, it doesn't tell you enough about his work—the details themselves are most important particularly for somebody who's interested, as I have been, in the war mentality and the wartime society.

What were your first reading experiences?

I enjoyed the Tom Swift and Rover Boys books tremendously. But the first work that made a real impression on me was a prose version of the *Iliad* given to me by an older cousin. I read that and reread it almost without stop and every term I'd make a book report on it. Beyond that I can't recall reading anything that I liked and I had a feeling then, which I still have, that most of the literature that we're taught as great literature is pretty uninteresting.

Will you give some examples?

Dickens. I've yet to read Dickens and I don't think I ever will. Shakespeare and Chaucer on the elementary and even secondary school levels are terrible things to throw at a child. The question is not only whether many of these works are suitable and relevant for elementary and secondary school but whether they have any relevance at all. I don't think they do, in many cases. When I had the Fulbright, I spent one term on Milton and one on Chaucer and one on Shakespeare and I came to the conclusion that Milton is pretty much of a waste. There's almost nothing he says that's pertinent or of any importance to us today, not only in terms of philosophy or attitude but even aesthetically. This kind of poetry is not for me and I don't think it's for us in our time.

What would *you give kids to read?*

I would probably concentrate on contemporary fiction—American novels of the last 20, 30, or 40 years, written in a contemporary idiom and fairly easy to comprehend. I'm thinking of something like *Catcher in the Rye* or *The Sun Also Rises,* or maybe *The Great Gatsby*—although I never liked Fitzgerald. But I would seek novels that are short, written in modern English, about Americans probably, and dealing with subjects, with problems, with characters that are recognizable today.

What kind of reading excites you now?

Let me preface my reply by saying that I don't read much. I read much less than the average college student. Mainly because I'm not much interested in literature, including my own. I'd much rather reread a book of Shakespeare criticism or Dostoevsky or pick up something like *The New York Review of Books* or *Commentary*. Secondly, I'm kind of a phlegmatic person—it's very hard to impress me. But an extraordinary accomplishment in almost any field will overawe me.

I have the feeling that if no more poetry were ever written, if no more painting were ever done, that civilization would really not be much poorer than it is today. Fiction is more important because it says more—it's something for mentality to grapple with. A good work of drama, a complex work of drama which we don't have anymore, offers the same kind of diversion. But many people lead happy and successful lives and never read or go to museums and I guess they're pretty intelligent as well.

So, at any rate, it's the extraordinary accomplishment that really gets me whether it's in baseball or horseracing or politics. Consequently, the novels that I really go for have a high content of originality. I'm not making originality and experiment synonymous with quality, but the experimental is what intrigues me.

Whom do you consider original?
John Barth, J. D. Salinger, Thomas Pynchon, J. P. Donleavy. I'm more interested in what they will do next than probably two dozen more successful, possibly more competent contemporary writers. Mainly because I *don't know* what they'll do next. I can almost predict what others of my contemporaries will do—what their next work will be about, how it will be structured. But writers like Salinger, Barth and Pynchon have the capability, the potential for doing something astounding. Now predictable genius is fine. One could predict what Bach would do. Given the 28th and 29th piano sonatas you can pretty much guess what the others would be.

Is fiction moving in any particular direction?
I see fiction moving in the direction of individualistic expression. By expression, I mean aesthetic expression primarily. Novelists today—at least those who interest me the most—don't belong to any kind of school. Their works will be unlike each other as I hope mine will be unlike theirs. We're similar only in the sense that we feel we do want to do our own work without being members of a certain school or certain philosophy. I don't think fiction is worth a damn as a means of propagandizing or expressing a philosophy.

Wouldn't you say that Catch-22 *makes extremely effective propaganda?*

I hope so. I hope it's persuading hundreds of students to avoid military service. But it took about ten years to write it and have it published, and if I had an urgent message to bring I would sooner send a telegram than to wait ten years to save the world or influence people.

Who influenced your political philosophy?

My political philosophy doesn't come from books—it comes from reading newspapers, from the social environment, from the kinds of friends you make. I find that with the exception of one person, who's a Republican, just about everybody I know either thinks as I do politically or doesn't think about it at all.

I was reminded of Kafka in the interrogation scenes in Catch-22. *Was he an influence?*

Kafka's *The Trial* was very much present. It's the idea of being charged with something and not knowing what it is, and being judged guilty and they'll tell him what he's guilty of once they find out what crime he's done and they're sure he must have committed some crime because everybody's committed some crime. The thing that inspired that was the congressional hearings that were going on then—this was the period of McCarthy and the House Un-American Activities Committee. We had state committees as well as loyalty oaths. But I did not attempt to reproduce Kafka as such. I wanted to create an impression of our society at that time and with a literary consciousness. That's why the book is replete with literary allusions and quotations or misquotations.

Which other writers influenced Catch-22?

Céline was a very strong influence in terms of literary style, particularly *Journey to the End of the Night.* Also Nathanael West and Nabokov's *Laughter in the Dark.* Faulkner's *Absalom, Absalom!* has a structure that I wanted to follow, and also an epic feeling which I try to get in my own idiom.

Can you think of specific influences in drama?

King Lear is to me the all-purpose play. It encompasses every kind of play, including *We Bombed in New Haven.* I can relate *We Bombed . . .* to much of *Lear,* in structure and philosophy.

Waiting for Lefty is interesting because it's really a very dated play now. I reread it after I finished *We Bombed* . . . I was very much aware of Odets's use of theater—his converting the theater into a union hall and converting the audience into members attending the union meeting. Well, *I* converted the theater into a theater. After I finished my play, I read Pirandello's *Six Characters in Search of an Author*—I had never read Pirandello—and I read a book on Pirandello and I came to the conclusion that there was nothing in the way of similarity except maybe a superficial thing here and there.

When I was preparing the manuscript for *We Bombed* . . . I was tempted to put in the stage direction, "The feeling should be like the stage setting in *Waiting for Godot*." I didn't—*We Bombed* . . . should be an independent book.

Literary Dialogue with Joseph Heller

George Mandel/1970

From *Penthouse* May 1970, 54–56, 59–60, 98. Reprinted by permission of the author.

Mandel: I understand you have been married 25 years.

   Heller: That's true, and I've enjoyed almost every minute of it.

   Mandel: Almost? Then there were periods that you did not enjoy?

   Heller: Yes. Periods of separation. There have been times when, because of my work, I have had to leave my home to buy a newspaper or get a bottle of milk. These moments apart from my wife and children are very difficult to bear.

   Mandel: I see. Have you ever been unfaithful?

   Heller: No.

   Mandel: Not once?

   Heller: Not once.

   Mandel: Have you ever been tempted?

   Heller: No.

   Mandel: Not once?

   Heller: Not once.

   Mandel: You're that much of a monogamist?

   Heller: No. That much of a liar.

   Mandel: If you *were* tempted, and you *did* give in to your temptations, would your wife object?

   Heller: No, she wouldn't object because she wouldn't know.

   Mandel: And if your wife did know, would she object?

   Heller: My wife wouldn't object, my daughter would.

   Mandel: You have one son and one daughter, and they are teenagers, is that correct?

   Heller: Yes.

   Mandel: Well this induces me to ask how you feel about the new morality.

   Heller: What new morality—sex?

   Mandel: Yes. I understand there's a new sex revolution that has us by the—

Heller: It certainly doesn't have us by the throat. And young people don't seem to be any happier as a result of it. I think the experience in the Scandinavian countries—where there has been unlimited sex for years—indicates that there does not seem to be a necessary relationship between total happiness and unrestrained sex.

Mandel: Do you think, as so many people maintain, that sex is clean and beautiful?

Heller: No, and I'm glad it isn't. If people want something clean and beautiful, let them go to bed with a bar of soap. As that eminent financier and movie director Mel Brooks once said, if sex is so clean and beautiful, why can't you do it with your mother?

Mandel: Maybe what's wrong now is the so-called sexual revolution. The best part of it is starting to be eliminated—the vice. What do you think of that?

Heller: I miss the vice. I think what many young people have lost and many middle-aged people—I mean people of my generation but not my moral rectitude—what they are losing by promiscuity is the sense of adventure that used to accompany copulation, which is now called lovemaking. I really don't like this idea of sex being respectable, or even universal. I'd rather it were reserved for just me and a few friends.

Mandel: Maybe there is hope in the maxi-coat. Do you think that this is a possible unconscious attempt on the part of the young to make sex sneaky again?

Heller: No, I think it is a conscious attempt to keep warm.

Mandel: But from this innocent attempt good things may come, longer dresses and a lot of seclusion for the female person.

Heller: I don't think that is necessarily a good thing. I like the female person.

Mandel: And I like your moral rectitude—which is said to be very apparent in both your novel, *Catch-22,* and your play, *We Bombed in New Haven.* On the subjects of your play and your moral rectitude, were you able to engage in sexual relations with any of the women in the cast?

Heller: Are you asking if the popular belief about stage people— about girls offering to do almost anything to get parts in a play—was true in my experience?

Mandel: I am asking about your experience with the women in the cast.

Heller: My experience in this respect was limited because there was only one female part in the play. I suspect that I could have established friendships with some of the boys in the cast, but I don't think my wife would have approved of that.

Mandel: Well, have you had any calls or letters from women or girls propositioning you since *Catch-22* was published?

Heller: I would say that the publication and the success of *Catch-22* has exposed me to a number of carnal temptations, all of which, with God's help, I have been successful in resisting.

Mandel: You did wish to resist them?

Heller: Of course. I have endeavored to resist them steadfastly.

Mandel: Because of your moral rectitude?

Heller: No, because of my wife. You must understand that not all the answers I give you are necessarily true.

Mandel: I will try my best to remember that. I hear the movie of *Catch-22* is soon to be released. Have you seen any of it?

Heller: No I haven't seen any of it.

Mandel: Have you heard about it?

Heller: I've heard that it's soon to be released. You just told me that.

Mandel: Anything else?

Heller: That it's exceptionally good. All that was photographed. But it will have to be cut down to about two hours.

Mandel: It will run that long?

Heller: Yes, between two hours and two hours and 15 minutes, which is a bit longer than the average picture. And this is much more than an average picture, from what I've been told.

Mandel: It sort of follows the pattern of your book. I remember that you had about that much footage in the novel too, and that you cut whole sequences out of it.

Heller: I cut out about 100—close to 200—pages, which was a shame, since they were all pretty good.

Mandel: I understand you are still selling pieces of it.

Heller: Yes. I'm selling unpublished parts of *Catch-22*. In fact I am writing more unpublished parts of *Catch-22*, since there seems to be a market for them.

Mandel: What is it called, this industry?

Heller: By-products, literary by-products.

Mandel: Right. I gather that there aren't many by-products of

Catch-22 which you aren't selling. Yossarian cookies, Joseph Heller sweat shirts. But the first *literary* by-product of yours that I can remember hearing about was index cards. Is there any truth to the story that you sold a bunch of index cards to somebody who was about to make a movie of *Catch-22*?

Heller: Yes. That goes back about six years. I had index cards, outlines, notes that I had used to keep track of the characters in *Catch-22*. The movie rights were owned by Columbia Pictures then and a different director was going to make it. He was very interested in having access to all this material. And I was very happy to sell it to him for a rather large sum of money.

Mandel: This included what?

Heller: Outlines, chronologies, character records, and even the dramatization of a number of scenes from the novel for a stage version I had started. The stage rights now belong to me again, by the way, as well as the TV dramatization rights—two additional literary by-products of *Catch-22* that I hope to market someday. It was a combination of outlines and masses of notes that I sold. And what I did sell, I did not sell, of course, in my original handwriting. I had it all typed because I sensed that the same material could be sold to other people, or donated to libraries, and that when the time came it would be worth more in the original handwriting.

Mandel: And, I recall, the time came that very year.

Heller: Yes. The original manuscript, along with subsequent versions and all the notes and other material that went into preparation of the novel, was given away to Brandeis University.

Mandel: It was very nice of you to give it to them.

Heller: I've been described before as being generous to a fault.

Mandel: That was certainly generous to your family if not to a fault, in the sense that giving the material to Brandeis saved you some money.

Heller: Well, there were some benefits to be gained in income tax deductions.

Mandel: While we have you in this honest family mood, is there any truth in the story that you once put your first-born up in the closet?

Heller: What are you talking about?

Mandel: I heard that you once did that.

Heller: Put my first-born up in the closet?

Mandel: On a shelf up in the closet.

Heller: For what reason?

Mandel: To upset your wife. Your wife stepped out of the room and you rushed to put your kid up in the closet. Your excuse was she couldn't crawl anyway. She couldn't get hurt. She was safe.

Heller: I don't recall this. I might have done anything to upset my wife. I am fun-loving at home. I like the sound of laughter, particularly my own.

Mandel: Is it true that in your pizza period, when you wouldn't let anyone in your apartment unless he brought a pizza, that you wouldn't let your own child come home to lunch because she didn't bring a pizza?

Heller: I don't recall it, but if she had come home during that period without a pizza, she would not have been allowed in. She was given money. Everyone in my family was given money.

Mandel: Given money to buy pizza?

Heller: No, not just to buy it, but to come home with the pizza, and if they didn't come home with the pizza they were either forgetful or had misappropriated the funds. I believe that children should have responsibility. They should be given chores to do at a very early age. I also believe that, if not every father, then this particular father should be indulged, not only by members of his own family but by strangers as well. There was an opportunity to combine both these principles. I wanted the pizza and they had to be taught responsibility. Both my children profited, by the way. They never come home now without a pizza for me, even though I've lost my taste for it.

Mandel: I'm glad to hear you acknowledge this, because I wouldn't want the inference to be made that my source for this story was a liar.

Heller: Who is your source?

Mandel: Your daughter.

Heller: My daughter doesn't lie. I think that's one of the things that's wrong with American youth today. They don't lie the way we used to and still do.

Mandel: Do you have problems with your children?

Heller: Oh, no. None at all. They may have problems, but I don't.

Mandel: Investigating among your family I learned that, although you may, as you called it, be generous to a fault, you haven't exactly spoiled any of them. I must confess that Lucy is the only one that hasn't complained.

Heller: Lucy is my best friend.

Mandel: For what reason?

Heller: Lucy is a dog. And I'm a man. And everybody knows that a dog is man's best friend.

Mandel: A remark about dogs leads to thoughts of politics. Have you ever thought of running for office?

Heller: I've been beseeched many times to run for high office. I know there is a big need for men like me in Washington, but I'm not interested.

Mandel: What was the highest office you were ever beseeched to run for?

Heller: President of the United States. But I haven't time for that. I have too many responsibilities.

Mandel: You don't feel duty bound to . . .

Heller: Oh, no, no. I really don't feel a free American has any duties or any public responsibilities. I believe the government exists to serve the people. I don't believe the people exist to serve the government. I think it's an obligation of people in the government to cater to us. That's the reason we have a representative form of government.

Mandel: You would call representatives of the people public servants?

Heller: Oh, yes. And they should be treated like servants, not like rulers. They are in office to serve, to administer to the needs of the country, by no means to be looked up to, certainly not on the basis of past performances. I don't want to be President or a Senator because I don't want to put myself in a menial position, frankly.

Mandel: You don't want to be President because you don't want to be a menial?

Heller: Yes, that's the main reason.

Mandel: You don't want people making demands on you and criticizing your speeches.

Heller: I don't want to have the obligation to make speeches, although I don't mind making speeches. In fact, I rather enjoy making speeches. But there is a serious danger that if I did run for President I would win, and I'd have to serve. There's no question in my mind that I could do a much better job in Washington than anybody in the last three or four administrations. I think anybody who knows me knows I can.

Mandel: I know you and I think you can and this leads me back to the original question. If those, especially the youth of the country, who are anti-establishment politically, asked you to serve, would your answer be no?

Heller: If they used the term "serve" the answer would be that I'm not a good servant.

Mandel: What if they asked you to lead them—as a dictator.

Heller: Well, perhaps. But I don't think I'd really be happy as a dictator. The hours would be long.

Mandel: Then may I take it that you are opposed to our form of government?

Heller: I'm not opposed to our form of government. I just don't think it works.

Mandel: Do you have any vision of what might work?

Heller: I really don't care about that. I think the British system works very well, but that is because the English are a superior people.

Mandel: How do you mean?

Heller: I think they are superior. The people in government are much better educated than our own, much more intelligent.

Mandel: Have you spent much time in England?

Heller: I've been there frequently over the years, and long ago I was a student there.

Mandel: An Oxford scholar, right?

Heller: A Fulbright scholar at Oxford.

Mandel: And you found the English superior politically as well as intellectually?

Heller: In England I think intelligent people go into politics. Here intelligent people are intelligent enough to stay out.

Mandel: What you are saying now, in effect, is that as a rule in America, under the terms of our way of life, inferior people go into politics?

Heller: I would say that is generally true. It is rare that a superior person, I mean morally superior as well as intellectually superior, is even sought after as a candidate.

Mandel: And even rarer that one will win. So Washington's loss, in this case at least, is literature's gain. Do you believe, as many people do, that *Catch-22* is the Great American Novel?

Heller: I don't know if anyone would call it THE Great American Novel. That assumes there can only be one. But, asked if it is *a* Great

American Novel, I would have to say, in modest deference to the opinion of the many people who hold that view, that it is. As a matter of individual opinion, I've kind of felt that to be true, even when I was writing it.

Mandel: You believe *Catch-22* is a Great American Novel of the past decade?

Heller: No. I believe it is *the* great novel of the decade. I would never quibble over the restriction of the word *American*.

Mandel: In how many foreign countries has it been published?

Heller: How many foreign countries are there? In every language from Formosan English to Russian plagiarism.

Mandel: Then it is *the* great novel of the decade indeed.

Heller: It is the only novel I can think of that was published in the early '60s and is more popular now than it was years ago. Many other novels sold more copies. *Catch-22* was never on the best-seller list—I mean in the original hard-cover edition. There were popular novels that sold more in paperback.

Mandel: You might say it's the only great novel that has sold more than 2,000,000 copies. How many copies does it sell now?

Heller: It still sells about 500,000 a year in this country in paperback. It still has a life in hard cover, about 4000 copies a year. In the first 12 months of publication I think it sold about 30,000 copies.

Mandel: Very healthy for a first novel.

Heller: But of course it doesn't compare with Jackie Susann. Or Mario Puzo, for that matter.

Mandel: But we don't want to discuss Mario and Jackie in the same dialogue.

Heller: I think Miss Susann might object.

Mandel: In paperback, what is the sales figure at this point?

Heller: Over 3,000,000 copies. It is in what is known as "sex book territory," now. With the possible exception of *Catcher in the Rye,* I can't think of another serious contemporary novel that has sold over 3,000,000 copies. It is into sex book territory with those figures and that is because it is a sex novel as well as a serious one.

Mandel: Well, we know there is a lot of good sex in it.

Heller: Oh, there is a lot of delicious sex in there. I wish I were writing those passages again today. I got a nice salacious pleasure out of writing the sex scenes because I identify strongly with whatever I am writing about. That's why I tried to make it as funny as I could—in order to laugh and make the work pleasant.

Mandel: Do you do a lot of laughing while you work?

Heller: Oh, yes, if what I'm writing is funny.

Mandel: Much of what you write is of a strong and painful nature. Does it ever hurt when you write?

Heller: Only when I laugh.

Mandel: Have you ever laughed so much you couldn't work?

Heller: Well, I don't work while I'm laughing. When I stop laughing. I go back to work. I like laughing more than working.

Mandel: That's very rare in writers. Most writers would rather write than laugh.

Heller: I'd rather laugh than work.

Mandel: Rather laugh than eat?

Heller: No, I would rather eat.

Mandel: I thought so. It's known that your eating habits are rather prodigious. I've even heard you referred to as The Animal.

Heller: Yes, some people call me that. And others have referred to me as the Locust—you, to name one. I like to eat. Some people call eating a sex substitute. But I incline toward the opposite view. I feel that sex may be a substitute for food. People repress their desire for food, and that repressed desire for food is sublimated and reappears as a sex urge.

Mandel: That is what you believe?

Heller: Yes. That's the reason there's so much secret eating today and so much public sex. Sex is no more complicated than a desire for a good meal, and much less injurious to the health. If people had bigger meals the divorce rate would probably go down. There would be much less adultery. People should eat more, not less.

Mandel: If they ate more there would be less activity in the bedroom, and thus more divorces.

Heller: I am saying a lot of divorces are caused by adultery. If people ate more, they would make love less. And that applies to adulterers too.

Mandel: Wouldn't this act against marriage? Husband and wife would spend less time making love to each other.

Heller: But they would spend more time eating together. For a writer this might be an important change. A writer can work with one hand

while eating with the other. It is hard to work as a writer when you are
making love.

Mandel: Both longhand and typing would be difficult.

Heller: I would guess so. I've never tried.

Mandel: In connection with these views, I would like to ask you if
your wife minds you eating.

Heller: Not as long as I'm fairly discreet about it.

Mandel: Does she object, then, to your having lunch with other
women?

Heller: My wife doesn't object because my wife doesn't know.

Mandel: Does she mind you eating with other men?

Heller: No, she's completely broadminded about that, and I eat rather
regularly with other men. At least once a week and sometimes more.

Mandel: I happen to know about that. These are the men that enjoy
calling you The Animal and have formed a kind of gourmet club to
watch you eat.

Heller: I would not put it that way. These gentlemen are too distinguished in their various fields for anything like that. They gather much
less formally than that to watch me eat. They eat also.

Mandel: If they're quick enough. Are they too distinguished to have
their names divulged here?

Heller: Oh, yes! Far too distinguished. Why, the noted financier and
film director, Mel Brooks, is one of them. And another is Mario Puzo,
the philanthropist. He'd be terribly embarrassed to find his name in this
sort of publication.

Mandel: The same Mario Puzo who wrote *The Godfather*?

Heller: Yes, the philanthropist. Every month he donates large sums
of money to needy casinos all around the world. We also have Hershey
Kaye, the manufacturing troubadour. We can't mention him either.

Mandel: Why not? Manufacturers don't care what they lend their
names to.

Heller: Well, despite the millions he gets from his chocolate business, Hershey wants nothing to do with it and composes bawdy songs
instead, like the classic "Johnny Come Tickle Me," and "Lulu Had a
Baby." Others in the group might object also if I mentioned their
names, like Ngoot Lee, the Chinese advertising expert.

Mandel: He advertises in China?

Heller: No, he *is* Chinese. But he tries to hide that.

Mandel: How?

Heller: By speaking Yiddish. He doesn't get away with it, how-ever—he speaks with a Chinese accent and fools nobody. Then there is Julie Green, the theatrical agent and raconteur, and Speed Vogel, the famous painter and downhill racer, and you.

Mandel: Me? Well, how would you characterize me?

Heller: I wouldn't. I assume your readers will be more interested in my character than in yours.

Mandel: You may be right. Do you find that successful literary activity, meaning a good day's work with lots of pages and good stuff, subdues or regenerates your appetite?

Heller: I am unable to answer that because I have never had a good day's work with lots of pages. I think in terms of hours or half hours. I have left my desk thinking this has been a good hour's work.

Mandel: And did it increase your sexual drives?

Heller: Well, I felt that having done a good hour's or half-hour's work merited some kind of reward and I was free to spend the rest of the day in pleasurable activities that included laughing, eating, love-making, and swinging. I mean swinging literally. I still like to swing in playgrounds. I like to push people on swings. Now some people might say that is a disguised form of sexual activity. I believe it's just a repressed urge for a hamburger and some potato chips.

Mandel: Which brings us back to the younger generation—I mean the potato chips, not the disguised urges. What would you say is wrong with current youth?

Heller: Nothing that wasn't wrong with previous generations of youth. In many ways they are superior. They have a better sense of what they want to do with their lives. They don't want to spend it the way we spend ours, which isn't all that intelligent.

Mandel: How do they spend their lives?

Heller: Many of them have not found what they want to do but certain studies among college students indicate that, unlike preceding generations, the most intelligent ones don't want to go into medicine and don't want to go into fields of applied science and don't want to go into business or industry. The ones who organize their education in the most practical ways are not those who score highest in intelligence tests or do the best academically in college. There is, for example, a greater interest in some kind of social work—vague, perhaps, but definitely

philanthropic—than there is in achievement and acquisition. There is a
trend away from success as a goal. If I were a young man today and
somebody asked me if I wanted to be Henry Ford or something analogous to Henry Ford in the future, or Watson of IBM or John D. Rockefeller, I would say no, and I would guess that that same question asked
of high school and college students would show the more intelligent and
accomplished ones also saying no. They would not settle for so little.

Mandel: Can you give an indication of some pursuits they might
prefer?

Heller: It would relate very much to the nature of the individual.
Playing a guitar, composing music, even if it is not good music, or
composing poetry, even if it is not good poetry, or simply traveling,
even producing nothing.

Mandel: But doesn't one grow old and friendless that way?

Heller: One grows old any way. One grows old faster working hard.
Work is not good, and labor is certainly not noble. Accumulating
money does give one power, but as an end in itself money is not good
enough for many people. It's not good enough for me. I wouldn't
change places with any of the millionaires I can think of today. I would
take their money if I could get it, but I certainly wouldn't work for it.

Mandel: Do you feel that what you are expressing now is in any way
unique to this generation?

Heller: I think there are more young people who feel this way than
there were in my generation, which came out of the Depression. I don't
know why anyone who has 2,000,000 dollars should spend even one
minute doing anything he doesn't like just to make a few million more.
And if making money is what he likes doing, the psychiatrists have an
explanation for that, too.

Mandel: Where does that leave someone who has no funds?

Heller: Destitute. He will have to do one of two things: he will have
to learn to live on a very low income level, which people can do when
they are young, or else he will learn that life is not always a matter of
doing what he wants to. There are conflicts and disappointments, and
people have to find some means of getting money if they want it.

Mandel: In other words he will have to come to the day when he
realizes that the only thing that's important in life is money.

Heller: That day shouldn't come until he's at least 30 or 40 or 50.

There are many young people who make as much money as they feel they need, then stop.

Mandel: Isn't this typical of youth in every generation?

Heller: I don't think it was typical of my generation; everybody wanted to go to work quickly and make as much money as possible, far beyond his needs.

Mandel: There are people who feel that earned money is much better than inherited or found money.

Heller: I think they are wrong. Inherited money is better. Much better. It is better for the character if one doesn't have to work for money.

Mandel: Do you feel hopeful that the unconventional young are an indication of something optimistic, that they can "save mankind"?

Heller: I don't know if they can save mankind or even if they *should* save mankind, and I don't think they're concerned with saving mankind. I think it is optimistic because it portends a renunciation of, or even a revolution against, certain traditional values which have the effect in any culture of really enslaving the minds and the emotions of each new generation. This is a break with values that have outlived the conditions that created them and are more stifling now than functional. It is not merely a questioning of values any more but a repudiation of them. I like the fact that they are dressing differently, wearing their hair long; it's the good old traditional American way, like Buffalo Bill and Kit Carson. I wish that certain people in Washington would let their hair grow a bit longer so that they would look more like Americans and less like Huns and Teutons. I like the fact that they are bent on pleasure and do want to do their own things, even though I might not like the things many of them choose to do.

Mandel: George Bernard Shaw said: "What was good enough for my father is not good enough for me." You agree with those children who share that viewpoint?

Heller: In all my speeches at colleges I never met a single kid who wants to take over the family business. No matter how big it is. Why in the world should anyone want to, especially if the business is big enough to keep going without him? Only the poor should have ambition.

Mandel: What I'm trying to get from you is whether or not you see this as an ongoing kind of thing, some kind of breakthrough in the American way of life or maybe the Western world's way of life and ultimately the world's way of life. Do you believe that there is a motion here which will carry on to the next generation?

Heller: Well, the 18-year-olds affect the 16-year-olds, the 16-year-olds affect the 14-year-olds. The numbers will increase of those young people who are setting their own fashions and philosophies, simply because of the ability of people to influence other people.

Mandel: That still leaves the question of whether they can support themselves.

Heller: Many of them don't have to support themselves, and if they don't have to I don't see why they should.

Mandel: But most of them have a *future* in which they will have to support themselves. What are they heading for with this self-gratifying attitude?

Heller: They'll be heading toward a form of employment which will also be self-gratifying, and they will select or find forms of work which will provide them with as much income as they need and will require no irrational sacrifices. If there is another Depression, then we're all in trouble. I don't think people should start working for money before they have to.

Mandel: What does this portend for society?

Heller: It is hard to answer that question without raising the question of how important society is or what direction society should go in. I don't know what society needs. I don't know who society is. I don't think anybody owes anything to society, not in a free country.

Mandel: How much do you know about the communes? Have you visited any?

Heller: No.

Mandel: Would you like to?

Heller: No. I might have to work.

Mandel: What if you were promised just leisure?

Heller: I'd prefer an invitation to the Plaza or the Beverly Hills Hotel.

Mandel: Would you *accept* an invitation from one of those hotels?

Heller: Yes, especially if I could go there with the people I'd meet at a commune.

Mandel: You would enjoy living with people of that kind under comfortable circumstances?

Heller: We would get along, there would be no hostility.

Mandel: What if the conversation became philosophical or mystical?

Heller: I would pack my bags and leave. I don't mind people doing their thing. I do mind them trying to justify it in intellectual or philosophical terms.

Mandel: Like the descriptions we get these days of consciousness-expanding experience?

Heller: Yes, they may or may not be true; for me, it doesn't matter. I have the same feeling about God—I don't care if he exists or not and I wouldn't change my way of life even if there were proof he did or didn't.

Mandel: You are expressing an agnostic attitude toward reality and I am glad to see you so healthy.

Heller: I realize that even if I received convincing physical evidence that there is a God and a heaven and hell, it wouldn't affect me one bit. I think the experience of life is more important than the experience of eternity. Life is short. Eternity never runs out.

Mandel: Now you are turning all of religion and philosophy backwards.

Heller: Because life is transitory, we ought to use it in our own special way.

Mandel: That reminds me once again of your play, which was so thought-provoking that it probably angered a lot of people. I understand it has been published in book form.

Heller: Yes, by Knopf and by Dell. It is being produced this year in more than 200 different community and college theaters, and now there's an off-Broadway production in the works as well.

Mandel: Several critics and some people I know in the theater think it is the most important play of the '60s.

Heller: And the '70s.

Mandel: You get good results for someone who would rather eat than write. Do you find writing a lousy occupation?

Heller: There are more writers than Presidents.

Mandel: Do you enjoy the work of any other writers in particular?

Heller: Living or dead?

Mandel: Either.

Heller: No.

Mandel: What are you working on now?

Heller: Another novel.

Mandel: Are you getting much done?

Heller: I'm moving along at my own pace. I might finish it this summer and publish in January but then again I might not.

Mandel: Putting all the elements together—how much time would you say you spent laughing on *Catch-22* and this new novel?

Heller: Well, I worked eight years on *Catch* of which I would say close to two years was spent laughing—this was in a five-day week. I don't want you to say I spent over 700 days laughing continuously. When I couldn't eat I had to find a food substitute. The amount of actual time I put into writing *Catch-22* was probably a matter of months, what with eating, and laughing, and even making love when I couldn't find food in the refrigerator.

Mandel: This novel is taking a little longer . . .

Heller: I have less time to work now because I don't have a job. When I had a job during the day, I was able to work on the book at night because I was too exhausted to leave the house for recreation and, having nothing easier to do, wrote the book.

Mandel: So it was really eight years of *nights,* in which you wrote, laughed, ate, made love, and took your dog for a walk?

Heller: I didn't have a dog then.

Mandel: Visited friends?

Heller: I didn't have any friends then either. Most of the friends I have now are fair-weather friends that came to me after I became famous and influential and they hang around hoping I'll help them and I am sure that if things go badly they will desert me in a second and go to somebody like Puzo or Jacqueline Susann. Friends are overrated anyway. I don't think people need friends. Acquaintances are more valuable—no obligations—you can drop them quickly. Nobody accuses you of dropping acquaintances but you can frequently be accused of dropping your friends. Strangers are nice, but once you get to know them you may discover things about them you don't like.

Mandel: Then they become acquaintances and you can drop them.

Heller: Strangers are a man's best friend.

Mandel: Do you have many strangers?

Heller: Yes, I'm on intimate terms with several.

Mandel: Are any of them women?

Heller: I don't know them that well, unfortunately.

Mandel: Would you like to talk about your new novel?

Heller: No.

Mandel: Not even the part of it that has already been published in *Esquire*?

Heller: No.

Mandel: You've been most helpful.

Heller: I try to be. Along with being generous to a fault, I am most often complimented for being helpful.

An Interview in New York with Joseph Heller
Richard B. Sale/1970

From *Studies in the Novel* 4 (Spring 1972), 63–74. Reprinted by
permission.

Richard B. Sale, an editor of *Studies in the Novel,* interviewed Joseph Heller on 14 December 1970.

Heller: I want to tell you I suspect your motives. I don't believe you're
taking all this trouble, coming to New York, to interview me.

Sale: Well, I planned to see the big pre-Columbian show at the
Metropolitan while I was here.

Heller: That's a little better.

Sale: Do you keep up with the criticism that's been written about
your work?

Heller: No, because I don't have access to the critical stuff. I sometimes hear about things on *Catch-22* that have been written in books,
but apparently there's no way of finding out about random chapters
which mention my writing. Someone is doing a casebook on *Catch-22.*
Most of those articles are unfamiliar to me; I just don't read them.

Sale: For some time now, critics have been playing with the notion
usually expressed by the phrase "the death of art." Is there some corre-
spondence between this idea and any ideas expressed in *Catch-22,* your
play, or the novel you're working on now? Is there a connection between the novel of the absurd and the death-of-art notion?

Heller: It certainly doesn't correspond closely because, in *Catch-22,*
We Bombed in New Haven, and *Something Happened,* I was and am
very much conscious of the art involved. I'm very much aware of character development, for example. In all my writing I have the desire to
communicate certain things effectively in aesthetic terms. To me this
desire involves an extraordinary amount of energy given to the details of
structure.

I have not heard anybody say that I put the death-of-art idea in any of my work, although they have said it about Samuel Beckett and some of the contemporary experimental novelists.

I'll say this about *Catch-22* and *We Bombed in New Haven:* Each of these works was founded on a metaphor, and the rest of the work was created to develop that metaphor. The whole concept was literary, aesthetic.

I don't believe in "the death of art." I don't think it is even meaningful when strictly applied to literature, for the writer who does genuinely believe—and Samuel Beckett comes close—in the absurdity of it really couldn't write.

Sale: Here's a companion idea. Ever since Coleridge's "Dejection" ode, there has been the notion that, at the same time the author is bemoaning the loss of his creative powers, he is producing his best work. He is at his strongest when he is most worried about drying up.

Heller: I'm not sure I know what you mean. I think writers have talent and may reach a height in a certain work, while in others they hit a point less than that height. In Shakespeare there are peaks and in William Faulkner there are peaks. Missing those peaks did not signify the death of their art. I think every writer that you or I know about, throughout history, tried to do the best he could at the time he was writing any given piece. That would include Shakespeare and all his carelessness. I think people who work at anything would rather do well than poorly, but that doesn't mean you can hit a home run every time up at bat. And if Coleridge was worried about his poetry, it was not because of a lack of interest in his art or a loss of ambition; it might have been that he had written himself out on certain things. If he had and was aware of it, he would have been very much distressed by it. Hemingway was constantly worried about such things. I'm not sure I've answered your question because I'm not sure I understand it.

Sale: I'm afraid I was confusing two different things. I was asking for an aesthetic answer to a psychological dilemma: how does the artist solve the problems of reality with an aesthetic work?

Heller: About reality. I think literature, except for a brief period in recent history—and that was a really brief period—has never been realistic. Starting with the Greeks and moving through the Renaissance to the present, there seems to me only a period of twenty or thirty years in which realistic literature was strong. "Realism" began in the nineteenth century with those American novelists that nobody reads right now, novelists like Frank Norris and that guy from Boston, W. D. Howells. It continued, trailing off, into World War II in such writers as James T. Farrell and John Steinbeck.

Apart from that time, literature has always been much larger than life, romantic, imaginative. And this impulse of writers is, I think, essentially sound. Writers have always brought literature up to a pitch larger than life. As soon as an author seeks a way of telling a story that is different from the mere narration of the events of history, he is involved in an act of the imagination. Even the French antinovel is an act of the imagination. It's a way of writing a novel that's different from the preceding way. Don't make me say what art is.

Sale: You said that any serious writer has to put strong emphasis on the structure of his work.

Heller: I don't think I said *any* serious writer; I said *I* did. I think what I meant was that any writer who doesn't regard his work, his writing, as being a form of art, comparable, let's say, to architecture, painting, or sculpture, is probably not serious. There must be attention given to form. There must be a sense of form. The writer must figure out the form a specific work needs to take.

Sale: Are you willing to describe the structural patterns of *Catch-22* in a brief outline, or do you feel that is the reader's job?

Heller: I think it's the reader's job. The structure in *Catch-22* is kind of self-evident though.

Sale: The reason I ask is that some commentators have maintained that *Catch-22* is structureless; one critic, Joseph Waldmeir, compares *Catch-22* with Ken Kesey's *One Flew over the Cuckoo's Nest*. He maintains that the Kesey book is commendably put together and that in comparison *Catch-22* lacks structure. I didn't think he made his point.

Heller: If one wants to look deeper than people normally do, he would see that nine-tenths of *Catch-22* is organized around three combat missions: the mission to Avignon, the mission to Bologna, and the mission to Ferrara. The first mission is the main one. The whole novel is a series of events that either deal with the missions or are outgrowths of events that happened on the mission. Now of course I was aware of this pattern; I had planned it at least a year before I began writing the novel.

The three missions have occurred before the time of the opening chapter, and they keep recurring. Milo's bombing of the squadron was something else that had taken place before the opening of the first chapter. Snowden was dead before the book begins; the death of Snowden keeps recurring.

There is more to this pattern of recurrence. Things happen twice or more. Yossarian flies over the bridge at Ferrara twice. The soldier in white appears twice. There is the chaplain with his *déjà vu* susceptibilities. Now all that is a pattern.

And this also is a part of the structure: I was very much aware that I was creating in the first, oh, four-fifths of the novel the effect of something being chaotic and anarchistic, and yet have the pieces come together much the way William Faulkner does in *Absalom, Absalom!*, *The Sound and the Fury*, and other works in which he deals with a large body of information presented in tiny fragments and then have the fragments connect toward the end of the book and give the whole picture.

The narrative line in *Catch-22* assumes a forward motion only toward the end of the book when Yossarian decides to desert. Then the narrative goes straightforward with the exception of one flashback, the description of the death of Snowden, told in realistic form. Even the flashback is handled in traditional, straightforward narration. But until Yossarian's decision there is almost no forward action.

Sale: Just circular motion?

Heller: Yes, ever-widening circles until that last section where Yossarian refuses to fly the final mission.

Sale: It's even possible that the dizziness created by the first two-thirds of the book would make the direct narration at the end seem phantasmagorical.

Heller: It took me about five years of planning and making notes and cogitating to get the effect that the book was unplanned, that the narration was spontaneous, just being spilled out on the pages as they approach. It takes a lot of care; it takes a lot of planning to make things seem unplanned.

Sale: And your payment is that you get panned for writing a structureless novel.

Heller: I must say that at this late date I don't think anything can be written about *Catch-22* that would give me displeasure or make me even want to thumb my nose. Now the first year it came out, those first reviews. . .

Sale: Many of the reviews had high praise for the book.

Heller: Yes, but I knew, and my agent and my editors and my family knew, eight or ten weeks before publication, that a really venomous review was scheduled for the Sunday [New York] *Times* book review section. Knowing it was going to be that kind of review, knowing in advance what was about to fall on my life, I walked around holding my breath and praying that they would not run it at all. They frequently commission more reviews than they can publish.

Sale: Was the actual review as bad as you expected?

Heller: It was a single-column attack. Well, not even an attack; it dismissed the book. What did happen took most of the sting out of it. On the Sunday it came out, the review was so small it was run way in the back of the book review section and very few people saw it. Except for the people who knew me. They were looking for it. I had to console them. They would call me up and say, "The sons of bitches." On Monday Orville Prescott, the reviewer for the daily *Times,* came out with a review that was an absolute rave. Then more people noticed it. The first year it did very well for a first novel; it sold about 30,000 copies, not enough to make the best seller list.

Sale: You copyrighted a portion of the book in 1955. What part was that?

Heller: In 1955 the whole plan of the book occurred to me, and I wrote the first chapter one morning. The next morning at my office I decided to have it copyrighted. I spent the week rewriting that first chapter and then gave it to my literary agent to submit for publication. I offered it to any publication which would print it as the first chapter of a book. And it was published in that year. I worked on the rest of the book until 1961.

Sale: Besides your work in advertising, what had you written before?

Heller: When I was an undergraduate at NYU—I guess I was twenty-three years old, a sophomore—I took a course in creative writing.

Sale: That was after the war?

Heller: I didn't go to college before the war. I did well in the course and submitted the stories I wrote to magazines. I guess it was a combination of a lot of good luck and very little creative talent, but I sold two stories to *Esquire* and two to *Atlantic Monthly.* One of those was included in the *Best Short Stories 1949.* I thought of myself as successful.

But what happened was that as I became a junior and senior and got better educated, I began to develop a critical sense and began to dislike those stories, realizing that they were mainly imitative. I stopped writing then. I didn't want to begin writing again unless I did something which I felt was peculiarly my own.

Sale: What kind of stories were those early ones? How would you describe them?

Heller: Oh, I would say to a large extent they were influenced by the stories that were appearing then in the *New Yorker* or *Esquire*. They were imitations of Irwin Shaw or Ernest Hemingway. Hemingway *seems* to be easier to imitate. I'm not saying he is, but only seems to be.

Sale: To imitate him well would be no bad trick.

Heller: It started with those. I've always been kind of good with dialogue, and Hemingway's stories are almost entirely dialogue. That was my early writing experience. Then I stopped for about three or four years, waiting for something to strike me that I felt was worth doing.

Sale: How is the work going on your new novel? When do you predict it will be published?

Heller: I don't predict anymore. Publicly I say six months because a year ago I gave my solemn word to my editor. I swore on my life, the life of my children and his it would be done in a year. Now I have to cut it down to six months, or he'll think I haven't been working at all.

But there's no problem. I just handed in another section of the book, and it's becoming a longer book than I'd planned.

Sale: Does what you said a moment ago about the writing of *Catch-22* apply to this novel? Do you know exactly where it's going to lead?

Heller: Oh, yes, I knew where it was going before I began.

Sale: I meant in the details of the work.

Heller: In the course of writing *Catch-22,* I felt it would be too short to make a novel.

Sale: And you ended with God's plenty.

Heller: Beginning this book, I thought it would be much shorter than *Catch-22,* but as I work, somehow my imagination produces more and more material. This may turn out to be a longer book than *Catch-22* and much different in this respect: its title, *Something Happened,* is ironic because *nothing* happens. There is almost no action in the whole book except introspection and recollection. It may turn out to be a longer book than *Catch-22* without any of the energy or humor.

Sale: That's an ominous prediction.

Heller: There is almost no humor in this book. It is a very bleak book, a melancholy illumination on the part of a man in his forties who looks at his past and looks at his present and tries to see some kind of future, and sees not much of any.

Sale: And what does he do?

Heller: He comes to the very pessimistic conclusion—as much as he can see at all—that there's nothing he will do. Not that there's nothing that can be done, but that there's nothing that he, being who he is, *will* do. And that's why I say that it's a very pessimistic and melancholy book. But so far, it's standing up very well.

Sale: And entertaining *you*.

Heller: Oh, sure.

Sale: Critics are always trying to categorize novels and novelists. They have tried with you and *Catch-22*. Yet there's not a book similar to *Catch-22* that I can think of which appeared around the same time. Or since then.

Heller: A few novels came out while I was writing *Catch-22* that seemed from the descriptions of them to be very close to it.

Sale: Did that scare you?

Heller: Oh, they scared hell out of me. I rushed to get those books and then when I read them I was kind of relieved. I'll tell you two books that came out while I was writing. One was Kerouac's *On the Road*. And it does have much in common with *Catch-22* as far as pacing goes, anyway.

The other book was *The Ginger Man*. When I read the review of *The Ginger Man* and Dangerfield, the hero, I said, "Oh, my God, there's Yossarian." If you can picture reading a *review* of the book and having Dangerfield described as a hero, you might understand why I saw Yossarian.

Yet it was reassuring in a sense. Here were books being written that were responding in similar ways to mine to conditions of breakdown of form, of narration becoming secondary to the emotions of the character and the ideas of the author, that is, the author's ideas being the same as those of the main character.

Sale: What is the history of *We Bombed in New Haven?*

Heller: *We Bombed in New Haven* began as a whim, meant to kill time. I was doing my novel in the daytime, and it had gone so beautifully that I felt in the evening I could afford the luxury of relaxation. Now one of the unfortunate consequences of my having spare time to use is that there's nothing I really want to do with it. I don't like television, I don't go to many movies, I don't go the theater often, and I really don't read that many books. So here I was in the evenings with a clear conscience. I began doing this thing.

In the evening I began to write. I can write plays very quickly because, as I said, dialogue comes easy to me. Description doesn't and the play has little description. And I can create the big scenes, farcical scenes, and confrontation scenes. Those are two things I do rapidly, and that's what plays consist of. So I just breezed along. When I finished the first act, I showed it to a Broadway producer and he said he would produce it. I said, "Fine, I'll send it to you." And along the way I met Bob Brustein at Yale, who I'd known years back. He wanted to put it on at Yale; the Broadway producer said okay, and it was done first at Yale.

It was a disastrous Broadway production. There were review problems again. Not bad reviews, just problems.

Sale: You've mentioned television reviews. Do television reviews affect the theatergoing public?

Heller: No, they have a slight effect. The only thing that has an effect on the New York theatergoer is the newspaper review, and it makes no difference who the reviewer is.

Sale: That is certainly not true with books. A book review in a newspaper would not make a best seller.

Heller: No, not only would the *Times* book review not do it, but what's called the "intellectual mafia" or the "red hot set" or the "Jewish mafia" which lives upstate and which includes reviews and commentaries would have no effect at all. They can help a book a little, but they can't make it go.

Sale: What does affect the success of a book?

Heller: I think what affects the booming of a book is the quality of the book itself, what the readers enjoy.

Sale: I'd like to think this is so.

Heller: Well, I think it's true, and I think it's true of *Catch-22*.

Sale: How does the word get around?

Heller: People read it and tell other people to read it. And I think that's as true of books like *Catch-22* as it is of books like *Valley of the Dolls*.

Sale: Can't the publisher advertise a book heavily for an extended period for a kind of cumulative sale?

Heller: They cannot boom a bad book. Now let me define what I mean by "bad." There are different qualities of books. Let's assume, immodestly, that *Catch-22* is good serious literature. There is also good inferior literature. We're talking about the popular novels like those of James Michener, Herman Wouk, Leon Uris. Within that category there are writers who are better than others. And then you can even get into a lower level of the sex novels. If a sex novel like *Peyton Place* or *Valley of the Dolls* becomes a very big seller, there may be forty of the same kind that don't attract any readers at all. Regardless of the category, even the pornographic, there are some books that do give pleasure to the audience—the audience for that kind of book—and others that don't. I think Jacqueline Susann's *Valley of the Dolls* must have given a lot of pleasure to people. Her second book didn't. It's not sold nearly as well in paperback.

What *can* happen with a book can't happen with a play. *We Bombed in New Haven* ran in New York about eleven weeks, and it lost nearly all the cash put on it. And yet more people saw the play in those eleven weeks than bought *Catch-22* in the whole first year.

Sale: Those are amazing statistics.

Heller: And the show was playing to a theater that was half empty during the week. That's a picture of the economics of the matter.

Sale: Has *We Bombed in New Haven* been performed frequently around the country?

Heller: Oh, yes, it's done on campuses all over the place and by community theaters too. I imagine every amateur production has been better than the New York production, where there was a great degree of self-consciousness on the part of the professionals. For example, the performance at West Virginia State College—the first act especially— was better than the New York production. And they didn't even have a drama school.

Sale: You mentioned that you are working on a playscript of *Catch-22*. Is that going to be an expensive production?

Heller: No, when I finish it, I'm just going to sell the rights directly to Samuel French. I never want to be personally involved in the pro- duction of a play again. I will write the script, and the script, like *We Bombed in New Haven,* in various places leaves things up to the director and the cast. They will be free to leave out or change scenes as they want. It should be that way because they have to take the rap for it.

Sale: What of the humor in your work? In any calculated way do you work toward a humorous climax in any given scene?

Heller: I tried very hard in *Catch-22* to take out anything that would only be of a humorous nature, that didn't contribute to the feeling of absurdity. The manuscript of *Catch-22* ran about eight hundred type-written pages. We cut out about a hundred seventy-five. The parts that were taken out—very little in the way of actual incident—were just as funny as what was left in. But I thought it was going on too long and none of it would be funny.

I don't want to be a humorist. Humor in *Catch-22* was not the end but the means to an end. And as I've said, in *Something Happened,* a different type of novel, I don't think there is any humor. It is a serious novel. And I've discovered, since I spoke to you on your campus last spring, that in mood and in tone and in many other respects it is not much different from the kind of novel Samuel Beckett wrote. Over the summer I read *Molloy, Malone Dies,* and in particular, *The Unnamable.* Both *Molloy* and *Malone Dies* are about the character writing. The mind is writing down the book you're reading as you read it.

I'm not Beckett but myself using a similar device. *Something Happened* is essentially about a man working in an office, a speech writer or a promotion writer, I never make it specific. The work is boring to him, he doesn't have too much to do, and he begins writing a book. And like the Beckett trilogy, every once in a while there is an allusion to the fact that he is writing now what you are reading.

Sale: Do you think it is dangerous to read authors you admire very much while you are writing? Aren't you afraid they'll influence the way you write?

Heller: On the contrary, I keep rereading them. At the beginning of *Something Happened,* I purposely made the style look almost like a Dick and Jane kind of thing in a children's reader. At that time, I started to read something by Faulkner but stopped because Faulkner's language was not what I wanted then. As I get into the book, the language becomes progressively more complex. But at the beginning, the character is disorganized, almost anally fixated and controlled.

Sale: Is the section that appeared in *Esquire* the beginning of the book?

Heller: Yes, that starts the breakdown. In spite of himself, he becomes more honest in his emotions, and you see this in the language and the sentences. At this stage of the writing I read Faulkner just to keep that stylistic possibility open. And I read Beckett and Dostoevsky because I want to absorb their language. I want to be immersed in that type of expression.

Sale: You've mentioned Dostoevsky and I think you may have mentioned Faulkner before. Looking back to the late fifties, do you think of anybody else?

Heller: Well, Nathanael West. Certainly Céline was a name I mentioned to you. Céline has no place in this new book. Faulkner, Beckett, and maybe Thomas Mann. I read *The Fall* again; the third-person narration there is similar to what I'm doing. I read *The Stranger* when I was working on the first part of the book.

Sale: That would work because of the stark simplicity.

Heller: Right, and I wanted it to be very simple. Now that it's more complex, I reread *The Fall* and I'm rereading Faulkner.

Sale: May we go back to *Catch-22*? Someone has called Yossarian the Innocent.

Heller: I would say it's a good description. Yossarian is innocent and good.

Sale: Why isn't he corrupted like everybody else? Like most of the people?

Heller: Most of the good people in *Catch-22* are not corrupted, not the sympathetic characters. Your question should be: how come he doesn't die?

Sale: How come he doesn't die?

Heller: Okay. He does when he goes away.

Sale: You didn't mean that.

Heller: No, I didn't mean that. How come he doesn't die? Because he does take his step to save himself.

Sale: That could kill him.

Heller: Well, if he kept flying missions, he could get killed. And if Yossarian is described as the perennial innocent, Orr is his counterpart, someone who is good but also has insights, so many insights that Yossarian lacks.

Orr is the most intelligent person in the book. You have to read it twice or three or four times to realize that throughout the book Orr is playing a game. He is advancing a false self so that even Yossarian feels sorry for him. And all the book long Orr has figured out his survival, and he knows that part of surviving is to conceal his real intentions. And all the book long he has two missions really: he is practicing being shot down, and he wants to protect Yossarian. He wants to leave him with a warm tent so that Yossarian will be able to survive the winter. Oh, and the third thing is to keep both intentions secret. In order to keep them secret, he lets himself be considered a dopey kid.

Sale: Have you really answered the question how Yossarian can stay pure?

Heller: Well, staying pure isn't so hard in this world. Most of the people I meet or I get friendly with—

Sale: The nice guy is victimized.

Heller: Yes, the nice guy is victimized. But I'm surprised by your question, because today, I think every campus has anywhere from forty to two thousand good people. One of the things in the book is the development, the birth of Yossarian's consciousness of himself as a moral being. Through most of *Catch-22* Yossarian feels all that he wants to do is survive the war. The colonels say, "You can go home." And he accepts it at first.

He has deluded himself into thinking that all he wants to do is survive. He has the opportunity and accepts it in despair. In the hospital he finds that he can't accept it because there's a moral life inside him. As scared as he is of dying, he doesn't want to live if it has to be in terms of calling those colonels by their first names. Being on a first-name basis with the Establishment. He would rather be a fugitive. It is an awesome decision.

You say how come he's not one of them? You remember on campus the day of the moratorium the girl who got up on the stage and made the speech about the principles of the young, the tragedy at Kent State, and the need to tell people these things. She was scared, but she made her speech. You see, it's not that hard.

Sale: She is a generation younger than Yossarian and may be partly shaped by him.

Heller: Well, he's my generation. In the fifties he was a little bit ahead of us. You know, what I do is nothing compared to what other people do, the young people in the world of protest. I think of Cassius Clay. He likes to be called Muhammad Ali, and I'll call him

Muhammad Ali. He and Dr. Spock, to give an example of a person younger than me and older than me, have taken steps which I haven't been called upon to take. And I don't know if I could if I were.

Sale: You've had your man Yossarian.

Heller: All I want to say is it ain't that hard. It ain't that hard to be good, you know, to take a stand on something.

Sale: Can we end with some comment on Yossarian's trip through Rome, that night of hallucinations.

Heller: I was aware of all the parallels in that chapter. I mentioned Raskolnikov twice and I mentioned Christ. But there is a danger in a work of fiction that's supposed to have been realistic of making too many allusions. I didn't want to in that chapter, but the reference to Raskolnikov is there for two reasons. One is that there is a kind of street scene that Dostoevsky creates so vividly in *Crime and Punishment* and other works. As I mention, Yossarian saw a man who was beating his dog with a stick like the man who was beating the horse with the whip in Raskolnikov's dream. For those who know Raskolnikov, who know Dostoevsky, they will see that it's that kind of scene. And also, the reader thinks on those as really surrealistic scenes describing surrealistic matter.

Sale: Which they are, aren't they?

Heller: Yes, but the chapter's called "The Eternal City." It could have fittingly been called "Crime and Punishment." You keep seeing crime after crime. With Aarfy's rape and murder of the girl, Dostoevsky was still on my mind. So was Dante. It was a trip to the underworld, a purgation from which Yossarian emerges. Remember the last episode there. It has to do with an old woman he doesn't help. He is guilty, and that is the dark beginning of his moral consciousness.

Notes on the Next Novel: An Interview with Joseph Heller

Brother Alexis Gonzales/1970

From *New Orleans Review*, 2 (1971), 216–19. Reprinted by permission.

Alexis: Are there any novelists who influence your writing? Who are they?

Heller: Kafka and Samuel Beckett are two of my most important novelists. Kafka did influence *Catch-22* and is influencing *Something Happened.* I was not familiar with Beckett when I wrote *Catch-22*; but I have since been amazed by certain very striking similarities in view and language-use in *Catch-22* and Beckett's early novels *Murphy* and *Watt.* This past summer, I read Beckett's trilogy, *Molloy, Malone Dies,* and *The Unnamable,* and found to my astonishment, that very, very much of Beckett's view and technique in these are present in *Something Happened.* And from here on in, the resemblances in *Something Happened* will be conscious and deliberate. And Kafka's view of the world too is present in *Something Happened.* The difference is that I try to present the same dilemmas and all the horror in situations that are not in any way abnormal or out of the ordinary.

Alexis: What about the contemporaries?

Heller: I think that compared to my present admiration for Beckett as dramatist and novelist, any admiration I might express for any of the contemporaries would be small by comparison. I think I would choose Philip Roth, John Barth, and J.D. Salinger as those whose works hold the greatest amount of interest for me at this time.

Alexis: Have you seen the film version of your book *Catch-22*?

Heller: Yes, I have, and I think it's one of the best movies I've ever seen. It isn't a photographed version of the novel. If it were it would be a very dreary motion picture as most film adaptations taken from plays and novels usually are. Many characters are left out, many episodes are omitted, as they would have to be. It is, after all, a very long novel with too many characters to make a successful movie. Things are com-

pressed, characters are combined. The effect is to create in cinematic
terms pretty much what I would have created had I set out to write a
screenplay, rather than a literary work. The spirit is there, the episodes
are there. The formula or relationships of humor to the morbid has a sort
of grotesque effect. The use of time, rather than sequential flow, exists.
It exists as a unity. The fragmentation of episodes as in the movie in
place of those values which only fiction has reflects the interior monologue, depth, pace, turgidity—these are really critical of a fiction
writer. Mike has used the camera, the color in a very strange way; I
have never seen anything like it. The use of light and composition in
some scenes becomes works of art, works like one can see in some of
the best museums in the world. The visual elements are the best I have
seen because they're not visual in their visual prettiness alone, they are
organic, they fit not only with the book, but they seem to stem from it,
and serve to constitute an organic whole. I've never seen a movie, I
think, that was so much of one piece, as *Catch-22*.

Alan Arkin as Yossarian is superb. He gives the best performance of
his career, and the best performance I can remember, and yet he does
not dominate the movie, but fits into the totality. These are things you
don't often find in a movie and which I regard as the only way to get a
faithful representation of a novel, which is really to exploit a novel form
or to forget the sequence of the book, forget the prose, but to take the
intention of the author, and the content of it, almost as if to decompose
it and put it back together in a new formula or structure, using the same
materials, working within a different medium.

Scenes in the movie which I thought Mike might have eliminated
from the beginning are included. These are very tough scenes, scenes
which I thought might be too strong for a movie. A scene, for example,
of Milo blowing up his own squadron. I would have suggested that he
leave that out, because in the novel it's almost an allegorical scene,
rather than a literal one, and I would have said that the audience would
not have believed it. In the film, however, it is vivid, frightening, and
totally credible. Mike has chosen those scenes which are very strong in
the book, and it's a good movie. Mike has done a good job . . . he has
done a much better job than I thought was possible.

He is a humorous man. If you had to work in this movie you'd have
two things you don't often get: a director who is an extremely literate
person, and a leading man who is also extremely literate, an intelligent

person. These are two people, Mike and Alan (I don't want to suggest that the others aren't, but I know these two fairly well), who have highly developed sensibility. They've read everything, just about; and they are very serious people. It's a pleasure to sit with them. You can get into a discussion of Bach's music or Marcel Proust; there's no allusion, no subject that we can come up with that they won't talk about.

Alexis: Did you go on location?

Heller: No. I had nothing to do with the movie.

Alexis: Did Buck Henry consult with you?

Heller: We had a meeting which at the time I thought was a kind of courtesy meeting. Mike Nichols called me and said that he'd like me to read the script. I read it, and met him at dinner. I told him all I liked about the script, and a few things that troubled me. I came away with the feeling that it was really a courtesy session. But when I met Mike a couple of weeks later in California, he made reference to some of my remarks, so apparently he did remember.

And also a quality of that version of the script that had troubled me had been edited out of it, as I felt it should have. And Nichols, once I got to know him better, I realized how sensitive he was, how much of a perfectionist, also. I felt that some of the lines of dialogue were kind of joke lines and superfluous. That troubled me. Anyway, they're all out of the movie. I don't think there's a superfluous moment. There's no searching for an easy laugh anywhere in the movie. Anyway he did remember some of the things I said.

Alexis: What was the budget? Did they go over?

Heller: It depends on what date they pick. I think what they tend to do is to take the starting date of shooting as the budget date . . . that is the day they send the first technician down . . . to an area. By that time, which was January, I think the budget was up to $13 million. Mike says $14.7 million. Other people say $18 million. I don't know who's right. I hope Mike is right. He's annoyed at the $18 million. I think originally, when they were at the talking stage, before they realized how good a movie Nichols wanted to make, they were speaking of about six to eight million dollars. Mike has said in other interviews that he would not have made a cheap picture out of *Catch-22*. In one meeting with people at Paramount he said it should either be done right or not at all, that they were going to have to spend at least ten to twelve million dollars for it. And he's done it right. The people don't understand, that in order to do something, one has to hold fast. It's difficult to understand why one minute on the screen can cost $300,000.00, because it might take five days to shoot that one minute perfect.

Alexis: Did you see the completed version, the one that will be released?

Heller: I saw the version that will be released apart from some improvement in the sound and perhaps some minute changes Mike might still want to make. I saw it on a Sunday, two Sundays ago. That Friday or Thursday the movie was sneak-previewed in Boston and editors of the college newspapers in the area were invited, and word had leaked out that *Catch-22* was to be shown at 8:00 p.m. and people began lining up at the theatre from 10:30 a.m. on and sat through whatever the feature was four or five times, and so many remained outside that they ran a second. The audience reaction there was everything that Nichols and the executives at Paramount and a number of movie owners in the area could have hoped for. They laughed at all the funny parts, were stunned, stone still at the serious parts, and there was considerable weeping. A person at Paramount who's in charge of campus publicity was there and he said that he had never before been part of a movie audience where college kids began to cry. It is possibly one of the most powerful movies I've ever seen.

Alexis: The Board of Censors has given *Catch-22* an "R" rating. What did they object to?

Heller: Well an R rating is better than an X rating. I think it barely escaped an X. I think they objected to a bit of bad language. There are a couple of sex scenes, but they're very tame. Alan Arkin is in bed naked, with a girl, naked, but they are covered and they don't make love. Thank God! There is also one quick scene of an act of love, and it's no more than a tenth-of-a-second long as Alan walks through the streets of Rome, the camera hits an alleyway, and there's a soldier and a girl there, and it's so quick that many people will miss it. It could have been that. There is some language, but I don't recall. I really don't know. I didn't know it was R rated.

Alexis: Have you seen Robert Altman's *M*A*S*H?*

Heller: No. Not yet. In New York you have to stand in line for hours to see a good movie. Ring Lardner, Jr., who did the screenplay for *M*A*S*H* I know very well. He knows the novel *(Catch-22)* very well. He was one of those who went to jail with the Hollywood Ten during the black list days of Senator Joseph McCarthy. These were men who could have pleaded the Fifth Amendment and suffered no penalty. I think Dalton Trumbo, Ring Lardner, Jr., I don't know about Abraham Polonsky, went to jail. They were ten, and they refused to plead the Fifth Amendment and decided to defy the investigation on the basis of the First Amendment, freedom of the press and speech, and they were found guilty and sentenced. I think, since then, there were some Supreme Court decisions which would have allowed that sentence to be reversed.

Alexis: Mr. Heller, could you comment on the present student protests?

Heller: I am in total sympathy with the students. I think indifferences and stupidity of the government administration has made it necessary to move from peaceful dissent to acts of violence. I hold the administration guilty, Nixon and Agnew particularly guilty for the shooting at Kent State. Agnew has been inciting to riot in every speech he makes, they are almost paraphrases of the Nazi speeches in Germany . . . the "rotten apples" that have to be separated from our society. It's almost a license to the local policeman or national guardsman to treat these students as they do. I think Nixon and Agnew are as guilty of the deaths of those four pupils . . . as the men who did the shooting. I think that any other course than this at this time would result in a loss of freedom in this society. The war is illegal. Nixon has not signed a declaration of war. There's an absence of a declaration of war. Nixon is a liar. He's a habitual liar, as Johnson was before him on this Vietnam war. Nothing he says has any right to be believed, but whether the troops will or won't be withdrawn by the first of July, I think it's a mistake he made, and he knows it, because they're apparently accomplishing nothing there anyway. But even apart from that, he's never sought a declaration of war for the Vietnam war and so consequently it's an illegal war. It's a moot point as to whether the Selective Service Act can be enforced and the government has carefully avoided any court case which would bring the legality of war into question. I think the students are the most hopefully refreshing thing in the country. I think they're doing the dirty work for a lot of middle-class respectable people like myself.

Alexis: Do you think these kids are the Yossarians that have sprung up and are doing what he would do today?

Heller: When I wrote *Catch-22* things were relatively calm in this

country. They are doing what he would do and what he should have
done in *Catch-22*. The possibility of such collective action, of such
widespread dissent was not really something to be considered in the
'50s. It just didn't take place, and there didn't seem to be any immediate need for it. This is an alternative that he doesn't consider in the
book. It's touched on very sparely in *Catch-22*. The idea of collective
action, when the character Dobbs wants him to become his accomplice
in an effort to kill the colonel and Yossarian declines. Later Yossarian
decides he must kill the colonel, that his salvation depends on it. Then
Dobbs won't do it. By the end of the book, there is no one left for
Yossarian to join with. I think undoubtedly that what Yossarian is
reacting against has come to be a reality in the past four or five years
and intensifies. He would be reacting to that and he would be out with
them, and I am all for it. I mean, there has been no act of violence yet. I
can't recall any except for the incident in New York where the building
blew up. I can't recall when somebody has been killed except by the
police or the national guardsmen. And anytime I read about these fire-
bombs going up in mysterious explosions all over the country I am
delighted, because I think that the enemies of this country are in Washington, and it's nonsense. The argument that all these protests encourage the enemy is nonsense, because the enemy is first Lyndon Johnson,
then Agnew, Nixon and Kissinger. They are the ones, I think, that are
the danger to this country, and they must be opposed in the only way
left for us to oppose them.

When Martin Luther King turned back from the bridge at Selma, he
lost the support of so many, particularly Eldridge Cleaver and the ones
who later became the Black Panthers because they had come down there
for violent confrontation, as Cleaver writes. This was an opportunity
to expose publicly the real nature of the opposition to the blacks in
Alabama who had been turned back from the bridge. There was a great
lessening of enthusiasm and a feeling of defeat. It is a fact that violence
and the terrorism that it suggests is, and always has been, an effective
weapon. And since the government is deaf, dumb and blind to the poor
attempts of persuasion—there is nothing left but violence or protest.
The protest has been met with indifference and contempt and insult, and
an enticement to more violence, particularly by Agnew's suggestions
that these people should be mistreated the way that the local authorities
want them to.

Alexis: Have you been involved in any peace marches or protests?

Heller: I have a daughter of 18, and she's been on peace marches and civil rights marches, but these have tended to decrease as they've been ignored. I've not been asked to to any extent. Yes, I think I was asked to go to Washington, to go in the parade. I couldn't come to Austin to make a five minute speech on the moratorium, it's a long way from New York, but in New York I would. I was on the last Washington march. I'm not considered a first stringer. They generally go for Norman Mailer first.

Alexis: Do you think *Catch-22* influenced today's college youth?

Heller: I don't think a writer's work of literature really influences people. It shapes them. It does confirm what they themselves might suspect. I think *Catch-22* is attractive to people today, because the people themselves are attractive. They themselves have certain thoughts, certain ideas, certain attitudes and they find them expressed in *Catch-22*. The same with Bob Dylan songs, the Beatles' songs have an appeal for them because they themselves can respond to it now, in a way that many people could not respond to *Catch-22* when it first came out, and do respond to it now. Many, many people said they couldn't read it, or were not interested in reading it past the first two pages, when it first came out, then tried again a few years later. There was a girl at Our Lady of the Lake, yesterday, I suppose she was about twenty, she said she couldn't read the book when she tried it about four or five years ago, then went back a year or two later, and she couldn't understand why she had trouble the first time. It's the prose style, hundreds and hundreds of people have called me and told me they started reading it and stopped because it was too confusing in the beginning. So many people have told me that that I think it's a valid criticism.

If I were doing the novel over again I would try to make the early chapters a little more coherent. I wanted to suggest confusion by being confusing, but not so confusing as to chase readers away, but I hear that less and less among people, for two reasons: now the novel has a reputation and people will have patience with a novel that has a reputation. Most good works of literature are not all pleasure. If you've ever read Thomas Mann or James Joyce or Marcel Proust. The novel isn't intended to be easy the way movies are. Movies are easy forms of apprehension. Plays are. If they aren't then audiences don't enjoy them. Plays and movies go at their own pace. You can't re-read them. I think cinema is close to being a sybaritic kind of entertainment, and I suspect that many people go to see many inferior movies only because they're too lazy to read a book.

Alexis: Do you go to movies or the theatre much?

Heller: I almost never go to the theatre. I go only if someone I know is connected with the production. And I go to the movies seldom. The kinds of plays I like are not produced anymore, and if they are they're produced off-Broadway in uncomfortable theatres and close before I get tickets. I did make it a point to see *Mahagonny* in New York because it's the first time it's been in this country, and I would go to see Samuel Beckett's plays, even though I'm not sure it's a pleasure to watch Samuel Beckett. Like fiction the theatre is not supposed to be pure pleasure. Movies are almost always pleasure.

Most movies I find, even the good ones, are somewhat shallow and thin. Even what passes for a serious movie is very thin compared to what passes for a serious play, and I think both are pretty thin and shallow in contrast to what can be said about a work of fiction. Movies I distrust very much because there's a kind of pandering that goes on to the popular taste and very often it's subtle enough so that the public is taken in by it. I think there's a considerable amount of pandering going on toward the young audience. They're not good movies. They are movies that deal with things the young people want. And they are movies which have a viewpoint which I know young people have. And the uncritical spectator will rate and appraise film only for those reasons, not because the film is particularly good, not because the screenplay is good, not because it's authentic, but simply because it has a scene with a hippie smoking pot, and a lovemaking scene which they identify with.

Alexis: What is the book you're working on presently?

Heller: It's titled *Something Happened*. It's about this executive 43 years old, married, with children, unhappy with his marriage, his children, his job, the condition of the world. But finds that at this point of his life what means more to him than anything else is to be allowed to make a three minute speech at the next company convention in Bermuda.

That's pretty much the plot of the novel. It's going to be very long unfortunately, because it's going to take me a long time to finish it. The title is ironic because *nothing happens* in the novel. There is no plot, no action. So far it's very successful, the two people with whom I've checked *Catch-22* out as I wrote in sections are rather astounded at how effective it is so far. If I can sustain this another four or five hundred pages I'm hoping to finish it this year, but I may be two or three months late. I worked on *Catch-22* seven years. This will be hard to measure in time, because the play, *We Bombed in New Haven,* took me away from the novel for two full years. I don't know where the time went. I wasn't working that hard on it. The thing I don't like about the play is that even though there isn't work to be done, the process of production commands one's whole attention anyway. And I would sit around for weeks or months at a time just raising a question or giving answers to a question and yet being unable to concentrate on any other kind of work. Working with so many people it does really become a collaborative effort, one in which the playwright and the script are not the most important elements.

Hanging Out

Robert Alan Aurthur/1974

From *Esquire*, September 1974, 50, 54, 64. Reprinted by permission of *Esquire*/The Hearst Corporation.

Okay, the word is out, proof in the form of ten-dollar copies of *Something Happened,* soon to be in your local bookstores: novelist Joseph Heller will not be America's most celebrated one-book author since Michael Arlen and *The Man in the Green Hat.* Faded from memory, if not completely forgotten, Arlen retired while he was ahead, lived the good expatriate life mostly in the South of France, remains at best a literary curiosity. Joe Heller, while perhaps dreaming of devoting his middle years to lazing on the Côte d'Azur, never considered quitting. Though almost thirteen years to the day will have passed between the publication dates of *Catch-22* and the second novel, Heller has been working—doggedly, slowly, steadily. *Slowly!* Thirteen years. Yet, because *Catch-22* was such a phenomenon, more than a book—a cause, a celebration, a definition, an anticipation of the insanity of Vietnam, a big but lousy movie (not adapted by Heller), a modest but marvelous play (adapted by Heller)—it never seemed that Joe Heller was out of the sketch. In reviews and studies of war novels, Heller and *Catch* were always produced as standards; he was constantly cited among the best and most original of the black humorists; he became defined as one of the great contemporary surrealists. Surely an artist. All a result of the one book.

More than a year ago, finding myself sitting around with Heller, having heard he was closing in on the finish of the second novel, and sensing a big moment to be recorded, I asked Joe on what day he planned to write The End. "August twenty-first," Heller said instantly. "What time?" I asked. "Three-ten p.m.," he said. Fine, I told him, I'll be there. Heller never blinked nor asked why, simply nodded. A shared awareness that significant moments in literary history deserve recognition. But, then . . . well, it turned out he wasn't even home on August twenty-first; then it got to be October; and on January eleventh, the day

100

Something Happened was finished, not I nor anyone was there to record the event.

Now it is midsummer, 1974, and one begins to hear that Joseph Heller has another big one. Without my help both *The New York Times* and *Newsweek* ran features to celebrate the completion of the manuscript; *Harper's Bazaar* called to confirm; the BBC sent a film crew for an interview. *Something Happened* is a Literary Guild main selection, a major paperback sale brews, foreign rights have been snapped up. Yes, a biggie, and so I call Joe to suggest I do a column. "The theme for your piece should be," Heller says, after agreeing to meet me the following day, "that [playwright Murray] Schisgal is halfway through the book and has nothing but good things to say about it." That's encouraging news. A mutual friend, Schisgal is known to be extremely grumpish, often hypercritical. I hustle to Schisgal's house for confirmation; is it true he's halfway through the book? Holding the yellow-covered bound galleys, Schisgal nods. "I had dinner with Joe last night and the night before," he says. Well, how's the book? Murray stares off thoughtfully. "I have never . . . not *ever* seen a man eat as much as Joe Heller," he says. But, what about the book? "Last night," says Murray, "we were put out of a restaurant when they had to close, and Heller was still on the first course." The *book*? "The book is brilliant," Murray says. "The man is a great writer. There are parts in here no other writer in the world could approach; he gets right down to the bone. The work in the first half is stunning, and Joe says it keeps getting better." A pause; and then, for no apparent reason beyond complete awe, Schisgal says, "Except for eating, I don't think Joe Heller likes to do *anything*. He leads a life of active boredom. He's the most bored man I know."

Joe and Shirley Heller, married for more than twenty-five years, own a summer house in the Amagansett dunes. It is raining heavily when I arrive, rain being appropriate underscoring for a meeting with a bored novelist. Joe comes out to meet me, accompanied by a bounding animal which, to a non-dogman, looks like a large poodle with a naked black tail. As we enter the house I remark that I've never before seen such a tail on a poodle. Heller is indignant. "Sweeney is a Bedlington terrier," he says; and then to the dog: "Did you hear what the schmuck called you, Sweeney? And he had the nerve to criticize your tail!" Sweeney couldn't care less, runs around the living room, a room that is tastefully neat, mostly white, pristine. There is a large Robert Natkin painting;

over the fireplace is a wildly colorful poster of an artist showing in
Menton; on another wall are three Matisse lithographs mounted in one
frame, discovered and bought by Shirley Heller. Bright, cheery, attractive, Shirley quickly assembles coffee, collects Sweeney, and both
disappear. On a tape machine a Mozart quartet plays at exactly the right
level—loud enough to be heard but not at all intrusive. Heller and I
settle into comfortable chairs, facing each other across a large coffee
table. Without prompting, Heller says, "You know, the opening section
of my book appeared in the September 1966 issue of *Esquire*."

Yes, I remember; he goes on. "The way it happened, I was carrying
the manuscript around with me, about forty pages, and I left it in a Horn
and Hardart's. In total paranoia I pictured some guy finding the pages,
rushing out and publishing it under his own name. So I told my agent to
submit a carbon somewhere quick to establish my copyright. Rust Hills
was fiction editor then, and he bought it. At the time I had a second
section of a hundred and twenty pages, but when I went back and
revised the first forty it grew to another hundred and twenty pages. Then
those two hundred and forty pages were revised to become more than
six hundred. In the original version, and you might find it interesting to
compare the *Esquire* piece with what I have now, my character's name
was Joe Slocum; he worked for a guy named Green, and he was offered
Green's job. The name Joe Slocum came from my then five-year-old
son. At dinner one night, when I first started the book, I said, 'What
should I call the guy in my new book?' and instantly my son said, 'Joe
Slocum.' So I did, but later I changed the first name to Bob to avoid
confusion with my own first name. In the finished book—there were
eleven hundred manuscript pages from which I cut about three hundred—Slocum has two bosses above him, and his chance is at a better
job.

"The same thing happened in *Catch*. The first time around there was
only one general, but when I began to like him I created another general, Peckem, to take over those qualities of rottenness I'd originally
given to Dreedle."

A man whose first job after his World War II Air Force service was to
teach freshman English at Penn State, who later worked in the advertising and promotion departments of *Time* and *Look* magazines, Heller
seems neither to know nor care where the art comes from; nonetheless

he appears to be fascinated by and quite involved with the schematics of his own work method. It's as if by examining his spontaneous creative process, a force which keeps him going in what often seems, at least to observers, an incredibly protracted pursuit, he will learn something important about himself. But not necessarily to try to change or effect anything. He spent seven years writing *Catch-22*.

"I missed my deadline by four years," he says. "Bob Gottlieb was a twenty-six-year-old editor, and I think I was his first writer. Not his first published writer, however, because I worked so slowly. It came so hard I really thought it would be the only thing I ever wrote. Working on *Catch* I'd become furious and despondent that I could only write a page a night. I'd say to myself, '*Christ, I'm a mature adult with a master's degree in English, why can't I work faster?*' But with the new book I was spared that anger and despair. My personal deadline was January first, 1969. Okay, so when I missed it by five years, it didn't bother me, knowing that was the way I worked, that's how it was. Actually, I took two years off to write the play *We Bombed in New Haven*, then came back to the book."

When I ask about the physical method, he says, "First I work in longhand on yellow legal pads. I'll do three or four pages, then think them over. I never go on unless I'm satisfied. One section of three pages eventually became more than six hundred with the same opening and closing sentences." He laughs. "I just filled in a little."

Heller types his own handwritten material, changing and revising as he goes. When he finishes a section, or "a book" as he calls it, he sends it off to a professional typist. In Amagansett he manages four work periods a day. "Before breakfast, then from ten till lunch. After lunch I'll work till I feel like going to the beach, and finally I'll get in a session in the evening. In the days when I was heavy I always gave out in the afternoon and had to sleep. I couldn't work."

Speaking of heavy. . . .

At fifty-one, Joe Heller is obviously a man in splendid physical condition, a trim one hundred and sixty pounds, but there was a time, just five years ago, when he weighed over two hundred. I tell Joe that as impressed as Murray Schisgal is with *Something Happened*, our playwright friend respects even more Heller's ability to hold down the weight despite his renowned eating habits. "The fact is," Heller says, "I was really a thin man who put on a lot of weight. I did fine till I was thirty; then I went to work for *Time* and got on all that expense-account food and booze. At the same time I quit smoking, when cigarettes went to twenty-four cents a pack, plus the cancer scare. So I put on fifty pounds. In those days I got named The Locust. Whatever was there I'd eat it. Even today, as long as there's meat on the table I'll continue to eat, but won't miss it if it's taken away. But when we did *We Bombed in New Haven* I saw a publicity picture of myself, noted all the double chins, and decided enough was enough. Only twice in my life have I ever shown willpower—when I quit smoking and when I took off the weight. The way I hold it down is by running three or four miles a day. I have grapefruit and coffee for breakfast, a light lunch, if any, and a *huge* dinner. Schisgal sees me only at dinner."

"Murray says you live a life of active boredom," I tell Joe. "Yeah," he says. "He says you're the most bored man he knows," I go on, and again, quickly, Joe says, "Yeah." A brief pause. "Somehow he's infuriated that there's nothing I do that I really enjoy. More to the point, there's nothing *he* does that I enjoy. Like, the other night he suggested we go *bowling*. I said he could bowl, and I'd watch. A lot of people seem to feel that if they're not in some kind of action they're missing something. Well, when I do nothing the time flies. It only goes slowly when I work. But if I have nothing to do it doesn't upset me. I no longer feel I'm missing anything."

At the risk of being cruel I ask if he's planning another book. "I have no idea at all," Heller says without rancor. "It would be so lovely to have another one working while I'm waiting for this one to come out. But I feel absolutely no necessity for it. I have enough income from the two books and my teaching."

With the mention of teaching, Heller becomes animated. "There *is* something I like," he says. "Teaching takes a lot of my time, and I enjoy it . . . a lot."

Heller has just finished his third year, with the rank of full professor, at New York's City College, teaching graduate and undergraduate courses in fiction. "The hardest thing to teach these people is that writing is hard work—and hard work for everyone," he says. "I've got a doctor who wants to give up medicine, a lawyer who wants to quit the law. They read the finished, published work and think that's exactly the way the writer dictated it." He grins. "Well . . . they're wrong."

Joseph Heller

George Plimpton/1974

From *The Paris Review,* 15 (Winter 1974), 126–47. Reprinted as "Joseph Heller" in *Writers at Work: The Paris Review Interviews, Fifth Series,* ed. George Plimpton. New York: Viking Press, 1981. Copyright © 1981 by The Paris Review. Used by permission of Viking Penguin, a division of Penguin Books USA Inc. A version of this interview also appeared as "How It Happened," *New York Times Book Review,* 6 October 1974, 2, 3, 30.

This interview with Joe Heller took place during the week of the publication of *Something Happened*—a literary event of considerable significance, since the novel is only the second of the author's career. The first, of course, was *Catch-22.* The fact that it has taken more than a decade to produce a second work of fiction seems of small concern to Heller, since he has evolved a definite and unique pattern of work that is not at all determined by deadlines and other arbitrary demands. He says he always wanted to be a writer. His earliest story was pecked out on a neighborhood boy's type-writer and ultimately rejected by the *Daily News* short-short story editor. His career moved at its own pace. He did no writing during his war years in Italy. His first accepted story appeared in *The Atlantic* (along with a companion piece of fiction by James Jones) in 1948. *Catch-22* wasn't published until ten years later. Heller has no illusions about the diffi-culty of making a living as a novelist. He tells his creative-writing class at the start of every academic year that even if every word a writer writes is published, he will almost surely have to supplement his income, usually by teaching (as Heller does), or perhaps by marrying money. The exigencies of such a career do not seem to have marked Heller himself. He sits very much at ease—an impressive figure (his consid-erable crop of hair seems to surround his face like a lion's ruff), trim (he keeps himself in firm shape by jogging and sticking to a strict diet), and with the detachment of someone talking about a third person he begins describing in a voice strong with the inflections of his native Brooklyn the unique process through which his novels have come to him. . . .

Heller: In 1962 I was sitting on the deck of a house on Fire Island. I was frightened. I was worried because I had lost interest in my job then—which was writing advertising and promotion copy. *Catch-22* was not making much money. It was selling steadily (eight hundred to two thousand copies a week)—mostly by word of mouth—but it had never come close to the *New York Times* best-seller list. I had a wife and two children. I had no idea for another book. I was waiting for something to happen(!), wishing I had a book to start. My novels begin in a strange way. I don't begin with a theme, or even a character. I begin with a first sentence that is independent of any conscious preparation. Most often nothing comes out of it: a sentence will come to mind that doesn't lead to a second sentence. Sometimes it will lead to thirty sentences which then come to a dead end. I was alone on the deck. As I sat there worrying and wondering what to do, one of those first lines suddenly came to mind: "In the office in which I work, there are four people of whom I am afraid. Each of these four people is afraid of five people." Immediately, the lines presented a whole explosion of possibilities and choices—characters (working in a corporation), a tone, a mood of anxiety, or insecurity. In that first hour (before someone came along and asked me to go to the beach), I knew the beginning, the ending, most of the middle, the whole scene of that particular "something" that was going to happen; I knew about the brain-damaged child and, especially, of course, about Bob Slocum, my protagonist, and what frightened him, that he wanted to be liked, that his immediate hope was to be allowed to make a three-minute speech at the company convention. Many of the actual lines throughout the book came to me—the entire "something happened" scene with those solar plexus lines (beginning with the doctor's statement and ending with "Don't tell my wife" and the rest of them) all coming to me in that first hour on that Fire Island deck. Eventually I found a different opening chapter with a different first line ("I get the willies when I see closed doors") but I kept the original, which had spurred everything, to start off the second section.

Interviewer: Was it the same process of "receiving" a first line with *Catch-22*?

Heller: Just about. I was lying in bed in my four-room apartment on the West Side when suddenly this line came to me: "It was love at first sight. The first time he saw the chaplain, Someone fell madly in love with him." I didn't have the name Yossarian. The chaplain wasn't necessarily an army chaplain—he could have been a *prison* chaplain. But as soon as the opening sentence was available, the book began to evolve clearly in my mind—even most of the particulars . . . the tone, the form, many of the characters, including some I eventually couldn't use. All of this took place within an hour and a half. It got me so excited that I did what the cliché says you're supposed to do: I jumped out of bed and paced the floor. That morning I went to my job at the advertising agency and wrote out the first chapter in longhand. Before the end of the week I had typed it out and sent it to Candida Donadio, my agent. One year later, after much planning, I began chapter two.

Interviewer: Is there any accounting for this unique procedure?

Heller: I don't understand the process of imagination—though I know that I am very much at its mercy. I feel that these ideas are floating around in the air and they pick me to settle upon. The ideas come to me; I don't produce them at will. They come to me in the course of a sort of controlled daydream, a directed reverie. It may have something to do with the disciplines of writing advertising copy (which I did for a number of years), where the limitations involved provide a considerable spur to the imagination. There's an essay of T.S. Eliot's in which he praises the disciplines of writing, claiming that if one is forced to write within a certain framework, the imagination is taxed to its utmost and will produce its richest ideas. Given total freedom, however, the chances are good that the work will sprawl.

Interviewer: Can you remember some other opening lines . . . ?

Heller: Well, people have always asked what happened to Dunbar, a character who disappeared in *Catch-22*. So I was thinking of writing a novel about him. The opening line I came up with was obviously cultivated by an advertising slogan for Bigelow rugs that was widespread at the time: "A name on the door deserves a Bigelow on the floor." My variation of it was, "Dunbar woke up with his name on the door, and a Bigelow on the floor, and wondered how he had got there. . . ." So it was a novel about amnesia, Dunbar finding himself in a plush office, not knowing the secretary's name, or how many people were working for him, or what his position was—and gradually finding out. It did not work. I couldn't take my mind past a certain point.

Interviewer: Do you have last lines that come along with those first lines?

Heller: I had a closing line for *Something Happened* before I began writing the book. It was "I am a cow." For six years I thought that was good. I had it on one of my three-by-five notecards. Then I wasn't all that happy with it, and finally I discarded it. But it seemed good at the time, and besides, I can't start writing until I have a closing line.

Interviewer: Once you have an opening (and closing) line in mind, what dictates whether you will continue?

Heller: I think writers move unconsciously toward what they think they can do. The two novels I have written, *Catch-22* and *Something Happened,* I chose to write and write in the way I did because of an instinctive feeling that I could handle the subject matter and the method of dealing with each of them. I have certain gifts. I can be funny—for one-half a page at a time, sometimes even more, though I wouldn't want to push my luck and try to be funny for ten. I can be humorous in several ways—with irony, with dialogue, with farcical situations, and occasionally with a lucky epigram or an aphorism. My inclination, though, is to be serious. But on the other hand, I cannot write an effective straightforward, separate narrative. I can't write description. I've told my editor that I couldn't write a good descriptive metaphor if my life depended on it. In *Catch-22* there is really very little physical description. There is very little in *Something Happened.* Bob Slocum tends to consider people in terms of one dimension; his tendency is to think of people—even those very close to him, his wife, daughter, and son and those he works for—as having a single aspect, a single use. When they present more than that dimension, he has difficulty in coping with them. Slocum is not interested in how people look, or how rooms are decorated, or what flowers are around.

Interviewer: Do you find it restricting to tell the novel through the limited persona of Bob Slocum?

Heller: It's true that I myself could have been much funnier, much more intelligent, much cleverer with words than Slocum is. But I must limit him, because if he had all my attributes he wouldn't be working for that company; he'd be writing *Catch-22.* Still, even though I can't have him talk like Nietzsche or Marcuse, I have unlimited possibilities with him as long as I can establish the personality of someone who is only sure that he is sure of nothing. He is utterly unset, undefined, ambivalent. Thus, I can put him into any frame of mind, have him react from just about any emotional perspective. The opportunities were not too few but too many.

Interviewer: Yes, but . . .

Heller: Besides, your question suggests that Slocum's function is to inform. I don't think, even as an author, that I have knowledge to give to readers. Philosophers might and scientists can. It's possible for me to express something that you can agree or disagree with, but certainly you will have heard it before. So I don't think the "what" distinguishes a good novel from a bad one but rather the "how"—the aesthetic quality of the sensibility of the writer, his craft, his ability to create and communicate.

I don't have a philosophy of life, or a need to organize its progression. My books are not constructed to "say anything." When I was at college, in every literary discussion there was always such an emphasis on "What does he say? What's the message?" Even then I felt that very few authors had anything to say. What was important to me was "What does it do?" This refutes, of course, the idea that the message is the objective of a novel. In fact, any "message" becomes part of the texture, stirred so much that it's as negligible as a teaspoon of salt in a large stew. Think of the number of artists who have done still lifes—a view of a river, or a vase of flowers . . . there is nothing about the choice of subject that is going to startle anybody. What will distinguish one still life from another is what the artist brings to it. To a certain extent that is true of the novelist.

Interviewer: What is your own feeling about Slocum?

Heller: I told several people while I was writing the book that Slocum was possibly the most contemptible character in literature. Before I was finished, I began feeling sorry for him. That has happened to me before. That's why there are two generals in *Catch-22*. General Dreedle certainly had bad qualities, but then there were certain characteristics I liked (he was straightforward, honest, not a conniver), and I found I didn't want to attribute certain unsympathetic qualities to him. So I invented General Peckem as a sort of substitute scapegoat. Very hard to like *him*. But as for Slocum, many of my friends to whom I showed the book found not only compassion for him but strong identification. That surprised me, but I suppose it shouldn't have. He *is* very human.

Interviewer: Does the reaction to your work often surprise you?

Heller: Constantly. And I rely on it. I really don't know what I'm doing until people read what I've written and give me their reactions. I didn't know what *Catch-22* was all about until three months after it came out, when people, often total strangers who had no interest in saying the right (or wrong) things to me, began coming up and talking about the book. It meant different things to them. I thought the chaplain was the second most impressive character in the book (after Yossarian). But it turned out to be Milo. Then, it surprised me that things in *Catch-22* turned out to be very funny. I thought I was being humorous, but I didn't know I would make people laugh. In my apartment one day I heard this friend of mine in another room laughing out loud, and that was when I realized I could be comic. I began using that ability consciously—not to turn *Catch-22* into a comic work, but for contrast, for ironic effect. I really don't think authors know too much about the effect of what they're doing.

Interviewer: Doesn't that bother you . . . that the author (you) has such a tentative grip . . . ?

Heller: No. It's one of the things that makes it interesting. I would only be nervous if I were told that what I'd done was no good and no one would want to read it. I protect myself from that by submitting the first chapter to my agent, and to my editor, and, after about a third of the book is done, to other friends. They can be tough on me.

Interviewer: Do you have an audience you keep in mind when you write?

Heller: Since writing is really performing for people, unconsciously I must have an audience I'm writing for—someone who is really me, I suppose, with my degree of sensibility, my level of education, my interest in literature. . . .

Interviewer: What sort of a discussion do you have with your friends about your work when it's in progress?

Heller: It's never a discussion. They simply tell me what they think is good or bad. I do not always believe them. I try not to talk about it to anyone for years. I think of writing as private enterprise . . . since so much comes from rumination. Nothing is more personal than one's thoughts; I think I'd prefer to keep it that way.

Interviewer: What are the best circumstances for this sort of ruminating?

Heller: I have to be alone. A bus is good. Or walking the dog. Brushing my teeth is marvelous—it was especially so for *Catch-22*. Often when I am very tired, just before going to bed, while washing my face and brushing my teeth, my mind gets very clear . . . and produces a line for the next day's work, or some idea way ahead. I don't get my best ideas while actually writing . . . which is the agony of putting down what I think are good ideas and finding the words for them and the paragraph forms for them . . . a laborious process. I don't think of myself as a naturally gifted writer when it comes to using language. I distrust myself. Consequently, I try every which way with a sentence, then a paragraph, and finally a page, choosing words, selecting pace (I'm obsessed with that, even the pace of a sentence). I say to myself what I hope to put down on paper, but I hope not aloud. I think sometimes I move my lips, not only when I'm writing, but when I'm thinking of what I'm going to be having for dinner.

Interviewer: How long can you keep at it?

Heller: I ordinarily write three or four handwritten pages and then rework them for two hours. I can work for four hours, or forty-five minutes. It's not a matter of time. I set a realistic objective: How can I inch along to the next paragraph? Inching is what it is. It's not: How can I handle the next chapter? How can I get to the next stage in a way that I like? I think about that as I walk the dog or walk the twenty minutes from my apartment to the studio where I work.

Interviewer: Do you put these ideas down as they occur to you?

Heller: I keep a small sheath of three-by-five cards in my billfold. If I think of a good sentence, I'll write it down. It won't be an idea ("have him visit a brothel in New Orleans"). What I put down is an actual line of intended text ("In the brothel in New Orleans was like the time in San Francisco"). Of course, when I come back to it, the line may change considerably. Occasionally there's one that sings so perfectly the first time that it stays, like "My boy has stopped speaking to me and I don't think I can bear it." I wrote that down on a three-by-five card, perhaps on a bus, or after walking the dog. I store them in filing cabinets. The file on *Something Happened* is about four inches deep, the one on *Catch-22* about the length of a shoe box.

Interviewer: Are there card files for unfinished work—like the Dunbar book you mentioned . . . ?

Heller: No. I don't unfinish anything I start, and I don't start—as I've said—until I see the whole thing in my head.

Interviewer: What are some of the other sources for material?

Heller: I pick up a lot from friends. Mel Brooks. George Mandel. Especially Mandel. He talked about his experiences in the war. Once, he told me about talking to an army psychiatrist who asked him about his dreams, and George made one up about holding a fish in his hand. That's a bit in *Catch-22*. I've picked up a lot from him. He had the oddest medical ailment at one time—a stone in his salivary gland. It's very rare. And we can conclude that it was a very *small* stone. Well, it turns up in the hospital scene about the mixed-up records in *Catch-22*. Just a year ago Mandel suddenly became aware that Schrafft's no longer existed in New York, and that the *World-Telegram* wasn't being published anymore—somehow he hadn't noticed—and he said, "My God, soon there'll be nothing left." That went down on one of those three-by-five cards and was used in one of Bob Slocum's digressions in *Something Happened*. He's been very helpful.

Interviewer: What about the influences from your reading?

Heller: Every once in a while I can identify an influence. There's a page and a half in *Something Happened* which I wrote during my Jamesian period . . . the use of the word "ah?" When Slocum tells the psychiatrist he doesn't have auditory hallucinations but thinks he smells excrement, the psychiatrist says "Ah?" a number of times. It's out of *The Ambassadors*. The influence is not especially pronounced.

Interviewer: What about personal contact with contemporary writers? Is that of use?

Heller: I don't think writers are comfortable in each other's presence. We can talk, of course, for five minutes or so, but I don't think we want to socialize. There's always an acute status consciousness relating to how high or low a writer exists in the opinion of the person he's talking to. I've noticed that the opening gambit in conversation between two writers—and I'm always very uncomfortable hearing it—is "I like your work." I've heard it so often. It's so condescending. What if the person had not done any work? He would not be spoken to at all. This sort of relationship is peculiar to writers—after all, our status is never challenged by anyone else, one's jeweler, or a dress manufacturer. No, I don't think two novelists who have enjoyed a high measure of success can exist into their middle years living close to each other if both

Heller: I have to be alone. A bus is good. Or walking the
Brushing my teeth is marvelous—it was especially so for C
Often when I am very tired, just before going to bed, while v
face and brushing my teeth, my mind gets very clear . . . and produces
a line for the next day's work, or some idea way ahead. I don't get my
best ideas while actually writing . . . which is the agony of putting
down what I think are good ideas and finding the words for them and
the paragraph forms for them . . . a laborious process. I don't think of
myself as a naturally gifted writer when it comes to using language. I
distrust myself. Consequently, I try every which way with a sentence,
then a paragraph, and finally a page, choosing words, selecting pace
(I'm obsessed with that, even the pace of a sentence). I say to myself
what I hope to put down on paper, but I hope not aloud. I think sometimes I move my lips, not only when I'm writing, but when I'm thinking of what I'm going to be having for dinner.

Interviewer: How long can you keep at it?

Heller: I ordinarily write three or four handwritten pages and then
rework them for two hours. I can work for four hours, or forty-five
minutes. It's not a matter of time. I set a realistic objective: How can I
inch along to the next paragraph? Inching is what it is. It's not: How can
I handle the next chapter? How can I get to the next stage in a way that I
like? I think about that as I walk the dog or walk the twenty minutes
from my apartment to the studio where I work.

Interviewer: Do you put these ideas down as they occur to you?

Heller: I keep a small sheath of three-by-five cards in my billfold.
If I think of a good sentence, I'll write it down. It won't be an idea
("have him visit a brothel in New Orleans"). What I put down is an
actual line of intended text ("In the brothel in New Orleans was like
the time in San Francisco"). Of course, when I come back to it, the
line may change considerably. Occasionally there's one that sings so
perfectly the first time that it stays, like "My boy has stopped speaking to me and I don't think I can bear it." I wrote that down on a
three-by-five card, perhaps on a bus, or after walking the dog. I
store them in filing cabinets. The file on *Something Happened* is
about four inches deep, the one on *Catch-22* about the length of a
shoe box.

Interviewer: Are there card files for unfinished work—like the
Dunbar book you mentioned . . . ?

Heller: No. I don't unfinish anything I start, and I don't start—as I've said—until I see the whole thing in my head.

Interviewer: What are some of the other sources for material?

Heller: I pick up a lot from friends. Mel Brooks. George Mandel. Especially Mandel. He talked about his experiences in the war. Once, he told me about talking to an army psychiatrist who asked him about his dreams, and George made one up about holding a fish in his hand. That's a bit in *Catch-22*. I've picked up a lot from him. He had the oddest medical ailment at one time—a stone in his salivary gland. It's very rare. And we can conclude that it was a very *small* stone. Well, it turns up in the hospital scene about the mixed-up records in *Catch-22*. Just a year ago Mandel suddenly became aware that Schrafft's no longer existed in New York, and that the *World-Telegram* wasn't being published anymore—somehow he hadn't noticed—and he said, "My God, soon there'll be nothing left." That went down on one of those three-by-five cards and was used in one of Bob Slocum's digressions in *Something Happened*. He's been very helpful.

Interviewer: What about the influences from your reading?

Heller: Every once in a while I can identify an influence. There's a page and a half in *Something Happened* which I wrote during my Jamesian period . . . the use of the word "ah?" When Slocum tells the psychiatrist he doesn't have auditory hallucinations but thinks he smells excrement, the psychiatrist says "Ah?" a number of times. It's out of *The Ambassadors*. The influence is not especially pronounced.

Interviewer: What about personal contact with contemporary writers? Is that of use?

Heller: I don't think writers are comfortable in each other's presence. We can talk, of course, for five minutes or so, but I don't think we want to socialize. There's always an acute status consciousness relating to how high or low a writer exists in the opinion of the person he's talking to. I've noticed that the opening gambit in conversation between two writers—and I'm always very uncomfortable hearing it—is "I like your work." I've heard it so often. It's so condescending. What if the person had not done any work? He would not be spoken to at all. This sort of relationship is peculiar to writers—after all, our status is never challenged by anyone else, one's jeweler, or a dress manufacturer. No, I don't think two novelists who have enjoyed a high measure of success can exist into their middle years living close to each other if both continue writing—I don't believe human nature can accept such a situation. The fact is there are few people with whom I would want to spend even a full weekend . . . to be in the same house or on a fishing trip with, unless I knew them well enough to go off by myself if I wanted to. I don't want to have to entertain them. In a novel you can't spend sixty pages writing about that sort of relationship.

Interviewer: You wouldn't go on a fishing trip with Bob Slocum?

Heller: No.

Interviewer: How close is *Something Happened* to your own experience?

Heller: Neither of my books was intended to be autobiographical. Both were based to a certain extent on experience—*Something Happened* is about someone who works in a company (which I have done) and who has a family (which I have), but it's also based to a great extent on my experience as an observer of other people and a reader of other writers. It's an imaginative work, after all—the most important ingredient in writing fiction is that *choice* is always available: *Who* will? *What* will? I told my wife and children years ago when they knew what *Something Happened* was about that they might think it was an exposé of their family life, and I told them—truthfully—that it was not about them. I did not feel (I said this half-facetiously to my wife) that she was interesting enough, or for that matter, that I myself was, to write a novel about.

I have had no experience with a brain-damaged child. But it turns out that the insecurity Bob Slocum feels not knowing how to deal with it is typical of parents who *do* have that experience . . . what's called "denial"—the refusal to accept the condition. Every time Slocum starts talking about the child, he starts digressing—and it's an accurate reaction.

Interviewer: How do you compare the two novels?

Heller: I think one difference between the two books is that *Catch-22* is concerned with physical survival against exterior forces or institutions that want to destroy life or moral self. *Something Happened* is concerned very much with interior, psychological survival in which the areas of combat are things like the wishes a person has, whether they are fulfilled or not, the close, intimate situations we have with our children when they're small and as they grow older, the memories we have of our relationship with parents as *they* grow older—these are some of the areas of disturbance in *Something Happened.* Of course, these areas are much more difficult to deal with than those in *Catch-22.* Given an Adolf Hitler, or inefficient or corrupt people, or people without sensibilities, we know what the dangers are, and we know what we must try to do. There's a line in *Something Happened:* "It was after the war that the struggle began."

Interviewer: How long did it take you to write the climactic passage about the "something" which happens at the end of *Something Happened*?

Heller: Two minutes. It had all been done years before sitting on that deck in Fire Island.

Interviewer: Do titles come to you easily?

Heller: There have only been a few. "Something Happened" turned up in the fall of '63 when I was walking with George Mandel past Korvettes or Brentano's and a kid came running past and yelled over his shoulder to another, "Hey come on, *something's happened*"—some sort of traffic accident I guess it must have been.

Interviewer: You've spoken about music being important while you are working?

Heller: It overcomes those noises that might distract me—a leaking faucet, my daughter's rock music in the other part of the apartment, or someone else's radio across the courtyard. I have tapes. I mostly listen to Bach, his choral music. Beethoven is OK; he's great, but Bach, for me, is the best.

Interviewer: What about the necessary disciplines of writing?

Heller: Well, I don't have social luncheons with people. By not having lunch with people it means that I do not have two martinis, which usually means the afternoon is not shot, since all I can do after two martinis is read the newspaper.

Interviewer: Still, a considerable amount of time . . .

Heller: I am a mysteriously slow writer. I say "mysteriously" because there is no accounting for it. I didn't start working on *Something Happened* until two years after that day on the Fire Island deck. In the meantime I started a musical comedy, wrote the final screenplay for *Sex and the Single Girl,* and then a television thing that turned out to be a sort of pilot of *McHale's Navy*—none of this especially serious stuff. Then the play *We Bombed in New Haven* took me away—not the writing of it (that only took six weeks) but the time spent working on the two productions. All this delay turned out to be for the better. When I went back to the two hundred and fifty pages I'd managed to get down on paper over those two years, I was able to write the book the way I wanted. I had learned more, and read more. The original forty pages became a hundred and twenty pages; the thirty pages of the second section became eighty; the seventy pages on the wife became a hundred—all of it much different in texture and mood from what I originally had in mind. It has happened with each novel. Originally, I didn't think *Catch-22* could be long enough to be more than a novelette. The addition became not padding but substance with a meaning and quality of its own. I missed my deadline for *Catch-22* by four or five years. I felt that it was the only book I was going to write, so I wanted to do it as well as I could. Actually, I wasn't ever sure I was going to be a writer. When I started *Catch-22,* I thought writing novels might be a useful way to kill time. I remember thinking that when I had the book one-third done and my agent was showing it to editors, that if they all had said, "No," I would not have finished the book. I don't have that narcissistic drive, the megalomania involved in spending years working on a book that no one is really interested in publishing. As it happened, there was no difficulty in finding a publisher. *Catch-22,* by the way, was the first novel I'd ever started.

Interviewer: Has success changed your attitude about living or writing?

Heller: I don't think so. And one reason is that it came to me so late. I don't think it's good to achieve too much at too early an age. What else can the future give you if you've already got all that your imagination has dreamt up for you? A writer is only discovered once in a lifetime, and if it happens very early the impossibility of matching that moment again can have a somewhat corrosive effect on his personality and indeed on the work itself.

Interviewer: It seems to be a peculiarly American dilemma.

Heller: It stems from a fundamental insecurity that afflicts successful Americans, particularly those who are self-made and have succeeded in a field in which there is a high element of risk. They never feel that they deserve their success, or that it is permanent; in fact, they seem to fear that their next book is going to cost them everything they've gained . . . sort of like doubling up at roulette . . . betting on the black five times in a row. Actors suffer the same way. They can't believe it when they are successful. They're positive that an angel looking like Claude Rains is going to appear and say that a mistake has been made and "We're taking it all away from you." I'm not immune to it myself. It bothers me tremendously. But I like to think I'm over the hurdle. If I had finished my two books by the age of twenty-eight, well, I'd have a lot to worry about. That's not enough. But two books at age fifty-one means that the next one won't be due until I'm nearly seventy. I can coast for quite a while.

Interviewer: Could you imagine not starting up again?

Heller: If I thought I might never get an idea for another novel—one of those lines dropping in that provides a whole book—I don't think it would distress me. I've got two books under my belt now. I would be content to consider that a lifetime's work, and I could just putter around and find other things to do. I've been very lucky. I've written two books that were unusual and unusually successful.

Interviewer: When did you begin writing?

Heller: I wanted to be a writer when I was in the sixth grade—of course I wanted to be one without working at it. I wanted to be published in the New York *Daily News,* which published one short story a day in those days, or in *The New Yorker.* I remember writing a story about the Russian invasion of Finland and sending it to the *Daily News,* which, of course, rejected it. I was eleven years old. All my writing was imitative of what I was reading: the magazines that my older brother or sister would bring home; what the circulating libraries carried out in Coney Island, where we lived—why, I think I can remember Jerome Weidman's work in the 1930s better than he does. In 1948, when my first story came out in the *Atlantic* and nearly won the "Atlantic First," I thought I was pretty hot stuff. About that same time, Norman Mailer's *The Naked and the Dead* was published, and he was on the cover of *Saturday Review.* We were about the same age—twenty-six or twenty-seven—and it put me in my place.

Interviewer: What about other fields of writing? Have you considered nonfiction?

Heller: I don't do nonfiction well, and since I work so hard at writing, I might as well concentrate on what I know I can do. I'm too conscious of myself as a writer to be a journalist. I'm a show-off. When I write, I want people to notice me and that I'm doing something different from other people. A journalist—at least the ones I admire—

is a writer who can make me forget his involvement so that I can concentrate on the subject of the piece, not the personality of the author. The journalist and the novelist have completely different intelligences. Journalists almost always compose on typewriters. They rarely do more than one draft. Somehow they think in terms of openings, development, conclusion—all in almost automatic sequences. I envy that gift. But if I had it, I'd be a journalist. You can't have it both ways.

Interviewer: Have you had any of those first lines come to mind since finishing *Something Happened*?

Heller: Dozens! I think when a book is finished and the editor likes it, and it's been handed in, an author goes through a period of nervous craziness. Some writers invest in Canadian uranium stocks; others change agents or wives or commit suicide. Some writers hear voices. It's not a good time in which to trust one's own judgment. The author has been too busy and intent. I remember one first line that came to me during this time was, "The kid, they say, was born in a manger, but frankly I have my doubts." It's not a bad line, but I wouldn't think a book would come out of it. . . . I did go further for a while, and I liked the idea, but it led me ultimately to remember Eliot's opening line about the Magi coming to the manger in, I think, *Ash-Wednesday*—"a cold coming we had of it"—and I gave it up after that. So I guess I'll have to wait around for another line to drop in. . . .

Joseph Heller: 13 Years from *Catch-22* to *Something Happened*

Seth Kupferberg and Greg Lawless/1974

From *Harvard Crimson* 11 October 1974, 3, 6. Reprinted by permission.

Last Friday writer Joseph Heller was in town for the Boston Globe Annual Book Fair, and agreed to an interview with *Crimson* editors Seth Kupferberg and Greg Lawless. Heller came to *The Crimson* that afternoon with his wife, and they were both relaxed and very friendly. The soft-voiced author of *Catch-22* and the just-released *Something Happened* was so responsive that on several occasions he began to talk before a question had been asked. Here follow some excerpts from the discussion.

Q: *I don't know where to begin. We can start—*

A: You don't have to begin at all. Whose idea was it to do an interview with me, the publisher's or yours? You don't have to worry. You ask the questions and if you don't get the picture let me know.

Q: *In your new book,* Something Happened, *the style is radically different from* Catch-22. *Do you see any parallel between the two at all?*

A: The only parallel there is the fact that each has a very conspicuous style which I felt was appropriate to the content of the book. With the subject matter in *Catch-22* I tried very much to make the style part of the content—maybe you found that yourself—the method of telling being as important as what's being told. I think that the same is true with *Something Happened.* What I want to tell in *Something Happened* is so much different in terms of emotions and viewpoint than *Catch-22.* The choice of style I think is very much different from the style used in *Catch-22* . . . and another thing, I certainly didn't want it to read like *Catch-22.* . . . Now you shut the machine off if you're not going to ask me any questions. Otherwise the tape keeps going . . .

[At this point in the interview Heller turned to speak to his wife, who expressed her desire to see Harvard Yard, despite his evident dis-interest.]

We can get somebody to drive you around Harvard Yard while . . . ah . . . this is going on . . . you want to go see a memorial to Kissinger, or McGeorge Bundy or Schlesinger? They've got statues for all of them: Galbraith Park, Schlesinger Square . . .

Q: *Christopher Lehmann-Haupt in his* New York Times *review the other day said that* Something Happened *would anticipate the seventies just as* Catch-22 *anticipated the rise of the military-industrial complex in the sixties. Do you believe that?*

A: No. *Catch-22* was written, not before you were born, but it was partly in outline before you were born. It was published in '61. And in '61 . . . ah . . . Kennedy was president. [Heller verified that Kennedy was indeed president then, and that there was an election in 1960, and continued.] It *did* anticipate—in the sense that it came before the Vietnam War—everything the Vietnam War brought with it, which was—it's not a phrase that I ever use—the 'military-industrial complex.' But it was there and certainly it grew with the whole morality of deception practiced by the executive in dealing with the American people and other nations, which often involves lying and distortion. But what I have to say about the military in *Catch-22*: I don't recall it being characteristic of the military in World War II. It *was* characteristic of the military during the Korean War, during the Cold War, and became manifest during the Vietnam War. It was just a perversion of all codes of honor that are being taught at Annapolis or in American military justice. Misuse of the FBI, the CIA, misuse of the courts, the attorney-general's office, and so forth. Political persecutions. Indictments would be started, trials would be carried out even though the chances of conviction were non-existent, or if convictions were achieved reversal was a certainty afterwards—I'm referring to the Spock trial, or the Ellsberg trial, the Ellsberg trial was a continuation of these things. All these cases are political. We all know that the Ellsberg trial was an attempt by the White House to discredit Ellsberg, or else to persecute him whether they got a conviction or not. Tying somebody up in a trial for two or three years is punishment, and it's a very great punishment. As I say, I don't recall *Catch-22* being characteristic, it *wasn't* characteristic of the military in World War II.

Q: *Why did you set the novel in World War II?*

A: Because I know World War II. I set it toward the end of World War II, the last few months, when Germany was not a factor. The dangers of *Catch-22* don't come from the enemy—they do as far as the flak goes—but the real dangers are the ones that continue after the war comes to an end. Yossarian's own superiors and their superiors are no different from the enemy. All right, *Catch-22* is about a person being destroyed by the war, about people in danger not from enemy forces, but from their own superiors from within the organizations of which they are a part. That is the truth of this country.

Q: *What did Yossarian do after he took off?*

A: I don't know. And I don't think that's really a bona fide question to ask about a book. My book ends with him taking off . . . ah . . . and I can live with the thing like that. I don't know about the reading public. I leave with him getting out of the hospital without being either captured or stabbed by Nately's whore.

Q: *But supposing he got to Sweden?*

A: That becomes a different book—

Q: *What would he do when he got there?*

A: He doesn't expect to get to Sweden, he makes that—I make that clear. He hopes to get to Rome and take his chances from there. What does he do when he gets there? That's not part of the book. He would probably have to go underground as a fugitive . . . wait for amnesty . . . or be captured and punished. As long as he's free, he's free. I saw his being free as perhaps inspiring in others a more critical attitude, an attitude of inspection. It's the same thing with the end of *Something Happened,* it ends where it ends. It's not like a nineteenth-century novel which in its last few pages tells what happens for the next fifty years in each of the characters' lives.

The last line of *Something Happened* is in a way very interesting: "Everyone seems pleased with the way I've taken command." And that's very interesting because it seems—if you know the character—he never feels secure in any situation. He *has* taken command, he's gotten promoted, he's doing very well. But his use of the word "seems" rather than "is pleased" is an indication that he's insecure, he's not sure just how pleased everyone is.

Q: *In* Something Happened, *how come you never named the company for which Slocum worked or either the daughter or the son?*

A: Or the wife. I don't know. The main reason is that I felt in this

book, it would be better if they were not named. I didn't even say what
they do. In *Catch-22,* where Yossarian has a first name, it's only used
twice in the thing—his nickname is used more often. He's never
described physically—Yossarian—other than being suntanned, and kind
of large in build. I don't know why it's that way. I think that in the
books I write I tend to lean away from action-packed kind of literal
realism.

Also, in terms of the character's mental operations—he, like many
men, when they think of certain members of their family never think of
them by name, or almost never think of them by name. The only one
who does have a name is the brain-damaged kid, and Slocum doesn't
think of him as a member of his family. That's why I decided to give
him a name.

Q: *Why did you choose this particular portrait of Robert Slocum, of
all the different ideas you might have had for a second novel?*

A: Well, listen: you don't get that many ideas. Sometimes you have
to tell people who want to be writers, who ask the question, "How come
you don't write one or two novels a year?" the answer is that novelists
just don't get that many ideas. If they get lucky they might get one that
can be developed into a novel. Writers don't have choices. Unless
you're writing for a newspaper, then you're assigned to write theater or
book reviews, or you interview a writer. Playwrights don't, novelists
don't really have a choice of what it is they're going to do. Different
kinds of writers might, you know—like Irving Wallace—if they can
choose from among current events like sex, or campus radicals.

I have to get an idea I can write. If I were going to class here, and I
were writing for a grade, which would mean my writing a novel, then I
would *pick* two or three things if they satisfied the instructor, and write
the best I were able to. But when you're on your own, when a writer's
on his own, he's lucky if he can get one good idea. He writes only for
himself, he's no longer writing for the faculty of a university. It takes a
long time. It takes me longer than most, but most novelists spend at
least a year or two on a book.

I wrote this book because I thought it would make a good book, and I
thought *Catch-22* would make a good book too. It looks like I was right
in the first case and it looks like I'm going to be right in the second
case. I could've been wrong. Imagine having spent, in my case, really
five years of hard work experimenting with ideas, with an idea in which

you have no confidence. I wouldn't be able to do anything about that. If I didn't feel very strongly about what I was doing, or I was doing it badly . . . I would give it up. The book wouldn't be very important to me.

I'm constantly testing out what I do in each section with my agent and with my editor, and they give me advice. It's never happened before that any book that I submitted was rejected or needed major editing. If they did reject it, I guess I would stop, because they'd probably be right.

Q: *Here's a catch-22 for writers: the more time you spend writing a book to satisfy yourself, the greater the anticipation on the part of your reading audience, and the greater their expectations.*

A: It worked that way with me but it probably won't work that way with most novels. It worked that way with me because *Catch-22* enjoys a remarkable longevity. There aren't many books that are so widely read after so many years. I can think of only two others that date from the same period that are still read by people with enjoyment, rather than any courses they might have to read them for. The other two are Ken Kesey's *One Flew Over the Cuckoo's Nest* and Kurt Vonnegut's *Cat's Cradle.* I cannot think of any others. Pynchon readers, I think, come mostly from courses studying contemporary literature.

Q: *Did you like the movie,* Catch-22?

A: I liked the movie very much. If you ask me if I liked it as an interpretation of the book then I would say that I think that's an invalid question. The movie was as good an American movie as I've seen. I was able to see the movie as it was in the making, and I didn't expect it to be that good. It's amazing what they've done with camera lenses.

Q: *Do you ever anticipate* Something Happened *going into film? Would you want it to go into film?*

A: No. I've made no effort to sell it. My agent has been told not to contact me about it at all until he has a very impressive offer he thinks I'll accept.

Q: *Where are you going from here? Any strong ideas?*

A: No. Not until I'm a little less busy, and I will be very busy for the next couple weeks. It's a very good feeling, as I've explained to you, it's nice. You really don't believe it's ever going to get printed on time, and then published, and then distributed, then to see it's out in the bookstores, in New York and here, and they're reviewing it. So many things could go wrong: there coud be a strike, there could be a war. [He looked at his wife in mock surprise.] What? You're not worried about any of this?

Mrs. Heller: I still can't believe it's finally out.

A: You really don't believe me. With *Catch-22* there was a paper strike, there was a copy-editor who misunderstood her instructions and rewrote whole paragraphs and changed the names, and made corrections. She missed the whole style. She'd edited—and very well— William Shirer's *The Rise and Fall of the Third Reich*. She was very good at that. Well, she took *Catch-22* and began making it historically correct; putting in dates where I didn't want dates. So all that happened during the four weeks she was working on it, all that was useless. Not only useless, but then I had to take out all her "corrections" and then send it back to somebody else—we wasted a week or two doing that. And then there was a strike after that.

But everything seems to have gone perfectly with this new book. And you can see that you've caught me in a mood of great emotional elevation: it's going to be successful, I feel I deserve it, and I love it!

After *Catch-22* was published I was down to a couple of parties, and some people complained about me to my editors, saying that I seemed to be enjoying my success too much. They had an idea that I was supposed to look like Thomas Wolfe, with this aura of suicidal melancholy.

Q: *I'm curious about the autobiography in* Something Happened. *I understand you spent a couple of years in advertising—how much of* Something Happened *is taken from your advertising career?*

A: It's less than was taken from my war experiences for *Catch-22*. What I got from that experience was some sense of the corporate operation. It was not mine—I enjoyed my job very much. I didn't stay nearly as long as Slocum does. I never aspired to as much as he does. I was not his age as when he's there. If I had one of my jobs and knew I was going to stay there for twenty or thirty years I might have gotten very depressed over it. But I was writing *Catch-22* and knew it was going to be published, and felt I'd get out of there when it was doing pretty good. So it's not autobiographical, but I was able to observe a good many people.

Q: *Is that where a lot of the characters come from?*

A: No. I wouldn't say that. I don't think any of my characters are based on anyone I knew . . . well, one character in *Catch-22* is based on somebody I knew. Hungry Joe is based on a guy who was named Joe Chrenko. But otherwise, characters—they tend to be general types. I tried to get a caricature, especially in the portraits of *Catch-22*, where you're given as predominant characteristics something that would be recognizable to the audience so they could see that person as being like someone they knew. It's one of the reasons I don't describe anybody too much physically in *Catch-22*. I tend to give them one or two or three outstanding, peculiar ironies. Then I hope that the reader will be able to fill in the rest of the picture. They were able to do that in *Catch-22*. I think it's pretty much the same thing for *Something Happened*. It doesn't attempt to be a complete history—it's not literal realism. If anything, it's psychological realism, and most everything is perceived or determined through Slocum's reaction to them. There's a high degree of what can only be called surrealism in this book; things that you know he's thinking but could not be literally true, even when presented to you literally. Even though he picks up the mannerisms of the people he's with, it's far-fetched to believe that he'd pick up the limp of a guy he works with and not be aware of what he's doing. So twice he walks into the house and his wife says, "You've been with Kagle today." (Kagle is Slocum's limping co-worker). And he says, "How do you know?" So he didn't know he's picking up a limp. Now that, I think, is surrealistic. I think a person might develop a strut or a swagger, that of somebody else with whom he associates, but certainly not a limp.

Q: *There's a strange sense of identity in your character. For example, when he picks up a friend's stutter. There's one passage where he's described as four different people.*

A: He imagines there's a person living inside his head, then another person who's watching those two, right?

Q: *Yes. And one unknown—*

A: "I know there's one more I don't even know about." That's what he says. "This last one never sleeps, and watches all three of us." What's your question? I have—

Q: *The idea of a quadriphrenic personality.*

A: Well later on in the book. These are signs that, I believe, are clinical symptoms of psychosis or schizophrenia. And what I have done by setting up another person in his head—which is the one that wants to kick Kagle, it's not him—it's almost suggesting the idea of a split personality, although it's not. But *he,* himself, is tending to somewhat because he's saying, "There's somebody inside me who wants to do these things that I'm ashamed of. I'm too nice a guy to do this." Then he has to create a third one, to supervise the other two. Then a fourth one that's watching everything—he never sleeps, never lets anything go too far. What I'm trying to do is set up again a process of alienation from oneself: "depersonalization," that's another clinical term.

And later in the book he has two passages in which he talks about how he's got a universe in his head, maybe three times, where he imagines multitudes of people lurking around in his head and, I think, some he knows and some he doesn't. They're the people he thinks about, the people who infest his dreams. Sometimes he thinks he wants to get them all out in the open, like a policeman, and line them up to see who they are. That's the kind of thing, I think, a schizophrenic would have. Except Slocum never is a schizophrenic; it's a schizoid formation, which normal people have, it's about being schizophrenic. And I'm using that deliberately.

Q: *What are you driving at with that kind of schizophrenic portrait?*

A: I don't know. I mean I can't say now. What I'm dealing with is a disorganized personality, a personality that can't be integrated in a way that the healthiest of personalities should be, the way more and more people I know about, people having trouble integrating their personality so solidly that there's never any anxiety, never any doubt or irrational feelings of inadequacy, never these kids that they can't understand. It's becoming harder and harder for people to achieve in their work, for a personal sense of identity or integration of personality.

Q: *William Faulkner talked about modern novelists in his Nobel speech and how they have to deal with conflicts of the heart, with pride, and love, and lust. And it seems here in* Something Happened *you're dealing with nothing more than a kind of middle-class angst.*

A: Well, it's not different from what I think Faulkner was talking about if we can understand what he meant. Faulkner's Nobel Prize speech is not really very intelligible to people now. At the time he made it the newspapers loved it because it had this language of sentiment and antiquity. I would think that Slocum is dealing very strongly in the same way that Faulkner's characters were. But I would not like to measure *Something Happened* against Faulkner's statement, in Faulkner's terms. You see, Faulkner is speaking romantically; we no longer speak romantically. We know that the only conflict the heart has is whether it keeps beating or not; if the artery gets a clot. We don't have conflicts of the heart, we have conflicts of the head. That's what I mean by his speech being romantic. What he means by conflicts of the heart can now be interpreted as conflicts of the mind, about the emotions. He was talking as if the heart were the center of the emotions, which was a great thing for song-writers of the thirties and forties.

And when Faulkner said at the end of his Nobel Prize speech that man would endure I don't think anybody today would take him seriously. Of course not writers, which isn't saying that it doesn't bother me. But I think it was *poetic* expression.

Joseph Heller: An Interview

Creath Thorne/1974

From *Chicago Literary Review: Book Supplement to the Chicago Maroon*, 3 December 1974, 1, 8. Reprinted by permission.

Joseph Heller at age fifty-one seems years younger. When I talked with him this fall a few days before the official publication of *Something Happened,* he was exhilarated by the very flattering advance reviews he'd seen of the book and its apparent financial success. In no way arrogant or conceited, he took my questions seriously, talked thoughtfully about writing. He is no Yossarian benumbed by the absurdity of his world. In his own words, his sensibility is "New York, Jewish, urban." As a writer, he prepares carefully, works slowly, finishes strongly. He has now written two remarkable novels, one of which, *Catch-22,* achieved nearly sacred status in the decade following its publication. His whole manner gives the promise of further important books to come.

Creath Thorne: In an interview you once said that when you were writing *Catch-22* you thought it was going to be the only novel you would ever write.

Joseph Heller: I didn't say I thought it was going to be, I thought it might be. I knew by then that I had become a very slow writer. I did have a contract for its publication before it was finished, and since it could have turned out to be the only book I would ever write I wanted it to be the best possible, and that slowed me down even more.

Thorne: What I was wondering was whether your sense of writing as a vocation or your sense of writing as a discipline changed after the immense popularity of *Catch-22.*

Heller: The financial success of the book, especially the financial returns of the motion picture sales, enabled me to leave the salaried position I had and devote myself to writing as an entire source of income, not just as a source of pleasure, which it had been and continues to be. It did not change my sense of writing as a discipline. If anything

127

it strengthened what stands I had. I try to be a very severe critic of my own work and usually am more severe than most people would be.

There's no hurry in writing for me. My method of work is to do sections. I do a section to my satisfaction, I mail it to my agent, he makes a copy and sends it to my editor, then each calls me up about that section and tells me what he thinks. With *Catch-22* and *Something Happened* they thought very well of the sections. So I had that encouragement. My editor knew that I was working because he would get 80 to 250 pages a year.

Thorne: Actual finished copy? Did you have overall plans of the books in mind before you started writing?

Heller: Yes. In fact, when I talk to students who want to write, I tell them not to start anything until they know how it's going to end and how it's going to get to that ending.

Thorne: Do you keep the plan of the book in your head or do you make notes?

Heller: In *Catch-22* I made charts of the details. I knew what the overall direction of *Catch-22* would be, but there were 42 or 44 characters, and I couldn't keep track of all of them. And I tended to get an overflow of ideas about it. I would write them down not to forget them. But with *Something Happened* the action and the activities were less complex, the characters were fewer. I was able to keep most of that in my head.

Thorne: Do you sit down and write every day?

Heller: No. In a loose way I try to. If I'm out late or if I'm going on a trip to the University of Chicago I usually won't for that day or the day after. When I'm teaching at City College I write in the mornings, which I prefer. It's an everyday thing, but I'm never guilt ridden if I don't work. I don't have a compulsion to write, and I never have. I have a wish, an ambition to write, but it's not one that justifies the word "drive."

Thorne: You mentioned teaching at City College. I wonder what your general impression is of the students you have. Are you impressed by their writings?

Heller: Of the undergraduates I teach, some show sure definite talent. Some show potential. And others don't. It takes a while before I am able to classify them. But even for those who don't, if they don't seem to display ability at that age for creative writing, then perhaps they come

away from the course with a set of standards and some ability to judge other people's writing.

I haven't had a class where I didn't have at least five people who wanted to learn to write and were willing to work very hard. And some have been writing for many years. It's easy to work with them, to try to accelerate their own development as writers and as readers. I try to steer them away from subjects they may use which are commonplace, trite, and sensational: a first sex experience, shooting heroin or cocaine, or a white person being screwed by a black person. It's all been done before.

Thorne: Do you see any connection between the teaching you do and your writing?

Heller: None at all. I almost see more connection between my former writing of advertising copy and my writing of *Catch-22*. There is no connection. The classroom situation is a classroom situation. It doesn't slow me down, it doesn't expedite things. Whereas, when I was working at the office job I had when I did *Catch-22*, if I put in a very busy day at the office I would be very anxious to get to my work. If I got sluggish at the office I would not feel like working.

Thorne: Then the movement of writers into academic jobs hasn't changed literature?

Heller: I don't think that has changed it. Literature is going to change anyway. It's becoming more and more an elevated and sophisticated type of artistic expression so that raw content is no longer enough for a work of fiction. Where it was in the thirties, forties, and mid-fifties when books that talked about screwing as screwing, or masturbation, or black-white sex relations were big successes. There the enormity of the content itself created a sensation for the book.

In 1949 in *The Naked and the Dead* Mailer couldn't use the word "fuck," he used "fug." But now, since anything goes, it's going to take a great deal of skill and insight for a person to make his work distinguished. That requires, I think, a great deal of educated experience. So I think that more and more you're going to find very well educated writers with graduate degrees. They will have to have some sort of income because most writers don't make enough money writing. The universities are very comfortable, congenial, and compatible for them.

I enjoy teaching college. It's a job I would like to keep. It's interesting. It seems worthwhile. I would think that here in Chicago someone like Saul Bellow . . . he still teaches, I believe. Right?

Thorne: A few courses.

Heller: All right . . . I think he does it because he enjoys it. I don't think he has to depend upon it for income. And I imagine I'm in the same position.

Thorne: I wanted to ask you about screenplays and articles. Do you consider them as important as your novels?

Heller: No. Nor is my playwriting as important as my novels. I am able to do certain things well and other things not well. I don't do articles well, unless they're humorous articles in the form of reminiscences. I do television script rewrites well and screenplay rewrites extremely well. I have never taken on a whole screenplay for myself and wouldn't want to. It would take too many months, maybe too many years to do.

I've adapted *Catch-22* to the stage and I've adapted one chapter, Clevinger's trial, as a one-act play. The adaptations were fairly easy. They required technique rather than original inspiration. My play *We Bombed in New Haven* required inspiration, but the writing was fairly easy. I think so much of playwriting is dialogue, and I do dialogue well. But a novel requires all kinds of writing: exposition, types of description, sustaining action. Techniques that can be used in plays to hide certain weaknesses cannot be used with success in a novel. I regard novel writing as very challenging, somewhat forbidding, engrossing work that really draws on all my powers.

Also, with the screenplay or television script, you're really a salaried employee writing something that someone else has commissioned. It is a question of giving them what they want. With a play that element is not so true because you are your own boss when you're writing a play. But with a play you are very much conscious of an audience and a need to keep that audience from getting bored or being contemptuous for even a second. So to me it is almost something of a performance, something being written with somebody else's tastes in mind. The novel is much less so.

Thorne: Have you ever wanted to write short stories?

Heller: I wrote short stories when I was an undergrad. That's pretty much how I got started as a writer and where my desire to become a writer changed from desire to ambition. I don't think I would do short stories again although I might. I don't have an idea for a new novel and what may come to me is an idea for a short story.

Thorne: *Something Happened* is so different from *Catch-22*. For instance, it is much more of an internal book . . .

Heller: Yeah.

Thorne: And it abandons the broad humor of that first book . . .

Heller: Yeah.

Thorne: Do you see yourself as permanently turning away from those things that you did with the first book or are you rather exploring different narrative possibilities?

Heller: I didn't want to write a sequel to *Catch-22* because I felt 1) there was no need to and 2) I would be ripping off something or doing an imitation; imitations are never as effective or as good or as genuine as the original. *Something Happened* is an internal book, almost totally introspective. It doesn't represent a change in literary philosophy. I got an idea for a novel that I thought I could work with and that would produce something that was worth reading, that was worth having in existence. I wrote *Catch-22* because it was the best idea for a novel that I could get at that time. *Something Happened* was the best idea I could get for a second novel. I don't know what the next will be. I do not want it to be about the same things the first two are.

Thorne: I wanted to ask you about black humor because when *Catch-22* is taught in lit classes it is usually grouped with those books.

Heller: Yeah.

Thorne: Do you see yourself as a black humorist?

Heller: Well, I don't think that I am the one to be asked that. I do think critics know more about literature and individual works of literature than the author does. And they certainly know more about genres of literature than authors do. How I see myself is not as important as how others see me. If they do group me with black humorists then I probably belong there.

I didn't like the classification when it first came up because I would find myself being grouped with writers with whom I felt my own work had little in common. I didn't like their works as well. But I think my judgment in that area should step aside for the judgment of other people.

Thorne: Do you see black humor as a significant movement in contemporary literature right now?

Heller: I think the literature of this period, say from '54 or '55 on, has been more imaginative and move vital, more significant and more intelligent than any in the history of the world. I do think there are more great American novelists at work today, more great American novels being written today than ever before. It's unfortunate that most of these will go unrecognized. They are so good and hardly any of them are read. There are so many of them that the culture can't absorb them, the newspapers don't even have enough space to review them.

Black humor is one very significant movement. The traditional, realistic novel is certainly still with us and doing well. But we have today a large number of gifted individual stylists whose works have very little in common other than the fact that they are written by someone who wants to write his novel his way. I am thinking of people like myself, Thomas Pynchon, John Barth, John Hawkes, Saul Bellow, Philip Roth, and perhaps a few dozen others whose names don't come to mind right now.

In the case of John Barth his novels don't even resemble each other, let alone other writers'. But these writers do seem to have in common a vein of humor. In most cases it's a signal to the reader that he ought not to take what is written too seriously, that he's reading nothing more than a novel about serious things. Of the people I've named, with maybe Saul Bellow as the exception, I don't think we think of ourselves as expounding the living important truths. I don't think there are any important truths that the reader is unfamiliar with.

Thorne: Do you think that stance is in any way a reaction to the modernist movement?

Heller: No, I don't think it's a reaction. It's what you might call a retreat from realism or an advance beyond realism. I like to regard a work of literature as a work of literature—as a symbolic masquerade for reality. The reality and our writing about the reality are two different things. There's something artificial in writing. Writing is different from life. A story about life is not the same as life itself.

In John Barth, for example, the writing itself is the subject of the book. In my books there is literal truth and there is imaginary truth, and hallucination is dealt with and fantasy is dealt with, interchangably and simultaneously. It implies a recognition on my part, an admission on my part, that I'm telling you a story and not handing you a hunk of experience.

The war situation in *Catch-22* came from my own experience, but the war that I am really dealing with was not World War II but turned out to be the Viet-Nam war. It's not literal. In *Something Happened* what I have is almost an abstraction of my corporate experience. I write in abstractions because the chance of my writing correlating with the experiences of somebody else is greater if the specifics are fewer.

Writing Technique Can Be Taught,
Says Joseph Heller

Ann Waldron/1975

From *Houston Chronicle* 2 March 1975, 14. Copyright © 1975 Houston Chronicle. Reprinted by permission.

Joseph Heller took 13 years to write *Something Happened*, because he rewrote it so much; he wrote inserts and then wrote inserts for the inserts.

Most of us agree that *Something Happened* was worth waiting for.

"Reviewers in New York hedged," Heller said in Houston the other day, "but out in the country, in Tennessee and Salt Lake City and Des Moines and places like that, reviewers loved it."

Heller's first novel, *Catch-22*, came out in 1961.

How did Heller, husband and father of two children, live during the 13 years it took to write *Something Happened*?

For one thing, he kept his job in the promotion department of *McCall's* magazine for a while after *Catch-22* came out. (He went around the country giving slide shows and talks that showed how advertising in *McCall's* would move a product. "I put as much creative effort into that in the daytime as I did into my fiction at night," he said.)

"I did occasional screen plays," Heller said. "And I had a fairly steady income from *Catch-22*. In 1970, *Catch-22* was sold to the movies, and I quit my job. Then I taught for a while, and I had an advance for *Something Happened*."

And all that time, Heller was writing and rewriting *Something Happened*.

"At first I could only work two hours at a time," Heller said. "Toward the end I worked eight or 10 hours. I write in longhand on yellow pads, one page at a time, or even three or four paragraphs at a time, a single piece of dialog at a time That's as fast as my imagination will take me. Then I rewrite compulsively. When I finish a section, I rewrite that section and then I type that section, and in the process of

typing, I cut and rewrite. Then I make penciled changes in the typed
copy and give that typed copy to a typist.

"The chapter about Derek, where Slocum loses control, that was four
and a half hand-written pages. The next day I started an insert and then
wrote an insert in the insert and ended up with 600 pages in that
chapter. I used lots of that section later, in other chapters. In fact, when
I finished writing that, I knew I could finish the book. The worst was
over. And when I typed that section over, I got chills."

Heller began to write his play, *We Bombed in New Haven*, because
the novel was going so well in the daytime that he had his evenings
free. He wrote the play at night and for a long time, until he got a
producer, it didn't interfere with the progress of *Something Happened*.

Then when the play went into production, he had to drop *Something
Happened* for two years.

Heller has a nice feeling of security about his work. He knows it's
good. But he's not arrogant. He just knows he's good. "The best thing
about literary acceptance," he said, "is being able to move people."

(He said he'd never see *Death of a Salesman* or *Our Town* wihout
crying or wanting to cry.)

"I knew *Something Happened* was long and I knew it was slow," he
said, "but I knew the reader would be indulgent because of *Catch-22*."
(*Catch* sold 8 million copies.)

Heller speaks of the hero of *Something Happened*, Bob Slocum, as
though he were a real person.

"Bob Slocum is asking for forgiveness for his actions, for his faults.
He's an unreliable narrator; he doesn't tell the truth. But he is able to
look at himself honestly, and the effect of this is to make other people
look at their selves."

Something Happened is indeed a work of the imagination, Heller
says. He is not as unhappy as Bob Slocum is.

"Absolutely not," Heller said. "My attitude is rosy, almost optimistic.
My life has been carefree for the last 12 years.

"And then my office jobs weren't like Bob Slocum's. The most
intelligent and well-informed people I worked with in my life were in
the advertising department at *Time* magazine. All the copywriters were
writing plays and novels and the people in the art department were
interested in serious art.

"It's been misunderstood, that I said Time is the 'company' in *Something Happened*. I wanted to use a company that was not harsh, but beneficent. I took Time for the book because of the six or seven companies that I worked for, Time was the most generous with vacations and pay and nobody was ever fired. I did not want to write a book about economic exploitation. I wanted a neutral corporation."

Heller teaches two writing workshops a week at City College in New York, with 20 students in the undergraduate class and 15 in his graduate group.

"I like big classes like that," he said, "because at City College, most of the students work as well as go to school and don't have time to write as much as students who don't work.

"Doctors and lawyers come to the graduate class, men who don't like their lives and want to become writers.

"You can't teach talent, but you can teach technique. All the students have some talent—they've been screened. If you have talent, development can be hastened. Mine was. I didn't go to college until I was 22 years old. After World War II, I went to New York University. My writing teacher was Maurice Baudin. Some of my stories were published in *Esquire* while I was still in college. Baudin pointed out my faults to me—he'd say throw away the first three or four pages, and he was right."

Heller has a daughter, 23, who is finishing up at NYU, and a son, 18, who is about to enter NYU. They're both interested in writing.

"They both retreated from writing when *Catch-22* came out," Heller said. "But they've started writing again. My daughter told me that *Something Happened* was so good she no longer felt she'd have to compete. She said she'd have to write something else."

Heller will take next year off from teaching.

"I won't get another idea for a novel until I have lots of free time," he said. "I've only had two ideas for novels in my life. The characters, the situation, the opening lines for those just came to me."

Heller was in Houston because he came to Dallas to lecture and read his work at Southern Methodist University. Then he came to Houston to visit friends and to publicize his book.

Joe Heller, Author on Top of the World

Charles T. Powers/1975

From *Los Angeles Times,* 30 March 1975, Part 7, 1, 12. Reprinted by permission.

Joseph Heller, famous novelist, author of *Catch-22,* a book of at least minor (perhaps major) classic stature, and *Something Happened,* now 6 months old and 6 months near the top of the *New York Times* best-seller list (long-range verdict still to come, preliminary reports highly promising), leaned to his left against the pull of a stuffed totebag of books and papers, looking shorter and altogether more professorial in blue blazer and tie than one might have expected. He removed his glasses and, in a voice like the slabs of his native Brooklyn, greeting his guides for the day.

Heller was in town, not to pump his new book (which doesn't need pumping) but as the guest of the students at USC, who had invited him to lecture. He spent most of the day talking, since that's what he was invited to do, and we spent most of the day listening. In general summary, it can be said that it is very pleasant to spend the day with a man who is on top of the world.

Joe Heller has arrived. From the first inspiration in the summer of 1962, it took 12 years for *Something Happened* to happen, and now, when coaxed, he will admit he believes his two books have established him as one of the important figures of American literature.

He enjoys it. He enjoys it when he and his wife go to the opera in New York and people recognize him standing in the lobby at intermission. He enjoys it when his old friend from Coney Island, author Mario Puzo, says, "Joe, you son of a bitch, you got it both ways. You wrote a good book and you're making money."

"It feels tremendous," he said at the end of the day, his voice hoarse from all the talking. "Absolutely tremendous. But it doesn't really change you. I still bite my fingernails. You've got to realize, too, that if there was never another novel written, the world would still go on. It wouldn't change anything, no one would care. But if there was no more television, everyone would go crazy in two days."

Between his first greeting and those final words, here is some of what
Joseph Heller had to say.

"Every once in a while I find nothing is bothering me and I get very
worried."

At lunch, with a small group of students following his lecture:

"I thought once about doing a comic novel with Henry Kissinger as
the central figure. The trouble with that idea was, ultimately, that
Kissinger will be forgotten and a man of almost no importance a very
short time from now.

"I think the people who really foretell the future in this country are
the newspaper columnists and political writers. About eight months ago,
you could see them begin to criticize him, and now columnists like Art
Buchwald and Russell Baker make fun of him and people have actually
begun to laugh at him. Right now he's a great joke, one of the genuinely funny characters in American life. But he won't last. That's why
I never went ahead with it."

"What scenes did you have in mind?" someone asked.

"I could have fun with just the 'Dr. Kissinger' business. Why do we
have to address him as 'Doctor'? It's like a Jewish inferiority complex.
I thought of some funny confrontations between Kissinger and John
Connally. (I don't care whether he's guilty or not, you gotta say Connally is a genuine personality.) You can imagine him looking at Kissinger and trying to figure out how he got all this power, and Kissinger all
the time afraid of Connally, looking into those hard little eyes imagining
Connally saying, 'We know what to do with you, buddy.'

"No, I don't see anything tragic about Nixon. In order to be tragic,
you've got to have a few things going for you. A tragic figure is a figure
of some stature. Nixon never had stature. I don't think anyone, even the
people he had with him, ever thought he had any stature.

"I never believed anything he said or did. Even when he told the
truth, he lied. In his own mind, there was no difference, no distinction.
There's no reliable source there, there never has been. You used to
hear about him being hard working, about his humor, his quickness of
mind, his intelligence. But there never has been any public evidence of
wit or humor or quickness of mind or intelligence. That's something
you can't buy in political life. One thing I feel very strongly about our

political figures is this: They get the image they deserve. No one is mistreated."

"What do you think of the novelist as journalist?"

"I'm objective about it and I don't know of any good novelists who write good journalism."

"You mean Norman Mailer?"

"I'll stand on that general statement. I don't know of a good novelist who is good as a nonfiction writer. I don't think you can do both. I don't think anybody can."

On the writers who have influenced him:

"John Hawkes. He might be embarrassed to know it, but I would say the influence of Hawkes' work was strong in the conception and development of a book like *Something Happened,* in which fear and terror and anxiety are so much a part, not of the abnormal but the normal life. (I liked the headline you had in the Sunday *Times*: 'An Extraordinary Novel About an Ordinary Man.') Hawkes is an important writer to me. He uses himself as an angleworm on a hook to go fishing inside himself for the deepest kinds of terror that exist in man.

"Samuel Beckett's novels would be an influence, although I was already into the book by the time I started reading Beckett, but once I got into him, I began using more heavily things I found in his novels, particularly *The Unnamable.* Dostoevsky's *Notes from Underground,* too.

On the type of writer he is:

"There are, loosely speaking, two types of novels. One is, I think, the realistic novel and one is—well, they have different names and the names change—but there is another kind of writer who deals with reality by looking at it through glasses with defective lenses. I feel a close alliance with, say, Hawkes, who creates an imaginary world. Although his book might take place in San Diego, it's not San Diego— and yet it is. Or in Germany. It's postwar Germany, and it's some- thing else. There's a similarity between Hawkes, John Barth, Thomas Pynchon, Kafka. And some of the work of Philip Roth and John Cheever moves away from realism."

What do you do with Kurt Vonnegut?"

"Vonnegut is an unrealistic writer.

"The work of those writers doesn't have much in common except in a very broad way. I can see only a very loose connection between my work and Thomas Pynchon, but I can see that Pynchon is not writing realism.

"I've tried hard in my books to create a certain sort of world. I've found that what people like in my fiction (or at least the people who correspond with me about it or talk to me) is the quality of surprise. That's what I like in the writers I admire: The ability to surprise is there. I mean, you can do anything you want to do if you do it well. You can set up any set of reference points of any set of rules you want. You have to remain consistent with those rules, but from there on, you can do anything you want, have any type of world you want, any type of character. So I think there's potentially more excitement and more room for experimentation.

"You get two things from that kind of writing. You get a closer look into the area of experience, looking at it beneath the surface. Now, a realistic writer will be able to come a certain distance with what people say and what they do and what their thoughts are. And the implication is that the writer often knows it all—he sees with clarity what his characters are thinking, what they're doing and why they're doing it. And that approach supposes that his characters would know what their own motivations and their own reactions are. To a certain extent, that *is* experience. But to another extent, we all know at some point that we really *don't* know what we're doing.

"And also, in this type of writing, there is an effort to make the form part of the content. I've tried to do it in both my books. Beckett said it—I was reading it the other day, an essay Beckett wrote about James Joyce. He was talking about the traditional view that form exists only to serve content, whereas with Joyce (and with Beckett and some others), form *is* content. And he said that Joyce's *Finnegans Wake* is not *about* something, it *is* something.

"I like to think of the books I write as being interesting in themselves, rather than just in what they say. It's like a painting. A Renoir nude is not telling you about the nude; the painting itself has an existence. Not because of what's in it. It's like what I try to do with my books. The book itself it is what it's about."

Later, in an informal session with about 20 students, most of whom presented the impression of being into postgraduate work:

"Is anybody here writing? Yes, no? How to get an agent? How I started writing? OK. I started writing by submitting short stories to magazines. All magazines. I would have been happy to have anything I wrote published. Once you get a few stories published, agents, good agents will look you up. It's hard to get an agent."

"What is an ending? I mean, how do you have an ending to a story?"

"I don't know what you mean."

"Well a lot of stories these days don't seem to have endings."

"An ending is an ending. I can't think of any stories that don't have endings. Maybe you're thinking of what is sometimes called 'The New Yorker story.' But even stories of a New Yorker type have an ending." He advised the student to read the James Joyce short story, "Clay."

"I found myself feeling very disturbed reading your book. At the beginning, I found myself hating Slocum (the central character in Something Happened), but after a while I found myself a silent accomplice."

"Do you have a question?" Heller asked.

"I was interested in your comment on that."

"Viewed from a distance, Slocum is a monster, but when you get close to him, you discover that he's not too much different from you and me. There are deliberate contradictions in what Slocum tells us about things, but toward the end, he loses his ability to keep a secret. But I really don't want to go into explicating the book."

"But what should I think of Slocum?"

"Make whatever judgment you want to make. I like the review in the New Republic. They said, 'Heller's book is about a son of a bitch named Bob Slocum.' They went on to call him a son of a bitch three times and a bastard once and end up saying, 'He's all of us.'"

"Why do you write?"

"Because I like to. Because it's the easiest way I know to make living."

A student asked about a detail in the book. "Was that conscious?" he said.

"Everything is conscious. In a serious book, I think you can assume that everything that goes in is conscious."

Some of the questions from the students and aspiring writers seemed to indicate the fond hope that Heller might somehow be able to provide for them the foolproof formula that would allow them to sit down and begin writing the great American masterpiece; all they needed was an explanation of the materials to use, whether to write with a pencil or pen or typewriter, and at what time of the day or after having eaten precisely the right balance of carbohydrate and protein over the previous week. "How did you form your routines?" one student asked, and Heller's answer, reduced to its essentials, seemed to be: Out of necessity. It wasn't magic.

And yet, riding back to his hotel, he admitted he had no explanation for the moment of inspiration for his new novel. It came, he has said, while he was sitting on the porch of a rented summer house on Fire Island. An opening line (later moved to the opening of the second chapter) simply dropped into his head. (The line: "In the office in which I work there are five people of whom I am afraid.")

The sentence suggested a universe, and in the three minutes that followed, he had the characters in mind, their names, the outlines of the story and, he insists, many of the key lines in the book.

"It's miraculous, I know," he said, turning around in the passenger seat as the car clawed its way through rush hour traffic. "It's a bit frightening, because if it doesn't happen that way again, I don't think I'll be able to write another novel. I have a friend who has gone around saying, 'Heller didn't write that book, he has a medium.'"

Other lines, possibly for another novel, have occurred to him, although he is not sure he trusts his medium, whoever or whatever it may be. Naturally, Heller is in no great hurry.

"There is one thing I've thought of," he said. "You can write it down and we'll see if anything comes of it.

"When I was growing up on Coney Island, in the summer months, fruit and vegetable peddlers would come around the neighborhood. From April to September. And the vegetables would change with the season. They were all Italian working in a Jewish neighborhood. They would go through the street and yell up, and the women would open their windows and if they wanted something, they would go down.

"The thing I remembered them yelling was this: 'If you got money, come down and buy. If you got no money, stay home and cry.' That was the line. I thought of a title even. 'Peddler's Cry, 1930.'

"I guess what I liked about it was its jocularity, but underlying the humor was a ruthless quality."

Heller turned around in his seat and faced the traffic.

"If you never see that," he said, "you'll know nothing ever came of it."

Playboy Interview: Joseph Heller

Sam Merrill/1975

From *Playboy* magazine, June 1975, 59–61, 64–66, 68, 70, 72–74, 76. Copyright © by Playboy. All rights reserved. Reprinted by permission.

In 1961, Joseph Heller, a 38-year-old advertising and promotion executive for *McCall's* magazine, finally completed the novel he'd been tinkering with in his spare time for the better part of a decade. The book was called *Catch-18,* a title that was later increased by four upon publication of Leon Uris' *Mila 18*—Heller's editors didn't think people would buy two novels with the same number.

They needn't have worried.

Catch-22's readership started as a small cult—the hardcover edition never appeared on a best-seller list—and expanded geometrically throughout the Sixties. Today, with sales over 8,000,000 and counting—it sold over 100,000 copies last year alone—*Catch-22* is the biggest-selling "serious novel" in American publishing history.

From the beginning, *Catch-22's* cult included some of the world's most distinguished, and disparate, citizens. Art Buchwald called it a "masterpiece." Philip Toynbee, in *The London Observer,* said *Catch-22* was "the greatest satirical work in English since *Erewhon*." And newscaster John Chancellor printed up bumper stickers that read, BETTER YOSSARIAN THAN ROTARIAN, referring, of course, to the book's protagonist, an Assyrian-American World War Two bombardier who wanted to "live forever or die in the attempt."

But when Yossarian went crazy, or seemed to, and asked to be grounded, he found there was only one catch: Anyone who was crazy could get out of combat duty. All he had to do was ask. But anyone who asked to get out of combat duty wasn't really crazy and had to keep flying missions.

Catch-22's spiraling insanity, which began to seem more and more sane as the Vietnam war dragged on, confused and irritated some early critics. But as readers became accustomed to the book's radical, time-warp structure, the complaints melted away and *Catch-22* passed through the invisible barrier that separates contemporary fiction from literature. And its title, symbolic of all oppressive tautologies, has become a part of our language.

In the fall of 1974, Heller finally released his long-awaited second novel, *Something Happened*. The new book, a stream-of-neurosis peek into the head of Robert Slocum—family man, corporate man, psychotic monster—has unleashed a fusillade of violently mixed reviews. *Time* and *The New Yorker* hated it. *Playboy* called it "the worst thing a writing giant can do to his loyal readers." Yet nearly three quarters of the critics viewed Heller's looping, memory-tape narrative as a dazzling, if depressing, literary tour de force.

The impassioned reviews, the mammoth book-club sale and the long, high ride on every national best-seller list indicate that once again Heller has produced a work to be treasured, despised and fought over for years to come.

The youngest of three children, Heller was born in Brooklyn in 1923. His father, a truck driver for Messinger's Bakery, died when he was five years old. The Hellers lived in a racially mixed residential section of Coney Island and young Joe did odd jobs while attending Abraham Lincoln High School, where he excelled at writing—and little else. After graduation, he became a file clerk at a casualty-insurance company (a job that re-emerged in *Something Happened* as the scene of Slocum's most agonizing sexual disaster).

After Pearl Harbor, Heller worked briefly at the Norfolk Navy Yard. At 19, he enlisted in the Army Air Corps. While bombardier Heller was stationed in Corsica with the 488th Squadron, 340th Bombardment Group, he flew 60 combat missions in a B-25 over Italy and France. After his discharge, as a first lieutenant, he enrolled in college on the GI Bill. He was graduated Phi Beta Kappa from NYU, received a master's degree in American literature at Columbia and studied English literature on a Fulbright scholarship at Oxford. While he was still an undergraduate, the most prestigious magazines in the country were eagerly publishing his short stories. By his senior year, he was already considered one of America's most promising young writers.

Then he stopped writing.

He taught freshman composition at Penn State for a few frustrating semesters, then got a job as a "copy and promo" man at a New York advertising agency. For the next ten years, Heller moved both vertically and horizontally in the promotion business: He did one long stint at Time Inc. and

Conversations with Joseph Heller

ended up at *McCall's*. During this period, he began writing again. In 1955, he published in *New World Writing* a story called "The Texan," which later became the first chapter of *Catch-22*.

The promising Young Turk of 1949 had been forgotten by the time *Catch-22* came out. The book might have been lost in the welter of first novels by nobodies except for the fortuitous accident of an interview with S. J. Perelman, published in the *New York Herald Tribune*. Perelman, asked if he'd read any good books lately, mentioned a title nobody had heard of: *Catch-22*. A spate of critical attention—some passionately pro, some viciously con—followed.

A $15,000,000 film version of *Catch-22*, directed by Mike Nichols, was the financial disaster of 1970. Nichols' budget was virtually unlimited (during production, he assembled the world's 12th largest bomber force). But the film sacrificed most of the book's humor in a vain attempt to establish a "story line"—something the novel didn't have to begin with.

Meanwhile, Heller continued to pursue his muse at a leisurely pace. As one close friend put it, "Joe likes to keep the rest of his life open, in case anything comes up." The summer after *Catch-22*'s publication, Heller had begun accumulating notes for a new book. Robert Gottlieb, his editor, took out a somewhat premature advertisement: "Joseph Heller is now working on his second novel, *Something Happened*. Publication date not set yet, of course—but look for it sometime before we get to the moon." As matters turned out, Neil Armstrong took his one small step for mankind long before *anything* happened for Heller's publisher. As Heller put it, he kept being "interrupted": Throughout the Sixties, he toured the country, speaking and demonstrating against the Vietnam war. He did several short stints as a Hollywood "script doctor" and in 1965 took a two-year sabbatical to write and produce a play, *We Bombed in New Haven*. Despite extravagant reviews, it did.

Thirteen years and six lunar landings after *Catch-22*, *Something Happened* was published and became an immediate international best seller.

Joseph Heller and Shirley, his wife of almost 30 years, winter in an elegant old courtyard building on Manhattan's Upper West Side and summer on the beaches of Long Island. Their two children, Erica and Ted, are grown and scattered. Along with his writing, Heller teaches fiction at the City College of New York. He makes few new friends, but the old ones seem to last. Some of them, members of what they call the Gourmet Club, have been meeting for dinner in New York's Chinatown at least once a week for the past 13 years. Fellow gourmets include Jules Feiffer, Mel Brooks and Carl Reiner (when they're in town), novelists Mario (*The Godfather*) Puzo and George (*Flee the Angry Strangers*) Mandel, playwright Joe (*Fiddler on the Roof*) Stein, adman Ngoot Lee, jeweler Julie Green and one Speed Vogel, occupation unknown.

At 52, Heller seems finally to have achieved it all: critical acclaim, popular success, a shucking of the dreaded one-book-author syndrome. So we thought it an opportune time to discuss life, literature and "the Snowdens of yesteryear" with the man whose wacky prescience had foretold a world of Vietnams and Watergates, and assigned writer Sam Merrill (whose "Mason Hoffenberg Gets in a Few Licks" appeared in *Playboy*'s November 1973 issue) to interview Heller.

Merrill reports:

"My first meeting with Heller took place at his summer home in Amagansett, Long Island, a quiet little seashore town about two and a half hours out of Manhattan. When I arrived, Heller was encased in a set of massive headphones, listening to Wagner's *Götterdämmerung* and reading Dickens' *Nicholas Nickleby*. While we chatted on the sun deck— eating Jarlsberg cheese and drinking French-roast coffee— Heller removed his shirt. His chest and legs were firm, tanned, supple. Only his neck looked 52 years old.

"Heller seemed leaner, more wolfish in person than on his dust jackets. And his speech was a curious but thoroughly engaging amalgam. The words—spare, epigrammatic, meticulously considered—were delivered in unreconstructed Brooklynese. While he spoke, a toothpick danced magically from one corner of his mouth to the other. He told me he'd learned that trick, employing the treacherous cupped-tongue technique, while giving up smoking in 1955.

"Chewing his nails and squirming around uncomfortably, Heller obviously had trouble sitting still for an interview. Yet he fielded each question patiently, his expression flickering between Stud Poker Gothic and Bittersweet Irony *Catch-22* Book Jacket Grin. He was a frequent and infectious laugher.

"Pulling out of his driveway that first afternoon, I caught a glimpse of Heller in my rearview mirror. He had begun to jog his daily three miles in a chilly, offshore fog that clung so close to the ground he was visible only from the waist up. The image reminded me of Kid Sampson, the young pilot in *Catch-22* who was sheared in half by McWatt's propeller.

"Subsequent meetings took place at the Central Park South office/apartment in which Heller wrote *Something Happened*. His work space was in farcical contrast with his two tasteful homes. A three-foot beer bottle, a broken stereo and a ruptured couch dominated a decor that could perhaps best be termed Flatbush Moderne. It soon became apparent that when Heller is writing, he simply does not *see* anything else!

"Our conversations started with his own involvement in the events described in *Catch-22*."

Playboy: How much of *Catch-22* is based on your own wartime experiences?

Heller: Well, like Yossarian, I volunteered for the Army Air Corps and became a bombardier. But I didn't try to avoid being sent overseas, as he did. I actually *hoped* I would get into combat. I was just 19 and there were a great many movies being made about the war; it all seemed so dramatic and heroic. I remember my mother weeping as the trolley car pulled away with me on it. I couldn't figure out why she was so unhappy. I felt like I was going to Hollywood.

Playboy: So you viewed World War Two as a kind of glorious crusade?

Heller: No, but I saw it as a war of necessity. Everybody did. Young people today don't know what it's like to fight in a war that makes sense to anybody. And neither did the people in my parents' generation. World War One and the earlier wars in Europe were as nonsensical as Vietnam. But Pearl Harbor united this country in a strong and wholesome and healthy way.

Playboy: About his war experiences, Yossarian complains that people he's never met keep shooting at him every time he flies into the air to drop bombs on them. We gather that you didn't feel persecuted.

Heller: At first, I was *sorry* when nobody shot at us. I wanted to see a sky full of flak and dogfights and billowing parachutes. War was like a movie to me until, on my 37th mission, we bombed Avignon and a guy in my plane was wounded. I suddenly realized, "Good God! They're trying to kill me, too!" War wasn't much fun after that.

Playboy: That sounds like the Avignon mission in *Catch-22*, when Snowden, the gunner, is killed.

Heller: It is, and it's described pretty accurately in the book. Our copilot went berserk at the controls and threw us into a dive. Then one of our gunners was hit by flak and the pilot kept yelling into the intercom, "Help him. Help the bombardier." And I was yelling back, "I'm the bombardier. I'm OK." The gunner's leg was blown open and I took care of him. After Avignon, all I wanted to do was go home.

Playboy: Was that because, like Yossarian, you began to suspect you were being sent on missions only to make your superior officers look good?

Heller: No, it was because I began to suspect I didn't want to die. But I was a good soldier and did as I was told.

Playboy: Did doing what you were told entail anything about which you're particularly sorry now?

Heller: No, but there was one low-level bombing-and-strafing mission I didn't happen to go on. They couldn't find any military targets, so they shot up everything that moved: women, children, animals. The men were in good spirits after that mission.

Playboy: If you'd gone on that mission, would you have machine-gunned women, children and animals?

Heller: I might have. There's something sexual about being in a *big* plane, with a *big* gun and having *big* bombs to drop.

Playboy: Aside from Yossarian, some of the other characters in *Catch-22* have become cult figures in their own right. Are any of them based on people you knew?

Heller: Just Hungry Joe. His real name is Joe Chrenko and he's now an insurance agent in New Jersey.

Playboy: Hungry Joe is the one who has screaming nightmares in his tent. Did Chrenko also run around Rome claiming to be a *Life* photographer so he could take pictures of naked girls?

Heller: Only once.

Playboy: Did he complain about the way you portray him in the book?

Heller: His only complaint is that I didn't use his last name. He feels it would have helped his insurance business.

Playboy: How about the rest of the characters?

Heller: They're not based on anyone I knew in the war. They're products of an imagination that drew on American life in the postwar period. The Cold War, really. I deliberately seeded the book with anachronisms like loyalty oaths, helicopters, IBM machines and agricultural subsidies to create the feeling of American society from the McCarthy period on. So when Milo Minderbinder says, "What's good for Milo Minderbinder is good for the country," he's paraphrasing Charles E. Wilson, the former head of General Motors, who told a Senate committee, "What is good for the country is good for General Motors, and vice versa."

But I resisted the temptation to make Milo a bloated plutocrat stereotype. And I moved away from the other kind of stereotype— William Holden or Tony Curtis as the con man who gets things done. Instead, I gave him a mental and moral simplicity that, to my mind, makes him a horrifyingly dangerous person because he lacks evil intent. Milo uses the credo of the National Association of Manufacturers and the chamber of commerce—but I gave him a sincerity those organizations don't have.

Playboy: How about Major Major, the timid officer whom nobody can get *in* to see unless he's officially *out*?

Heller: He's drawn from the McCarthy period as well. An Army dentist, Captain Peress, had been promoted to major, even though he refused to sign loyalty oaths. Toward the end of the Army-McCarthy hearings, when he had little else to do, Joe McCarthy kept asking who had promoted Major Peress. I took a paragraph straight out of the news reports and slipped it into the chapter about Major Major, who was promoted by an IBM machine. When he becomes suspect because he studied English history—wasn't American history good enough for him?—people start running around Washington, asking, "Who promoted Major Major?"

Playboy: And ex-Pfc. Wintergreen, the enlisted man who really runs the Army?

Heller: Wintergreen came out of both my military and my corporate experience. In a large corporation, the way to get ahead is often to get in with mail clerks and secretaries of important people. Careers can be made or broken simply by tearing up certain memos, and in the Army, although I was an officer, the only people I was afraid of were the enlisted men in the orderly room. They could process or not process

my requests, take me on or off combat duty. In my dramatization of
Catch-22, there's a line that doesn't appear in the book. Wintergreen
says, "I was going to cancel the Normandy invasion, until Eisenhower
committed more armor."

Playboy: Getting back to Yossarian, are any other of his experiences
like yours?

Heller: His encounter with Luciana, the Roman whore, corresponds
exactly with an experience I had. He sleeps with her, she refuses money
and suggests that he keep her address on a slip of paper. When he
agrees, she sneers, "Why? So you can tear it up?" He says of course he
won't and tears it up the minute she's gone—then regrets it bitterly.
That's just what happened to me in Rome. Luciana was Yossarian's
vision of a perfect relationship. That's why he saw her only once, and
perhaps that's why *I* saw her only once. If he examined perfection too
closely, imperfections would show up.

Playboy: Murray Kempton once wrote that, although *Catch-22* is
often considered a radical book, the only aspect of Yossarian's behavior
that deviates from traditional morality is his "appreciation of lechery."
Do you consider yourself a lecher?

Heller: No.

Playboy: So much for that. Returning to the war for a moment—

Heller: I assume you'll be returning to my sex life later on.

Playboy: In detail, if you insist. But for now, you said World War
Two seemed glamorous to you, like a movie. Don't you think young
people during the Vietnam era were more sophisticated than that?

Heller: Wars are still initiated by a certain type of professional
soldier whose ambition it is to act out fantasy scenes from war movies,
and they're still fought by very young people who have no more exciting life to lead. One very practical reason war seemed glamorous to
me was that the standard of living was higher in the Army than in
Coney Island. I ate better and had more money in my pocket than ever
before. And when I got home, I went to college on the GI Bill. In the
face of so many advantages, death seemed like a relatively minor
drawback.

Playboy: But the country was just coming out of the Depression then.
America was prosperous when we entered Vietnam.

Heller: Not *all* Americans were prosperous. The Vietnam war
found many blacks and Latins in the same situation I was in after Pearl

Harbor. They could see no future in the ghetto; the Army offered travel, education and money.

Playboy: Is that why the antiwar movement was largely a middle-class affair?

Heller: It's one of the reasons. Middle-class draftees in the Sixties suffered economic deprivation. They could travel all over the world anyway. They were going to college anyway. They had good jobs waiting for them. But, of course, the antiwar movement was ideologically based, also. The people who were aware of how we had stumbled into Vietnam were the ones who wanted us to get out.

Playboy: What do you mean by "stumbled into Vietnam"? Don't you see our involvement in that war as based on *some* reason or idea?

Heller: No, I saw—I *see* the Vietnam war as an extension of the Cold War that began in the late Forties and ended with the decline of the domino theory soon after John Kennedy's death.

Playboy: But if the Cold War ended in the mid-Sixties, why did we remain in Vietnam until 1972?

Heller: For *no reason at all.* That's the point! We often continue believing in things—and this is true of religions as well as ideologies— long after the circumstances that gave rise to the beliefs have disappeared. The belief in stopping communism wherever it threatens to advance simply carried over into another culture long after the *reason* for the belief disappeared. We weren't fighting communism in Vietnam. We were fighting culture lag.

Playboy: Eventually, Yossarian deserts an Army that doesn't make sense to him. Do you feel at all responsible for the guys in Vietnam— and apparently there were a lot of them—who went over the hill after reading *Catch-22*?

Heller: If anyone accused me of being the operative force in any specific desertion, I would deny it. I don't believe one book can shape an attitude or an action. But if I *was* responsible for people's running away from the war, then I evaded that responsibility consistently.

Playboy: In what way?

Heller: Often, while I was speaking publicly against the war, young men would ask me, "What would *you* do?" or "What should *I* do?" I always avoided those questions, because it would have been easy for me to give them the answer they wanted: that I *wouldn't,* and they *shouldn't,* serve. I, however, was not facing prison or exile.

Playboy: But Yossarian *does* desert, and you approve of his action.

Heller: Yes, and I would have gone further than Yossarian. I would have condoned *any* method of avoiding military service in Vietnam—including the one Yossarian rejects as being corrupt.

Playboy: You mean publicly endorsing the war in order to be sent home a hero?

Heller: Yes, and others Yossarian doesn't even consider, like using influence or buying a deferment. I don't think anybody should ever be compelled to fight in a war whose objectives he does not endorse.

Playboy: But to paraphrase Major Major, what if everyone felt that way?

Heller: Then, to paraphrase Yossarian, I'd be a damn fool to feel any other way.

Playboy: Do you prefer an all-volunteer Army?

Heller: I have no fear that a professional Army is going to be out of touch with civilization. Conscripts have never exacted a softening effect on the military.

Playboy: Do you still feel, as you did when you were 19, that World War Two was a necessary war?

Heller: The fact that the political and economic survival of this country was at stake is no longer as important to me as it was. But, yes, I still feel it was a necessary war. *Catch-22* was criticized because Yossarian justifies his participation in World War Two until the outcome is no longer in doubt. It offended some people, during the Vietnam war, that I had not written a truly pacifist book. But I am not a true pacifist. World War Two was necessary at least to the extent that we were fighting for the survival of millions of people.

Playboy: You mean the Jews?

Heller: Jews first, then blacks, then the whole sequence of extermination that was operating in Europe.

Playboy: As a Jew, do you have any special feelings about Israel's survival?

Heller: That's a difficult, confusing question. Emotionally, I have a strong attachment to Israel, even though I've never been there and have no desire to go. A year ago, I was certain Israel would be sold out.

Playboy: Now you're not so sure?

Heller: Strategically, I'm beginning to understand why this country has stood by Israel for so long. In case any type of mischief becomes necessary, Israel would be the only reliable ally America would have in that part of the world.

Playboy: When you say mischief, are you talking about a possible oil war?

Heller: If the flow of oil is seriously interrupted, or the price raised again, Western civilization will be out of business. There'll be no alternative but to go in and take the oil—that is, if we still can. But Italy hasn't the navy or air force to take even Libya. France can't do it. Germany certainly can't. England can't. So it would be up to us. And Israel, which was disposable a year ago, would become useful again. We'd need a friendly place to land our airplanes, tie up our boats and see that our soldiers get laid.

Playboy: Do you suppose an oil war would unite America?

Heller: If you mean in the way World War Two did, no. That war presented a unique set of conditions and I don't think we'll have another war like it—so we might as well give up hoping and resign ourselves to peace. Even in the Revolutionary War, there were huge sections of the population that didn't want to separate from England. I have a feeling they were right, that we'd be better off if we were a part of England.

Playboy: Why?

Heller: We'd have a better form of government. The parliamentary system would be a vast improvement over what we have now. Our Constitution looks good on paper and probably worked quite well with 13 colonies and about 72 registered voters. But now there's too much distance between the citizen-voter and his elected representative. He doesn't know *I* exist, and I wish *he* didn't. And with over 200,000,000 people, the Presidency has become a kind of public-relations enterprise for the party in power.

Playboy: But do you really *care* about politics? In 1972, you said you hadn't voted for a President in 12 years.

Heller: Then I voted for McGovern.

Playboy: Why?

Heller: Nixon made me do it.

Playboy: Has that experience changed you?

Heller: Yes. Now I'm *never* going to vote again—for anybody. The smartest people in Washington are the political reporters. They write about their inferiors.

Playboy: So, generally, you'd say American politics attracts a low class of people?

Heller: Yes, with one exception. There is a type of person who is occasionally attracted to politics for idealistic reasons and, once elected, does a creditable job. This is the gentleman who already has as much money as he wants and aspires to public office for reasons that have little to do with personal ambition. I may be naïve, but I felt Averell Harriman was in that class.

Playboy: Would you include Nelson Rockefeller?

Heller: I would exclude Nelson Rockefeller. There's a vicious, emotional quality to *his* ambition. But I would include Elliot Richardson and Archibald Cox. These are people who aspire to high position out of boredom.

Playboy: So you prefer a sated dilettante to a dedicated reformer?

Heller: Yes, and I feel safer with someone who inherited his money than with a self-made man. I think people like Roosevelt and Harriman and Stevenson are better suited to public office than the "sun-belt" millionaires who surrounded Nixon. The self-made man scares me. He attaches too much importance to his own personal accomplishments and yet is never really secure with people who are born into the highest order of society. Truman was an exception. He wasn't a social climber. Eisenhower was.

Playboy: Essentially, then, your ideal public official would be someone like Rockefeller or Kennedy.

Heller: But *not* Rockefeller. Or Kennedy. The Kennedy Administration was like a bunch of spoiled fraternity brats celebrating after having bought a campus election. They cavorted around, pushing each other into swimming pools. I think Johnson was more entertaining than Kennedy—until the Vietnam war escalated and his Administration collapsed. I've been delighted to see how dismally Kennedy's people have fared politically since his death. They were a disagreeable bunch. Even John Kenneth Galbraith seems to be a man without principles— or, if he *has* any, they are of only joking importance. Otherwise, he wouldn't be so friendly with William Buckley. You get the impression that although the two may disagree over a minor concern like the world's economy, when they get down to important matters like yachting, they are still in the same club.

Playboy: What have you got against Buckley?

Heller: I feel sorry for anybody who has to tangle with Buckley. Even though his reasoning is defective, he carries off a debate with so much *élan* that he makes the argument itself almost superfluous.

Playboy: Do you think Rockefeller will be the next President?

Heller: I don't think he'll let *anything* stand in his way. Rockefeller is so desperate for success he is in a position of virtually groveling for the Presidency. He has now lost the only favorable quality I ever saw in him: the poise, the aplomb of the gentleman born to wealth.

Playboy: Is there anyone you'd care to see elected President in 1976?

Heller: No.

Playboy: How about yourself?

Heller: Oh, no! I believe the Government exists to serve the people, not the other way around. Hence, the term public servant. I wouldn't want to be President, because I wouldn't want to put myself in a menial position.

Playboy: So you like the notion of a benevolent aristocrat in politics. What about a hard-nosed reformer?

Heller: I don't like the way reformers react to our political process. They have a difficult time realizing they must compromise or remain outsiders.

Playboy: In other words, they don't become corrupt quickly enough?

Heller: Exactly. A member of a legislative body who does not prostitute his integrity at the earliest possible moment is doing a grave disservice to his constituents. Unless he cooperates with the "inner circle," he'll never get his bills passed and the people who elected him will suffer.

Playboy: Do you think there is a better system of government in the world than the one we broadly call Western democracy?

Heller: No system offers greater personal liberty; the citizens of the totalitarian countries of the left and right enjoy less freedom than we do. But Johnson and Nixon were frightening because they demonstrated that an American President—even in a democracy, without Government censorship—is capable of waging a one-man war. That would not be possible in Russia, which is a dictatorship run by committee, or in China, where there are several powerful men.

Playboy: Is that power inherent in the Presidency, or did we just happen to elect a pair of megalomaniacs?

Heller: The power to exercise dictatorial control over the military is manifest in the office. A President can make war in a moment of personal panic or insecurity and no one in Congress will stop him.

Playboy: But Congress claims to have learned its lesson from Vietnam. Wouldn't it now be tougher on a President who asked for war powers?

Heller: If another President faked another Gulf of Tonkin incident, there would still be only about two Senators voting against the resolution, and they'd be tossed out in the next election.

Playboy: Shortly before his resignation, some people close to Nixon worried that he *would* push the panic button, try to mobilize the military in his defense. Others described his mental state as "serene." Do *you* think he was insane?

Heller: I would say no. Nixon had a very powerful sense of his own weakness. He doubted his abilities to an extent that could be called neurotic. Some people who repress their self-doubts overcompensate with a form of egotism. It is interesting that Nixon was never able to do that. His mechanism of repression never functioned well enough, so his self-doubts were always on his mind. He could never convince himself he was a superior person, and consequently was afraid people would observe how weak he felt. At the end, as you say, people in Washington were frightened. There was a *suspicion* that Nixon was insane. And certainly during his farewell speech, he took leave of what is customarily called sanity. He was not in touch with the situation or with himself. But I believe that was a temporary aberration. The real Nixon was a pathetic, fearful man who spent his life prophesying his own failures and living up to his own prophecies.

Playboy: His self-doubts aside, do you think Nixon is an intelligent man?

Heller: Throughout Nixon's political career, there is no evidence of *any* superior qualities. He had little intelligence, no gift for understanding a situation—and hasn't yet left us a single sally or epigram worth quoting.

Playboy: How about Johnson?

Heller: At least Johnson had a sense of humor. His jokes were apparently very cruel, but they *were* jokes. And Johnson was shrewd. He had a quality of strength missing in both Nixon and Agnew.

Playboy: Is that quality of strength evidenced by any political figures today?

Heller: William Simon, Nelson Rockefeller, John Mitchell. Their strengths are apparent.

Playboy: Do you believe public figures show us an accurate portrait of themselves in the media?

Heller: They can't avoid it. I think Gerald Ford, for instance, has lived up to the image he projected while being considered for the Vice-Presidency.

Playboy: What image is that?

Heller: That of the party hack with very limited intellectual gifts— a family man, team player, Rotarian. Every recent change in American politics has been for the worse and Ford will not prove an exception. A year ago, it was hard for me to imagine anyone worse than Nixon. But Nixon, because of the self-knowledge of his own small nature, may prove to have been less dangerous than Ford, who lacks that self-knowledge. Ford is a lot like Milo Minderbinder. Thinks of himself as a good guy, and God knows what devastation may result from that misconception.

Playboy: Some of the political changes you mention have come about through assassinations. Do you believe in any of the assassination-conspiracy theories?

Heller: No. But not because I have too *high* an opinion of human nature to believe there are people in this country willing to develop assassination plots; I'm convinced such people exist. However, I have such a *low* opinion of human nature that I don't think the conspirators would be capable of keeping a secret. If I were involved in a conspiracy that pulled off a difficult caper, there are a few people I would want to know about it. And each of them would tell one or two more. People are boastful. I could be wrong, but applying the same logic, I told Bob Woodward recently I didn't believe there was really a "Deep Throat," the guy who was the secret informer for his Watergate investigation.

Playboy: What was Woodward's response?

Heller: He was understandably offended. So I asked him if he had revealed Deep Throat's identity to at least one person who didn't *have* to know. He said he had, which was a very human answer, and that convinced me my theory was correct. Because that one person, being at least as human as Woodward, would have told one other person, who, in turn, would have told one or two more. The informant's identity would have become public knowledge within days.

Playboy: Then why would he invent such a character? To lend validity to otherwise unsubstantiated reports?

Heller: I believe Woodward and Bernstein's reporting was *better* substantiated than they themselves were willing to admit. I believe they had *many* sources inside the Government, and the best way to protect them all was to create one person who didn't exist.

Playboy: Woodward and Bernstein are currently stars of the college lecture circuit. That's a role you've filled twice—during the Sixties, as the author of *Catch-22* and one of America's leading antiwar spokesmen, and again recently, since the publication of your new book, *Something Happened.* Do you find that students have changed much since the war?

Heller: For the record, the Vietnam war is still being fought. But if you're asking if college students have changed much since the draft was abolished and most American forces pulled out of Indochina, I'd say there has been a decline in political action and interest.

Playboy: Why?

Heller: There are two conditions that must exist simultaneously to excite political activity in *any* population. First, the issues must be important and, second, one must know *exactly* how one feels about them. For college students in the Sixties, the war and the draft met those conditions. Today, though the questions are important, there is no clear-cut sense of what to do about them. So we are back to a normal state of political interest—practically none.

Playboy: We haven't talked about your own college experience. After you completed your wartime tour of duty and were shipped home—

Heller: Shipped is right. I was so terrified on my last few missions, I made a vow that if I got out of that war alive, I would never go up in an airplane again. The guys who were in a hurry to get home flew back across the Atlantic. I waited for a boat.

Playboy: How long did your antiflying vow last?

Heller: Until 1960, when I got stuck on a train for 24 hours. Suddenly, falling out of the sky didn't seem like such an objectionable alternative.

Playboy: What happened next, after you were literally shipped home?

Heller: I met my wife, got married, entered college on the GI Bill, did graduate work at Columbia and Oxford and began writing seriously. And reading.

Playboy: After reading something you liked, did you find yourself saying, "I wish I'd written that"?

Heller: No, but with some authors I found myself saying, "I could have written that if I'd thought of it."

Playboy: For instance?

Heller: I felt I could have written the plays of Clifford Odets. Unfortunately, Odets had already written those plays.

Playboy: Odets? That's not your style!

Heller: I didn't have my style then.

Playboy: But you *were* being published. Even as an undergraduate, your *Esquire* and *Atlantic* stories made you one of the country's most promising young writers.

Heller: Those stories were written while I was taking a creative-writing course at NYU in 1946. After the war, everyone who could write dialog was copying Ernest Hemingway and John O'Hara, and everyone who couldn't was copying Irwin Shaw. It took more talent to copy Shaw, because he used language better. My stories were as imitative as the rest.

Playboy: Imitative of whom?

Heller: I was writing *New Yorker*-type stories, stories by Jewish writers about Jewish life in Brooklyn. By the time I was a senior in college, I'd done a little more reading and I began to suspect that literature was more serious, more interesting than analyzing an endless string of Jewish families in the Depression. I could see that type of writing was going to go out of style. I wanted to write something that was very good and I had nothing good to write. So I wrote nothing.

Playboy: Did you formally "give up writing," or was it a day-to-day thing?

Heller: I formally gave up writing those trivial stories. In fact, I haven't written a single short story since. But I formally *began* looking for a novel that I could consider important.

Playboy: You mean you didn't come home from World War Two with *Catch-22* rattling around in your head?

Heller: As I've said, *Catch-22* wasn't really *about* World War Two. It was about American society during the Cold War, during the Korean War, and about the possibility of a Vietnam. I didn't get the idea for

Catch-22 until I had read many more writers. Louis-Ferdinand Céline's *Journey to the End of the Night* was the book that touched it off. Céline did things with time and structure and colloquial speech I'd never experienced before, and I found those new experiences pleasurable. It was unlike reading Joyce, who did things I'd never seen but that weren't pleasurable.

Playboy: How did Céline's book touch off *Catch-22*?

Heller: I was lying in bed, thinking about Céline, when suddenly the opening lines of *Catch-22* came to me: "It was love at first sight. The first time he saw the chaplain, Blank fell madly in love with him." I didn't come up with the name Yossarian until later, and the chaplain wasn't necessarily an *Army* chaplain. He could have been a *prison* chaplain. Ideas of plot, pace, character, style and tone all tumbled out that night, pretty much the way they finally appeared in the book. The next morning, at work, I wrote out the whole first chapter and sent it to my agent, Candida Donadio, who sold it to *New World Writing*. I was so excited I couldn't wait to begin chapter two.

One year later, I did.

Playboy: You're not one of the world's fastest writers, are you?

Heller: By the time I began *Catch-22,* I'd become *so* slow I suspected that might well be the only book I'd ever write.

Playboy: Is one of the reasons for your breath-taking lack of speed the fact that you insist on doing all your own editing?

Heller: If it weren't for the fact that I do practically *none* of my own editing, I'd never finish *anything at all.* As I submit sections of a manuscript to my editor, Bob Gottlieb, I indicate areas that might be cut. Then we discuss them and a decision is reached. That's the ideal situation for me, because without an editor I could trust, I'd still be in the middle of *Something Happened,* cutting out a section one week, putting it back the next, getting nowhere. I'm a chronic fiddler.

Playboy: Don't you think this business about lines "coming to you in bed" is rather unusual?

Heller: Yes.

Playboy: Did *Something Happened* start out that way, too?

Heller: No, I was sitting in a chair when the opening lines of *Something Happened* came to me.

Playboy: And where was that chair?

Heller: On Fire Island. *Catch-22* had been out for a while and was doing pretty well but wasn't near the best-seller lists. I wanted to quit my job writing promotional copy, but I had a wife and two kids to support. I wanted to do another novel but had no ideas. I was worried. Then two sentences came to me: "In the office in which I work, there are five people of whom I am afraid. Each of these five is afraid of four people." In a dream, a kind of controlled reverie, I quickly developed the characters, the mood of anxiety, the beginning, the end and most of the middle of *Something Happened.* And I knew Bob Slocum, my protagonist, intimately. Eventually, a better opening line came to me: "I get the willies when I see closed doors," and I wrote the first chapter around *that* line. But I kept the original to lead off the second part.

Playboy: Do your closing lines come to you the same way your opening lines do?

Heller: Yes. The closing line of *Catch-22* came to me on a bus.

Playboy: How about the closing line of *Something Happened*?

Heller: For six years, I had what I thought was going to be the closing line of *Something Happened* on an index card. The line was, "I am a cow."

Playboy: "I am a cow"?

Heller: It seemed good at the time and, besides, I can't start a book until I have a closing line.

Playboy: Have you a new book in mind?

Heller: Several prospective openings have come to me. But I've been too busy to develop them.

Playboy: Would you be willing to try out some possible openings on us?

Heller: All right. People have always asked me what happened to Dunbar, a character who disappeared in *Catch-22*. That question intrigues me, so I considered writing a novel that would begin: "Dunbar woke up with his name on the door and a Bigelow on the floor and wondered how he had got there." It was going to be a novel about amnesia. It went nowhere.

Playboy: Any others?

Heller: "The kid, they say, was born in a manger, but frankly, I have my doubts." I liked that line for a while, but nothing came of it, either.

Playboy: Can you produce these on command?

Heller: I have to be bored. I'm going to Mexico for a couple of weeks with the hope of achieving perfect boredom. New York is distracting. I suffer from a nervous impulse that makes me find excuses to call my publisher.

Playboy: Since *Something Happened* is one of the biggest money-makers Knopf has ever had, they must always be glad to hear from you. Why would you need an excuse to call them?

Heller: I always need an excuse, because I can never bring myself to reveal the true nature of the call.

Playboy: Which is?

Heller: To prevent them from forgetting about me.

Playboy: Don't you think that's a somewhat unrealistic fear?

Heller: *I* don't think so. I also fear that a day will go by in which nobody in the whole country buys a copy of the book. I once mentioned this to the people at Knopf and they laughed, as though such a thing were totally out of the question. But I need constant reassurance that my publisher remembers me and that Americans are still buying books.

Playboy: Besides striving to achieve perfect boredom, you're teaching. Why? Presumably, you don't need the money.

Heller: I teach fiction writing at City College in New York to students who are either very interested or drop the course. I believe I'm known as a hard marker. Money is no longer a primary consideration, but I enjoy the feedback I get from the better students.

Playboy: For some reason, we have difficulty relating to the idea that Joseph Heller still grades papers.

Heller: That strikes me as a little fishy, too.

Playboy: Have you considered giving up teaching so you could spend more time on your writing?

Heller: If I gave up teaching, I would have no time at all for writing. When I was working on *Catch-22*, I had a demanding job during the day. I was too tired to go out at night, so I wrote *Catch-22*.

Playboy: You wrote *Catch-22* in the evenings?

Heller: I spent two or three hours a night on it for eight years. I gave up once and started watching television with my wife. Television drove me back to *Catch-22*. I couldn't imagine what Americans did at night when they weren't writing novels.

Playboy: You're not into TV, then.

Heller: There's nothing I like on television. I used to watch ball games.

Playboy: Are you a sports fan?

Heller: Not anymore. My wife and I went through a period of going to hockey games. We haven't done that for a while.

Playboy: When was the last time?

Heller: Nineteen fifty-four.

Playboy: How about football, baseball, basketball?

Heller: I'm not a football fan, but I *was* a fan of the football strike last year.

Playboy: Were you sympathetic with the players' demands?

Heller: I never found out what their demands were. I just like it when things erupt. That's why I was sorry to see Nixon resign. Impeachment, like the football strike, was a pleasant change in the news. Otherwise, it's just laws and wars, winning and losing, elections and touchdowns. I like it better when something happens.

Playboy: What would you do with your time now if you weren't teaching?

Heller: I'd probably run amuck in Rome. When a writer is between books, he needs responsibility to keep him from making a fool of himself. Authors go through a period of craziness between books. Some invest in uranium stock, others change wives and agents. Some commit suicide. It's worse when you're young. Luckily, I was 38 and pretty well set in my ways when *Catch-22* came out. I had a good job and a nice apartment. If I'd been, say, 27 and living in a cold-water flat, my marriage would have broken up, I would have bought an estate in East Hampton I couldn't afford and, to pay for it, I would have started a second novel too soon.

Playboy: Do you think success is more damaging to a writer than failure?

Heller: Both are difficult to endure. Along with success come drugs, divorce, fornication, bullying, travel, meditation, medication, depression, neurosis and suicide. With failure comes failure.

Playboy: In balance, which is more beneficial to one's spiritual health?

Heller: Failure.

Playboy: Which do you prefer personally?

Heller: Success.

Playboy: Do you have any unfulfilled ambitions?

Heller: Most of the things I've wanted in life I've either gotten or stopped wanting. *Catch-22* fulfilled all my fantasies but two: It didn't

make me rich and it wasn't on the *New York Times* best-seller list. But in critical and popular esteem, it exceeded my wildest dreams.

Playboy: Do you ever tire of reading and rereading your own work?

Heller: No, I learn a lot from reading my work aloud, as I do on college campuses. I read sections of *Something Happened* at the University of Michigan recently and learned that for it to have remained a best seller as long as it has, it must be reaching a wider, older audience than *Catch-22.* I got a great response from the students with those passages dealing with Slocum's children. But during parts about his office, about fearing old age, there was silence. The attention was there, but the magic was gone.

Playboy: During the 12 years it took to write *Something Happened,* you were no longer working as an adman, so presumably you wrote during the day. What was your schedule like?

Heller: I wrote for two or three hours in the morning, then went to a gym to work out. I'd have lunch alone at a counter, go back to the apartment and work some more. Sometimes I'd lie down and just *think* about the book all afternoon—daydream, if you will. In the evenings I'd often go to dinner with friends.

Playboy: We've heard that you and your friends invented a game called Scapegoat and you played it fanatically while you were writing *Catch-22.*

Heller: I and a few friends—George Mandel, Mario Puzo and some others—redesigned a board game played with a deck of cards. It's a good gambling game.

Playboy: Did you, in fact, play fanatically?

Heller: I don't know what you'd call fanatic. We'd stay up all night three or four times a week—

Playboy: That's what we'd call fanatic.

Heller: We were all writing novels at the time. It was a good release.

Playboy: Would you tell us how it's played?

Heller: No.

Playboy: Most writers will do anything for money before they become successful; but you rewrote the screenplay for *Sex and the Single Girl* after *Catch-22* came out. Why?

Heller: For the money. They paid me $5000 a week. I wish somebody would offer me $5000 a week to work on something right now. I'd take it.

Playboy: Did you work on any other films?

Heller: *Dirty Dingus Magee* and *Casino Royale*. Charley Feldman, a nice but very nervous man, was producing *Casino Royale* and he traveled all over the country, hiring writers to do various scenes. He wanted to make sure he had enough material. Woody Allen later told me that he and I both did versions of the same scene.

Playboy: Few film makers have the luxury of choosing the Woody Allen or the Joseph Heller version of a scene. Which one ended up in the movie?

Heller: Neither. Feldman threw them both out.

Playboy: What was it like working on *Sex and the Single Girl*?

Heller: It was an enriching experience. Natalie Wood didn't want to do the picture, but she owed it to Warner Bros. on a three-film deal. And Tony Curtis needed the money to settle a divorce. That's what I like best about the movie industry: the art and idealism.

Playboy: Did you participate in the film version of *Catch-22*?

Heller: No, because I was experienced enough in film making to have virtually no hope that *Catch-22* would become a good film. And if I had participated in making it, I would have been compelled to care how it turned out. So I refused generous screenplay offers.

Playboy: Did you like the film?

Heller: It was OK, but I can never get the image of Buck Henry, who did the screenplay, out of my mind. I imagine him tearing through a dog-eared copy of the book while moaning, "Oy, vay, there's no *plot* here!" But when they were getting ready to shoot, I became friendly with Alan Arkin and Mike Nichols. They were so concerned about doing "justice" to the book—which is, of course, impossible in *any* film—that I found myself rooting for them.

Playboy: But the picture bombed. Do you think it deserved its bad reviews?

Heller: I think if the same film had been foreign, in black and white, without stars and based on an unknown novel, it would have been a major critical success. This is not a comment on the quality of the film but on the consistency of film reviews.

Playboy: Do you find that there is an exceptional thrill in seeing your work performed?

Heller: It's intoxicating, misleading. It appeals to the basest parts of one's mental anatomy. I love it.

Playboy: Your play, *We Bombed in New Haven,* opened to worshipful reviews. Several critics called it the most important play of the Sixties—

Heller: And the Seventies.

Playboy: But it was not a commercial success. Why?

Heller: Because it made people feel guilty, made them accessories to murder. People like to walk out of a theater feeling virtuous.

Playboy: Do you admire the work of any writers in particular?

Heller: Hawkes, Barth, Céline, Beckett, Pynchon, Faulkner, Shakespeare. . . .

Playboy: You have a pile of Dickens novels lying around.

Heller: This year I'm alternating between one Dickens novel, or biography of Dickens, and one contemporary book. Last year I did that with Jane Austen. The year before that, Henry James.

Playboy: Sounds as if you're catching up on your schoolwork.

Heller: When I was in school, I had neither taste nor patience. Now at least I have patience.

Playboy: How, in your view, does contemporary American fiction stack up against that of other countries, other periods?

Heller: The health of American literature is excellent. Unlike the movie business, which cannot make money with serious works, there is enough of a market for good literature in this country to support many novelists who are not commercially minded. I would put Updike, Cheever, Vonnegut, Bellow, Mailer, Baldwin, Roth, Styron, Malamud, Barth, Pynchon and Hawkes in that category. And there are perhaps 15 or 20 more I haven't mentioned, who will never speak to me again. There is a reading public in America that wants good, challenging books. That public is one of our national treasures.

Playboy: What about the rest of the reading public and the "popular" authors they support?

Heller: There are two kinds of people doing what we'll call popular fiction. One kind is the hack, the producer of quick pornography, quick mysteries—opportunistic books. The hack knows he is writing junk. The other kind may not be an "intellectual" writer but believes that he or she is producing works that are as good as anything that has ever been written. This type of writer puts as much effort into the work as Beckett or Mann or any conscientious writer does. The readers of that type of book are not to be looked down upon, either. They're reading what, to them, is good literature.

Playboy: What authors would you put into this category?

Heller: I'd rather not mention names.

Playboy: Oh, go ahead.

Heller: Jackie Susann, Erich Segal, Irving Wallace.

Playboy: Do you—or did you—know any of them personally?

Heller: I know Irving Wallace. He may not write the type of book I enjoy reading, but he starts work at six in the morning and puts as much effort and energy into *his* type of book as I put into mine. Anyone who wants to usurp Wallace's position with his particular readers is, literally, going to have to get up pretty early in the morning.

Playboy: Have you read *Love Story* or *Valley of the Dolls*?

Heller: No, but I know people who read *Love Story* and were moved by it. They might have been embarrassed afterward, but there apparently was something in that book—a legitimate reading experience—that I can almost guarantee was quite difficult for Segal to achieve. The proof is that it is not as easy to imitate these people as it looks. Even Segal himself can't seem to do it. I know a woman who was envious of Susann's success, felt she was brighter, more talented, and tried to write a *Valley of the Dolls* type of novel. In spite of her lavish advertising campaign, the book did not succeed. The more intellectual writer is likely to have a hack attitude toward that type of story and not spend enough time with characterization and detail.

Playboy: What about your old friend Mario Puzo? Where does he fit in?

Heller: After two intellectual novels that did not sell, Mario did attempt to write a popular book and succeeded. But *The Godfather* was not an imitation of any particular author or style, and I don't believe he approached the work with a condescending attitude. Perhaps he *is* an exception.

Playboy: Have you ever attempted any hackwork?

Heller: When I was an undergraduate publishing in the *Atlantic* for $200, I figured I might as well publish in *Good Housekeeping* for $1500. So I tried to write what were then called women's stories and never came close. I'd send off first drafts with the feeling I was doing hackwork, whereas the people who were writing *good Good Housekeeping* stories were rewriting them eight, ten, 12 times.

Playboy: Could you select one theme that you think connects all your writing?

Heller: The two novels are so different. I put everything I knew about the external world into *Catch-22* and everything I knew about the interior world into *Something Happened*. But in both books I am concerned with the closeness of the rational to the irrational mind, the location of reality.

Playboy: Reality is particularly difficult to locate in *Something Happened*. For example, in the scene in which Slocum discusses his problems with a psychiatrist. Afterward, the reader discovers that there is no psychiatrist.

Heller: Slocum tells the psychiatrist he never has hallucinations. The psychiatrist replies, "What would you call this?"

Playboy: In mapping that boundary between rational and irrational, you often employ humor. Why?

Heller: I'm inclined to be serious about most matters, yet jokes keep coming to mind. This disturbs me.

Playboy: Why?

Heller: Because humor comes too easily and I'm suspicious of things that come easily.

Playboy: Your conversation seems similar to your writing, in the sense that it careens between the serious and the farcical. Could this be "the Heller style"?

Heller: Perhaps. . . . Perhaps there is more truth in that than I realize. I wasn't aware that *Catch-22* was a *funny* book until I heard someone laugh while reading it. The experience was pleasant but also unsettling. As I said, I'm suspicious of comedy.

Playboy: Do you consider comedy trivial?

Heller: Yes. I can spend an evening with the best comedian and love every second, have a very *good* evening, but it's not going to affect me or change my life.

Playboy: And that's your definition of triviality—whether or not something changes your life?

Heller: A good novel will permanently alter the way I think. Nothing else does that for me.

Playboy: Earlier, while disclaiming responsibility for soldiers in Vietnam who deserted after reading *Catch-22*, you said one book couldn't shape an attitude or an action. Now you seem to be con-tradicting yourself.

Heller: I don't believe one book could convince a "good soldier" to go over the hill. Perhaps one book could convince a soldier who was thinking of it anyway, and perhaps a group of books could, over a period of time, completely change someone's way of thinking to an extent that would be impossible after reading only one book. But one book *can* change or expand my way of perceiving the world. A comedy routine cannot.

Playboy: When you say one book, do you mean only fiction, or do you read nonfiction, too?

Heller: I'll read a nonfiction piece about something I'm interested in. I read the newspaper.

Playboy: Are you interested in New Journalism as an art form? What's your opinion of Tom Wolfe's style?

Heller: I used to read Tom Wolfe in the *New York Herald Tribune* and wasn't even aware he *had* a style. He writes about interesting subjects, so his work is interesting. But for me, reading nonfiction is like going to the movies. Trivial.

Playboy: How much did you and Gottlieb cut out of *Something Happened*?

Heller: About 150 pages.

Playboy: And from *Catch-22*?

Heller: Nearly 100.

Playboy: What kind of material was it?

Heller: Adjectives and adverbs.

Playboy: *Catch-22* is a big, third-person novel in which you had 60 very different characters to play around with. But in *Something Happened*, everything is related through Bob Slocum, a psychic cripple. Didn't you feel cramped working through such a limited persona?

Heller: T. S. Eliot said that when one is forced to write within a certain framework, the imagination is taxed to its utmost and will produce its richest ideas. Given total freedom, the work is likely to sprawl.

Playboy: You spent eight years working on a book you *thought* was going to be called *Catch-18*, then just before publication, you were told to find another number. Did you take it hard?

Heller: I was heartbroken. I thought 18 was the *only* number. It took two weeks to select 22. I don't like to rush into things.

Playboy: When did you know that you'd "made it"?

Heller: Made what?

Playboy: Status.

about the external world into *Catch-22* and everything I kɪ.
interior world into *Something Happened.* But in both books
concerned with the closeness of the rational to the irrational ɪ
location of reality.

Playboy: Reality is particularly difficult to locate in *Somethiʌ.
Happened.* For example, in the scene in which Slocum discusses his
problems with a psychiatrist. Afterward, the reader discovers that there
is no psychiatrist.

Heller: Slocum tells the psychiatrist he never has hallucinations. The
psychiatrist replies, "What would you call this?"

Playboy: In mapping that boundary between rational and irrational,
you often employ humor. Why?

Heller: I'm inclined to be serious about most matters, yet jokes keep
coming to mind. This disturbs me.

Playboy: Why?

Heller: Because humor comes too easily and I'm suspicious of things
that come easily.

Playboy: Your conversation seems similar to your writing, in the
sense that it careens between the serious and the farcical. Could this be
"the Heller style"?

Heller: Perhaps. . . . Perhaps there is more truth in that than I
realize. I wasn't aware that *Catch-22* was a *funny* book until I heard
someone laugh while reading it. The experience was pleasant but also
unsettling. As I said, I'm suspicious of comedy.

Playboy: Do you consider comedy trivial?

Heller: Yes. I can spend an evening with the best comedian and love
every second, have a very *good* evening, but it's not going to affect me
or change my life.

Playboy: And that's your definition of triviality—whether or not
something changes your life?

Heller: A good novel will permanently alter the way I think. Nothing
else does that for me.

Playboy: Earlier, while disclaiming responsibility for soldiers in
Vietnam who deserted after reading *Catch-22,* you said one book
couldn't shape an attitude or an action. Now you seem to be con-
tradicting yourself.

Heller: I don't believe one book could convince a "good soldier" to
go over the hill. Perhaps one book could convince a soldier who was

thinking of it anyway, and perhaps a group of books could, over a period of time, completely change someone's way of thinking to an extent that would be impossible after reading only one book. But one book *can* change or expand my way of perceiving the world. A comedy routine cannot.

Playboy: When you say one book, do you mean only fiction, or do you read nonfiction, too?

Heller: I'll read a nonfiction piece about something I'm interested in. I read the newspaper.

Playboy: Are you interested in New Journalism as an art form? What's your opinion of Tom Wolfe's style?

Heller: I used to read Tom Wolfe in the *New York Herald Tribune* and wasn't even aware he *had* a style. He writes about interesting subjects, so his work is interesting. But for me, reading nonfiction is like going to the movies. Trivial.

Playboy: How much did you and Gottlieb cut out of *Something Happened*?

Heller: About 150 pages.

Playboy: And from *Catch-22*?

Heller: Nearly 100.

Playboy: What kind of material was it?

Heller: Adjectives and adverbs.

Playboy: *Catch-22* is a big, third-person novel in which you had 60 very different characters to play around with. But in *Something Happened*, everything is related through Bob Slocum, a psychic cripple. Didn't you feel cramped working through such a limited persona?

Heller: T. S. Eliot said that when one is forced to write within a certain framework, the imagination is taxed to its utmost and will produce its richest ideas. Given total freedom, the work is likely to sprawl.

Playboy: You spent eight years working on a book you *thought* was going to be called *Catch-18*, then just before publication, you were told to find another number. Did you take it hard?

Heller: I was heartbroken. I thought 18 was the *only* number. It took two weeks to select 22. I don't like to rush into things.

Playboy: When did you know that you'd "made it"?

Heller: Made what?

Playboy: Status.

Heller: I knew I'd achieved *something* the first time someone I'd heard of but never met invited me to a party by naming all the famous people who were going to be there and indicated that those famous people were being invited at least partly on the basis that *I* would be there.

Playboy: Any other times?

Heller: Yes, when I bought a car recently. I didn't haggle, but if I had, I felt I could have gotten a sizable discount.

Playboy: Just because you're Joseph Heller?

Heller: No, because I'm a friend of Mario Puzo. I had to go around shaking hands with all the Italian salesmen. Status isn't all gay parties and caviar.

Playboy: The title of *Catch-22* has passed into the language as a slogan, a concept. How do you feel when you see and hear it in everyday life?

Heller: Good, proud. Again, that is something that appeals to one's basest instincts—an appeal I, for one, find irresistible. But I don't always like the people who use *Catch-22* or the way it is used. James St. Clair, Nixon's attorney, tried to get away with it before the Supreme Court. He made the argument that you can impeach a President only if you have evidence that he committed a crime, but you can't collect criminal evidence against a President. One of the Justices had to play Yossarian and say, "Wait a minute. You lose me there."

Playboy: Do you think *Catch-22* is a radical book?

Heller: Its structure is more radical than the content. The morality is rather orthodox—almost medieval. With the exception of the aforementioned "appreciation of lechery," the seven basic virtues and seven deadly sins are all in their proper place.

Playboy: How about *Something Happened*? Would you consider *that* radical?

Heller: Yes, but again, only in structure. The first and third person are fused in a way I've never seen before, and time is compressed into almost a solid substance.

Playboy: Most of the reviews of *Something Happened* were quite good. But some were terrible.

Heller: Apparently, I don't write books people like a *little*.

Playboy: Were the reviews better or worse than you expected?

Heller: Three out of four were favorable—better than I expected. I think most of the negative reviews and most of the positive reviews were good.

Playboy: How can a bad review be good?

Heller: Most negative reviewers either found the book repetitious or found Slocum not a sufficiently interesting character to warrant such a detailed examination. Those are valid opinions. The reviewers analyzed the book carefully. That's all any author can ask and far more than most authors receive. *Playboy* published the only review I think of as being snotty. It wasn't really a review, just a paragraph that dismissed the book in an insulting way.

Playboy: *The New York Review of Books* accused you of over-weening ambition. It said *Something Happened* was a failed sequel to *Catch-22,* a sort of Everyman in war and peace.

Heller: That review, along with some others, couldn't resist the temptation to compare the two works, taken together, to *War and Peace.* They said *Catch-22* was perhaps the definitive book about war, but that *Something Happened* was *not* the definitive book about peace. But it wasn't *my* hypothesis that Slocum is the Everyman of his genera-tion. In fact, I'd *never* write a book in which the leading character was not a very distinct personality. I've said many times that I thought Slocum was perhaps the most contemptible character in all literature. Yet people have found him pathetic, even sympathetic. This surprises me. All these reviewers now claim to have loved *Catch-22.* Where were they when *that* book came out?

Playboy: At least *The New Yorker* was consistent. Its reviewer hated both books.

Heller: Consistency may be overrated as a virtue.

Playboy: There's never much physical description in your writing. Is it that you don't want to distract the reader or that you think descriptive writing is trivial?

Heller: Neither. I admire writers like Updike and Nabokov and Vidal, who have great powers of observation. I just don't seem to respond to visual stimulus. I once told my editor I couldn't write a good descriptive metaphor if my life depended on it. Every once in a while, I figure I'd better put in some visual description, but a flushed face and white shingles are usually as far as I get. Recently, someone told me my nephew has blue eyes. I said I'd never noticed. The boy is 28 years old.

Playboy: There is a minor character in *Catch-22* named Scheisskopf.

At one point, someone refers to him as a Shithead, with a capital S. Since *Scheisskopf* is German for shithead, it works like a pun, though it looks as if the capital letter were a typographical error. Was that intentional?

Heller: Yes, and you're the first one to comment on it. I've waited 14 years for someone to pick that up. I've blabbed it to a couple of people *myself,* but nobody's *asked* about it.

Playboy: Are there any other so-far-undetected jokes in *Catch-22?*

Heller: There is one more.

Playboy: Any chance you'll tell us what it is?

Heller: No chance at all.

Playboy: *Catch-22* has been translated into all the Western and many Eastern languages. Is there a special pleasure in knowing you are read world-wide?

Heller: Yes, but there's a certain queasiness that goes with it. I can never be sure about what's *in* those foreign editions. They *look* like *Catch-22,* but who knows? I got a rather unsettling letter soon after the book came out. It said: "I am translating your novel *Catch-22* into Finnish. Would you please explain me one thing: What means *Catch-22?* I didn't find it in any vocabulary. Even assistant air attaché of the U.S.A. here in Helsinki could not explain exactly." I suspect the book lost a great deal in its Finnish translation.

Playboy: You've been married to your first and only wife for nearly 30 years. To what do you attribute this unusually successful marriage?

Heller: I didn't say it was successful. Maybe we just don't quit easily. I know many people whose marriages have ended for reasons that I don't think are serious enough. If everyone were to end a marriage because of disappointments or dissatisfactions or moods or temporary attractions, almost *no* marriage would survive.

Playboy: Slocum says he would leave his wife if she had an affair. Would you?

Heller: That falls into the realm of imagined experience.

Playboy: Can you imagine leaving her?

Heller: I think you may now be slipping into the tendency to assume that a novel is a personal statement rather than a work of literature. *Something Happened* seems to invite this sort of thing. While my agent, Candida Donadio, who knows me as well as I know myself, was read ing *Something Happened,* she found herself continually saying, "Joe wouldn't do *that*!" I had to keep reminding her it was fiction. Now that we're back on the topic of sex, I'll have to remind you to ask another question.

Playboy: OK. In *Something Happened,* Slocum says he can't run off with a 19-year-old girl because after two hours he won't have anything to say to her. He claims he is unable to fall in love and that is what keeps his marriage together. Is that your feeling, too?

Heller: I would generalize and say that my imagination, like Slocum's, keeps me from making foolish mistakes.

Playboy: Slocum says his fantasies are worthwhile only as long as he remains inert. Do you have any cherished fantasies you feel would be ruined if you acted upon them?

Heller: Shirley and I often discuss moving to the south of France. But then I start thinking about getting a new driver's license, and what will happen when it gets cold and we have no one to talk to? And what are we going to do if we want a good piece of salami? I end up realizing that I like to live in a city that I know pretty well, among people I know pretty well, and the only place on earth that fits that description is Manhattan. But the south of France continues to be an appealing fantasy for us as long as we do nothing about it.

Playboy: Have you any fantasies that are closer to home?

Heller: Well, sometimes I think about moving out of the city, but it always takes the form of going to New Hampshire and living next door to J. D. Salinger. But, of course, if that happened, Salinger would immediately move to Montana. There I'd be, stuck out in the country with nobody to talk to.

Playboy: You claim you're fond of young people, yet you once locked your daughter out of the apartment. Why?

Heller: That was during my Pizza Period, when I didn't let *any* people in unless they were bringing me a pizza.

Playboy: We've heard that you have an insatiable appetite. Is it true that some of your closest friends, members of the famous Gourmet Club, call you The Animal?

Heller: It's not a club and we are not members. But, yes, the non-members do call me that.

Playboy: You are apparently quite an expert on food. In the February *Playboy Interview,* Mel Brooks, fellow Gourmet Club nonmember, quotes you as saying that 1000 years ago, there may have been egg in egg creams.

Heller: I belong to the catastrophist school of egg-cream history, whereas Mel is a steady-state theorist. When Mel is in New York, we spend a lot of time together searching for egg creams.

Playboy: Yossarian was orally fixated and, in *Something Happened,* Slocum sees the deterioration of American life in terms of food. Nothing tastes as good as it used to. He remembers the day he found out about a former girlfriend's suicide by recalling not his sorrow but the taste of the sandwich he ate afterward. Do you share the oral fixations of your two protagonists?

Heller: Possibly. But I also believe that young people today will never know the taste of a good seeded roll or a mellow roll. They will never know good ice cream, good butter, good whipped cream—the stuff they spray out of cans isn't whipped and isn't cream. This is a legitimate measure of the deterioration of our standard of living.

Playboy: How did the Gourmet Club start?

Heller: Thirteen years ago, Ngoot Lee, the famous Chinese advertising man, began cooking dinner for a group of us once a week. Then Ngoot became successful and decided cooking put him in a subservient position, so we began going to Chinese restaurants instead.

Playboy: We didn't know there were any famous Chinese admen.

Heller: Ngoot cunningly hides his nationality by speaking Yiddish.

Playboy: We've talked about your devotion to food. Are you a drinker?

Heller: Yes, but never alone. If I'm at a party, I'll drink all night. I'm known as a nice drunk. I get very funny.

Playboy: Do you think most writers like to drink?

Heller: I can't speak for most writers. But most people I know who *are* writers don't like to drink as much as I do.

Playboy: Are you into any other drugs?

Heller: No, and I don't think drugs are valuable to a writer. They might distort your perceptions in a way that enables you to *see* more, but the ability to coordinate what you're experiencing with the very acute discipline of writing will be absent.

Playboy: Do you have vivid dreams?

Heller: Sometimes.

Playboy: In color?

Heller: No, black and white.

Playboy: Have you used your dreams in your work?

Heller: Almost all of Slocum's dreams are my own: ones in which he must get from one place to another and can't; he's in school and has to take a test, but he can't find the classroom. Freud himself had a recurring dream about not being able to pass an exam. When I was teaching at Penn State, I used to dream I was in the classroom with 15 minutes left and I couldn't think of a single thing to say. It was terrifying.

Playboy: What else terrifies you? Do you believe in hell—or God?

Heller: I don't care if there's a God or not.

Playboy: What if Ralph Nader came up with a scientific study that *proved* there was a God and a heaven and a hell? Would that alter your behavior?

Heller: No. The experience of life is more important than the experience of eternity. Life is short. Eternity never runs out.

Playboy: Is there any special way you'd like to be . . . remembered?

Heller: Remembered? In order to understand that question, am I to assume you have euphemistically deleted the word death?

Playboy: We were hoping you wouldn't notice.

Heller: It is impossible to predict or control how you will be remembered after your death. In that way, dying is like having children: You never know what will come out. In Beckett's *Endgame,* he asks his parents, in effect, "Why did you have me?" and the father replies, "We didn't know it would be you."

Playboy: Yossarian wants to "live forever or die in the attempt," and Slocum wants to "outlive the Rockies." Do you fear death?

Heller: I fear death, nursing homes and vaccinations.

Playboy: Snowden's secret, which Yossarian learned when the young gunner's guts slithered out through a flak wound over Avignon, was that "the spirit gone, man is garbage. . . . Ripeness was all." Can you bring yourself to contemplate that inevitable transition from spirit to garbage?

Heller: I've come to look upon death the same way I look upon root-canal work. Everyone else seems to get through it all right, so it couldn't be too difficult for me.

Joseph Heller in Conversation with Martin Amis

Martin Amis/1975

From *The New Review* 2 (November 1975), 55–59. Reprinted by permission of the author.

Currently you're averaging one book every decade or so. It's easy to get an image of you hanging about the place polishing three lines a day, like Virgil. And yet your prose, for all its deliberateness, doesn't sniff of the lamp. How do you write? Are you just slow, or do you get clogged?

Well, one of the problems is that I think—and write—pretty much like I talk: slow and not very coherent. I don't have an instinctive command of a literary language, I don't think with a literary language. What I have to do is use my natural form of writing—which is as conversational as writing a letter to a friend or talking to him on the telephone—and then go back and liven it up some, make it more polished and considered. Then I have to go back *again* to check that it's still spontaneous and conversational. I write maybe thirty lines a day. I have a two-hour work-stand which I can sometimes stretch to two-and-a-half if I'm in the middle of a dialogue and know how it's going to come out. But if I worked any longer than that the prose would lose what polish it has and become sloppy, imprecise and diffuse. So it's 10 to 12 in the morning, except in the final stages, when some of the tension and insecurity lifts and you can complete the last third or quarter much more rapidly. At the moment I'm working pretty briskly on a third novel, and I think I'm going to like it. I'm in the habit. I started writing it ten months ago and I have 50 typewritten pages, which is three chapters, and a handwritten version of the fourth. When I get back, in about two weeks, I will read through what I have and I think I will like it enough to go ahead with it. It will be a short book, a funny book, more in keeping with the lighter novels of Evelyn Waugh and Kingsley Amis than with the gloom and anxiety of *Something Happened*—much closer to the comedy of *Catch-22*, but without that book's pessimism and "philosophical" underpinning. A departure.

A departure from what, exactly? In what senses, if any, are Catch-22 *and* Something Happened *the products of the same preoccupations? On the face of it, of course, they are radically dissimilar books. One is about war; it is lurching and surrealistic, full of heightened characterisation and grotesque incident. The other is about peace; it is intimate, glazed, monotone—you might even say that the point of* Something Happened *is that nothing ever happens in it. Do you think it possible to argue, though, that both novels are largely about the same thing—in short, going crazy? Yossarian, the exploited and flak-shocked hero of* Catch-22, *virtually has madness thrust upon him, whereas Bob Slocum, the shabby, furtive, lugubrious ad-exec hero of* Something Happened, *has to cope only with the more self-willed horrors of peace, and seems therefore to be creating and generating madness from within. Does this make any sense to you as a link between the books?*

I would say that madness is certainly a component of both books, but it is not what they are "about." And, again, they look at madness quite differently—one in a stylised, literary way, the other with total realism. I think madness is present only thematically or symbolically in *Catch-22*. With the exception of Dunbar, who has after all taken a bad knock on the head, I can't recall there being anybody too close to what might be called a state of psychosis or breakdown. Yossarian, yes, on those occasions when he suffers some kind of shock and goes into hospital in a state of what I call hysterical anxiety. But he soon recovers and then comes out and does go back to combat.

I assume you're being paradoxical? Or do you say this in order to anticipate, and so pre-empt, a literal-minded reading of the book? By almost anybody's standards, everyone in Catch-22—*except Yossarian—is irretrievably insane. But no doubt you'd reply that they are merely mild eccentrics reacting sanely to the insanity of war.*

Yes and no. I do regard them as eccentrics, and very heightened eccentrics, but they're in that novel to achieve a less literal (and more literary) effect than that of mass-hysteria. I wanted to recruit a cast of eccentrics or "types" who would have virtually no precursors in the tradition of realistic fiction. They would be the caricatures produced by war: Hungry Joe would be one type, and Dobbs would be another, and Orr would be another, and the Colonels would be others. Their various mental conditions were just part of realising an idea rather than pro-

ducing a commentary on deracination. I regarded them as cartoon
eccentrics, not real people intended to represent mental aberration and
collapse. You'd have to be suffering from a compassion problem to use
up much time feeling sorry for them.

In Something Happened, *on the other hand, psychological accuracy
(and particularity) is of basic structural importance—it is used to shape
and present the whole argument of the book. Bob Slocum's knowing but
guileless narration, with its flashbacks, blocks, traumata and repressions, is surely meant to be as revelatory of perverse and wayward
mental states as the therapy sessions of Alex Portnoy. Or would you say
that Slocum's neuroses are the appropriate responses to the anxieties of
peace?*

Bob Slocum is certainly very close to madness, and madness is a very
real thing in *Something Happened.* It is written from the point of view
of someone so close to madness that he no longer has the ability to
control what to think about. There are passages in the book where I
strongly indicate that Bob himself no longer appreciates the distinction
between what is and what isn't; as narrator, Bob transcribes his own
auditory hallucinations, so that parts of the dialogue are in fact imagined
conversations. No, the threat of madness is vividly real for Bob, which
makes the world of *Something Happened* entirely different from that of
Catch-22. Something Happened is about the processes of Bob Slocum's
mind, underlaid, from my point of view, by what knowledge I do have
of psychology, psychiatry and psychotherapy.

*Doesn't it make you at all nervous to subject a novel to a psychiatric
schema? Psychological accuracy is after all not the same thing as
literary shape. Don't you think that by your fidelity to Bob's thought
processes, which are necessarily often ponderous, hectoring, irrelevant,
obsessive and repetitive, you might be in danger of making the book
those things too? For instance, it made the book longer than it perhaps
needed to be. A lot of reviewers over here complained about the length,
suggested convenient cuts, and so on. Does this bother you?*

People say it's a long book. That's an accurate statement. The book is
long. The same criticism was made of *Catch-22* when it came out, by
the way. The initial reviews of *Catch-22* in the States were mostly very
unfavourable—people said that it wasn't a novel, that it shouldn't have
been published, that it was too long. Too long for some and not long

enough for others. It is a long novel. As for *Something Happened,* I can
justify its length the same way I can justify the whole book—by the
psychological nature of Bob Slocum. Slocum is a person whose memory
is fixed obsessively on three or four stages of his life; in his thoughts he
keeps returning to those moments, and also longs to recapture the
happier periods in between that he can't recall any more. That's not
unusual in the workings of human minds—we remember our humilia-
tions and feelings of unhappiness for a lifetime, I think.

But to answer your previous question, I wouldn't go so far as to say
that I followed a psychological structure. That's not how books get
written. Psychological accuracy is what you end up with if you're
fortunate, not what you set out to achieve. In fact, many of the nuances
of Bob's thought and speech habits, which I put in just because I
thought they'd be effective, were later pointed out to me by psycholo-
gists and linguists as being of psychological significance. For instance,
the only member of Slocum's family who is given a name in the book
(the rest are "my boy," "my girl," "my wife") is the brain-damaged
younger son, who is given the rather stark name of "Derek." I'm told
that people in Bob's state will habitually name things which they want
to dissociate themselves from, and not name things which they love and
want to protect. Similarly, Bob's use of infantilisms—phrases like "I
get the willies" and his habit of putting "ha, ha" in parentheses after
every one of his despairing jokes—was also later pointed out to me as
being typical of Bob's condition. Satisfying though all this may be,
however, I think it's hardly more than a lucky accident so far as I'm
concerned. Probably I don't write novels the way other people do. I get
an idea, and the only thing that attracts me about that idea is that I think
it would make a good novel. The subject-matter itself doesn't attract
me, though in the absence of that subject-matter I wouldn't proceed.
I didn't choose war as the subject of *Catch-22* and I didn't choose
whatever is the subject of *Something Happened.* I just feel very lucky
to get an idea for a novel that I think I can write.

*Regardless, then, of extra-literary considerations? Again several
reviewers over here found themselves gratuitously disgusted by Bob's
brutal and sickly ways—or ways of thought. Why write 570 pages about
a monster? seemed to be a fairly well-represented view. Caroline
Blackwood in the TLS, I remember, as well as calling the hero "Bob"*

throughout her review, also called him mean, sick, chauvinistic, etc. Perhaps they felt that you identified with Bob, endorsed him as a character.

Well, readers were more sympathetic to Bob than the reviewers were—or even than I was—and this shores up my feeling that the author's conception of what he is doing is no more accurate than the reader's. Or even less so: I would believe in the collective impression of an audience being a more accurate description of a book than any critique. As it happens, I myself thought of Bob as an incredibly contemptible person for whom I had no conscious sympathy whatever when I was writing about him. I mean, the way I have him behave is *awful*. So I was surprised when handing in the early sections to my agent and my editor and a few other people, to have them react instantaneously with phrases like "poor Slocum," "poor Bob," and to be so thoroughly moved by the unhappiness he was experiencing. That took me by surprise at first, but by now I feel sorry for him myself too. I have a better understanding of Bob now than I had when I was writing about him. He's not evil or corrupt, after all; he tries like hell to get on with his family, and his behaviour at his work is close to irreproachable. When he behaves badly he feels bad. And anyway it's not what he does so much as what he says and thinks: that's what causes the problems.

You could, mind you, extend Bob's roll-call of sins to include the most heinous of all: murder. As well as all the venial stuff—the sneaky office politics, Bob's extreme callousness about the "idiot" Derek, his routine nights of lies and booze and sex—there comes a point in the final pages of the novel where you make it very tempting to infer that Bob has taken the life of his elder son, the member of his family he loves most, as an act of vengeance. Bob's boy has been run over; Bob rushes up to him in the street and sees his son's face and body covered in holes with blood pouring out of them; through some desperate protective instinct Bob picks him up and hugs him violently in his arms—and we later learn that the boy died from asphyxiation, and not from his superficial injuries. Fair enough. But by this stage you've made it clear that Bob's boy has begun to move away from Bob and that Bob bitterly resents it. Immediately before the accident you have Slocum say:

I want my little boy back too.
I don't want to lose him.

I do.
"Something happened!"

Something has happened at last, as Bob is summoned to the scene of the accident. The incident could hardly be more cruelly ironic; but don't you think that this would have to weigh with a strictly moral reading of Bob and your attitude towards him?

It is part of it, and to be candid with you it is a part that I was not aware of consciously when I wrote it. I suppose it got in on the level of psychological understanding rather than deliberate intention. Again, it took somebody else to point it out to me. I got a letter from Bruno Bettelheim, in which he explained that Bob is about to lose the main love relationship in his life, and that the incident described in the book would be credible psychologically as Bob's wild attempt to *preserve* that relationship. I was surprised, too, to see that I had prepared for such an interpretation in the text immediately before the incident. When Bob mislays his boy on the beach he says, "I could have killed him," and by this stage the sheer suspense of Bob's anxieties is getting too much for him to bear: "I wish whatever's going to happen would happen already," he keeps thinking. Yes, it's part of it.

So far as I know none of the British critics noticed the implication, though it would certainly have fuelled those of them who feared for Bob's—and your own—spiritual hygiene. However, I'd take it that you would dismiss moral objections to the book as essentially extra-literary objections.

Well, I'd be very upset if I were accused of writing an immoral book. There is a high moral content in *Catch-22* and I think an extremely high moral content in *Something Happened*. It's quite specific in *Catch-22*— I made it easy to tell the good guys from the bad guys. At the end of the book, with the war almost won, Yossarian finds that the moral of the life of action is to desert from it, and with my sanction. You might disagree with me, in that we can argue, but there is morality involved and I know what I'm doing. It's my idea of conscience and it coincides with Bob's idea of it in *Something Happened,* in which an extremely exacting, at times peremptory, conscience is at work throughout. When Slocum does something wrong he feels guilty about it. In fact, he feels guilty without knowing what he's done wrong, and feels guilty sometimes even when he's done right. I think that Bob's own retributive thought processes, as established in the body of the book, supply all the moral the book needs.

Yes—and how can you punish a reprehensible character anyway? You can either have him tritely punished or improbably converted, and who is going to believe that any more? What you do need to do, though, and I think you do this very clearly in Something Happened, *is to establish your detachment, or disinterestedness, with regard to your narrator. But with general readers as much as critics the narratorial "I" has a habit of becoming* you. *Like Bob, you worked for several years in an advertising agency; and, like him, you have a boy, a girl, and a long marriage. I know you started to write about Bob with feelings of contempt for him, but it's certainly possible to write a novel out of a nugget of self-contempt. Did people assume that there was a good deal of self-revelation in* Something Happened? *Is there any?*

People certainly thought there was. When I handed the early sections of the novel in to my editor at Knopf he would say things like, "Joe, this is so fucking convincing, but I *know* you don't feel this way." That kind of reaction was so common that when a magazine wanted to take an excerpt I wouldn't let them have it; it was the chapter about Bob's wife and, read in isolation, I thought it might cause considerable embarrassment to *my* wife. In fact, the book is written in the *manner* of self-revelation: everything in it is meant to be self-revelatory, but it's not me who's being revealed. I used plenty of my own experience in it, but the mind the book is about is not my mind. And maybe I succeeded here to an extent that goes beyond the point of what might be called commercial caution, because everybody made it pretty clear what a harrowing experience it was to read the book.

Some final questions. I spoke earlier of "the horrors of peace" in Something Happened *being equivalent to the horrors of war in* Catch-22. *At one point Slocum says, unnervingly: "It was after the war, I think, that the struggle really began." How widespread is the malaise of inertia and anxiety in present-day America? At another point Slocum says, "I've got the decline of American civilisation . . . to carry around on these poor shoulders of mine." Is Bob bluffing? How much have he and America got in common?*

In many ways they're very much alike, Bob and America. I did not intend Bob to be symbolic of, or representative of, the upper echelons of American life, though not in any obvious or over-rationalised sense. Things are simplified by war, at least they were by World War Two. It was easy for every American to know what to think and what to do after Pearl Harbour. You knew who the bad guys were and who the good guys were and you had some idea of the dangers involved. If Slocum had been in Yossarian's war, it would have been morally and emotionally very simple for him. You're either afraid or not, or only a bit afraid, or so afraid that you can't go into combat. But the struggle of what to do with yourself after the war is more complicated for somebody like Slocum—or even for somebody like Kurt Vonnegut, who reviewed the book sympathetically in the Sunday *Times*. It's the end of what other people have called the American Dream, the wastelands that await the person who succeeds. Affluence combined with leisure does seem to produce clinical neurosis in a great many Americans. I grew up in what was called the Depression mentality. College had a different function than it has for the people going there now. The idea was to go to work as quickly as you could, advance as quickly as you could, get into the professional classes and win salary raises and rapid promotions. By doing this you would be handsome and sane, your wife would be beautiful, your children would be healthy and happy. Having achieved what we were told to strive for, we find that we're middle-aged and unstable, our marriages are likely to be unsatisfactory, and our children are miserable. And then there's nowhere else to turn. Remember when Slocum says, "I wish I knew what to wish"? That's the problem for people who have a choice of things, but no longer know what things they want to wish for.

Catching Joseph Heller

Barbara Gelb/1979

From *New York Times Magazine*, 4 March 1979, 14–16, 42, 44, 46, 48, 51–52, 54–55. Reprinted by permission of the author.

To Joseph Heller, death has always been a laughing matter. He was 5 when his father died suddenly, and he remembers the day of the funeral as a party. He was petted and crooned to and fed cake and candy. He was considered too young to understand grief, and for years he never heard his father's death mentioned, nor did he ask. Twenty-five years later, having confronted his own death on 60 missions as a bombardier in World War II, he began writing *Catch-22*, the funny and shocking novel about death in war that was to turn him, after the book's completion eight years later, into an aging prodigy.

Some writers are born to the tragic view and learn to embrace it, saying, as Eugene O'Neill did, "Life is a tragedy, hurrah!" Others, like Heller, acknowledge the tragedy, but hold it at arm's length, laughing in its face. (Death is a party, ha ha.) Heller grew up with this odd and isolating concept. His mother would chide him, in response to an oblique joke, "You have a twisted brain." And it was no more than the truth. Grimacing, Heller chose to nourish the twist and perfect the strangled laugh. His joke is the comedy of despair.

Heller continues to laugh about death. The joke is at the core of all of his writings—his long second novel, *Something Happened*, his play, *We Bombed in New Haven*, and his about-to-be published third novel, *Good as Gold*. In all four of his works, death is present as an event and a foreboding. In each, the climax is precipitated by the death of someone close to the protagonist—who always survives, gasping with gratitude.

Readers in the millions have laughed with pain and recognition at his wicked social satire, and have moaned (a favorite Heller verb) over the wayward wretchedness of his trapped nonheroes; literary critics here and abroad applaud his daring and his ferocity, analyze the gallows-grimness of his comedy and often, in passing, chide him for his languor and the paucity of his *oeuvre*.

185

Writing in his own sweet time, Heller has managed to produce one of the smallest bodies of work ever to be taken seriously. Eighteen years have passed since *Catch-22* was published, and in spite of a more recent success five years ago with *Something Happened*, Heller is still known best (in many quarters still known *only*) as the author of *Catch-22*. This is a little unfair, because *Something Happened* is a maturer, more searching book than *Catch-22*. It is as inventive and daring in form, but goes far beyond the cipher characters of the first novel. The central figures in *Something Happened* have been plucked from Heller's own anxiety-beset life and pinned down, naked and squirming, for Heller to dissect with pitiless glee.

But a dazzling first success is not easily followed, especially if it turns out to be a literary phenomenon such as *Catch-22*. The book's title has become part of the language, is embedded in dictionaries and spoken daily in the dialogue of frustration. The phrase has made its way even into the archives of the United States Supreme Court as a footnote to a dissenting opinion regarding a court martial, by no less a jurist than Potter Stewart. With eight million copies in print and with translations in more than a dozen languages, the book has created Heller as cult hero and brought him international glory of a kind that few authors—even those who have written several best sellers—ever manage to attain.

Something Happened took Heller 13 years from start to finish (with two years out to write and produce his play). It was an arduous journey of creation—the tragicomedy of an intelligent, middle-aged man named Slocum, a corporate misfit, morbid, tender, loving, oversexed, self-pitying, self-aware, choking with directionless rage, subject to grotesque nightmares and savage waking fantasies, trapped forever in infantile anger over his father's death (and desertion). Slocum, often voicing Heller's own most revealing thoughts, reverts obsessively to his fatherless childhood, saying, at one point: "I don't remember much about my father. I did not grieve for him when he died; I acted as though he had not gone, which meant I had to act as though he had not been."

Inclined at times to regard himself as a wounded bird ("Poor me," Heller-Slocum sighs), Heller set out to write a third novel that would spill less of his blood, gallop to completion, appeal to everyone's baser instincts, and, in his words, make him richer and more famous than he deserved. But, as happened with both of his earlier novels, *Good as*

Gold became a longer book than he intended, and somewhat more
personal. It is about the decline of the cities, particularly of his own
well-loved New York; about the disintegration of family life (and the
abandonment of the elderly), which he deplores without ever having
experienced; and about the failure of our political leaders. "No one
governs," Heller says. "Everyone performs. Politics has become a social
world."

Good as Gold reflects Heller's cynical and somewhat narrow view of
national politics (he has not voted in 12 years.) Depicting a coarser,
more openly hostile family than that of *Something Happened*, the new
novel bears down hard on the academic life, which Heller came to
regard askance when he was a college teacher. His overall intention in
Good as Gold was satirical—but the book is, in fact, a burlesque.

Good as Gold is being issued with all the ballyhoo accorded an
anticipated best seller; Heller's publisher has a very large investment
in the book. Now able to command royalty advances in the high six
figures, Heller has earned more than $1.25 million from his two earlier
books. His contract for *Good as Gold* virtually guarantees him an
additional income of at least a million dollars from the combined hard-
cover and paperback sales. So far, he seems to be having his joke and
making it pay.

If Heller's bleak comedy and warped viewpoint are money in the
bank for him and his publishers, they are also—as neuroses—a fertile
mine for psychoanalysts, who find his work to be succulent with
Freudian innuendo. Heller is an accurate and largely instinctive docu-
menter of such aberrations as your everyday Oedipus complex, your
sneaky, masked phobia (about closed doors, for instance) and your
devious, unconscious defense mechanisms, such as laughing at death.
When alone with his paper and pencil, and in the guise of a Yossarian
or a Slocum or a Gold, Heller does reveal fears, vulnerabilities, strong
attachments, sorrows and even, occasionally, joys that he cannot bring
himself to acknowledge in his personal relationships.

Outside the solitude of his writing, he is a largely hidden man, locked
into a pose of tempered bellicosity (sometimes not so tempered); he
masks his feelings with mockery and laughter. In this pose he can at
times be extremely entertaining. He can also turn offensive. It is dismaying to realize that the pose is intended to conceal a dreadful malaise.
Only his immediate family and a handful of intimate friends are aware

of the seething feelings that Heller prefers not to examine—that, in fact, he denies exist. He really believes in the magic of denial.

Throughout his life, Heller has been spinning himself a cocoon, layer over layer. This enables him to joke not only about death, but about all the other phantoms waiting to pounce, the instant he lowers his guard. He worries a lot about heart attacks, strokes and cancer. He is nearly 56 and his friends are dying. A compulsive dieter and jogger, who quit smoking 25 years ago, he has slid into his midlife crisis, biting his nails ("nibbling and gnawing away aggressively, swinishly, and vengefully at my own finger tips," whines the deliciously craven Slocum in *Something Happened*).

Heller fears the loss of his talent. He fears to embrace his fame or to dissipate his money. (He believes he will never have another idea for a novel, that he will be left destitute in his old age and that he will be introduced to someone who will not recognize his name.) He fears the emotional commitment of love and is embarrassed to feel any such stirring.

"I can let myself feel for people and I can let myself stop feeling for them," he says, quite sincerely. "It's easy, it's a skill—like an ability to draw."

Some people find Heller prickly and forbidding. If they were dogs, they would understand the tenderness below the surface. Dogs adore him; he lavished his love on pets until his second dog, a sweet-faced Bedlington terrier named Sweeney, died of cancer two years ago. If you are not a dog, it takes patience and perseverance to discover Heller's tenderness. I met him five years ago and it has taken me all this time to begin to understand the cause and source of his shielding laughter.

It happened that Heller and his wife, Shirley, to whom he has been married for 33 years, were coming to dinner on the day that Sweeney's illness was diagnosed as fatal and the decision made to put the dog to sleep. Heller, who knew I loved *Something Happened*, had by then begun to include me among the half dozen or so of his friends to whom he showed bits of his work in progress. I had him eating out of my hand when I mentioned that I had been struck by his novel's evocation of O'Neill's *Long Day's Journey Into Night*—a cruelly *funny Long Day's Journey*, but nonetheless weighty, as the play is, with guilts and ghosts and paternal sin.

When Shirley Heller called to explain about Sweeney and say she and Joe would be late for dinner, I remembered an evening a few months earlier when I had been a guest of the Hellers. He had cradled Sweeney in his arms as he saw me out on that occasion, and I was astonished when he held up the dog's paw and said, in dulcet tones (to the dog), "Wave goodbye to Auntie Babawa, Sweeney baby."

But even his love of dogs is not sacred. He will turn a joke against himself, just as readily as taunt his worst enemy or best friend. Once, during Sweeney's reign, Shirley Heller, who is her husband's most appreciative audience (and sometimes his crooked straight man), suggested going to a romantic movie that was being advertised with the invitation "See it with someone you love." Heller grinned wickedly. "I'd like to," he said, "but I'm afraid they won't let me in with Sweeney." It is Shirley Heller who tells this story. She is as adept as her husband at self-mockery.

The evening Sweeney's fate was sealed, the Hellers arrived at my apartment looking glum. Shirley appeared stricken even as she was laughing at her husband's wisecracks. She is the only person I've ever known who can laugh and cry at the same time, and is, therefore, the perfect Heller heroine. As for Heller, he told me later, "I broke down in the vet's office, inconsolably and uncontrollably." He forswore ever owning another pet. He had devoted a lot of time to walking Sweeney and grooming him, and there is now another small hollow in his life.

Heller's buried feelings are so fragile, his nerve ends so raw, he can survive only by trying to fool himself: What you don't know can't hurt you. It is a documented neurosis and it stems from his childhood. His talent for abnegation has been a matter of mild concern to his friends for years.

"I never knew anybody so determined to be unhappy, so suspicious of happiness," Mario Puzo says. Puzo, one of Heller's longtime friends, grew up Italian in Manhattan's Hell's Kitchen, rather than Jewish in Coney Island, as Heller did. But he shares with Heller an impoverished, immigrant background and the resultant street smarts and street scars.

"Joe is afraid to be happy; if he's happy, he gets unhappy," Puzo says. "Control over his feelings is important to him. He's so concerned about controlling his life, he can't have fun. Actually, I can even see him changing into a wild man, but it would be in a very controlled sort of way."

Puzo was thinking of the sort of outrageous (but just within the bounds of safety) behavior Heller sometimes indulges in. Once, at a cocktail party (to which Heller had gone with a friend reluctantly), he introduced himself to a couple of doctors as a fellow physician who specialized in geriatric illnesses. Heller, who reads everything about health, had been boning up on the subject as a hedge against his own imminent disintegration (imminent ever since he turned 30, calculated that his life was half over, and began to fear he had no future). He challenged the doctors knowledgeably, declaring, among other things: "If you study Menninger on mitosis, you foretell diagnosis." He was not quite convincing enough and the doctors began to feel affronted.

Sometimes, seeing that he is being taken amiss, Heller stops in time. On other occasions he either does not recognize the hostility he is incurring, or chooses to ignore it. In this case, the friend with whom he had gone to the party stepped in protectively and explained to Heller's victims that "Joe is just kidding; it's the way he is with everyone."

Heller did not miss a beat. "I make such efforts to alienate people," he said, still speaking to his boiling victims, "and this guy [his friend] comes along and wipes out all the bad will I've created." He walked away, laughing.

He was up to the same tricks as long as 30 years ago, when he was a Fulbright Scholar at Oxford, along with another ex-G.I., Edward Bloustein. Bloustein, now the president of Rutgers University, recalls that Heller "was then as he is now."

"I had a distinct sense of the strength of this guy, the compulsion for perfection, his attitude toward language," he says. "Joe was sometimes amusing and often sardonic. But he had and has a very biting humor that sometimes distresses me. His humor is delivered so deadpan, people misinterpret it and can feel insulted. This happened often when I was with him in England. I would take the people aside and explain Joe to them, and then they would find him the attractive man he is."

Heller forces himself to socialize—sometimes to help the sale of his books, sometimes out of boredom—and it is possible for him, aided by two or three martinis, to have much fun on such occasions. What he prefers, though, is the conversation of his friends, particularly if they are on his own wavelength of outrageous and ribald humor. Mel Brooks, the movie man and a sometime friend, says, "Joe plays the best verbal Ping-Pong of anyone I know. The ball will be returned with a spin on it, always. He has a Talmudic tenacity in argument."

But he is a closet recluse. He sees the same old friends week after week, never seeming to tire of the basically boring, second-rate China-town meals (from which wives and girl friends are barred) that he shares greedily with a basically unglamorous, comfortable Gang of Four. The gang expands to include Puzo and Brooks and one or two others when they are in town, but more often consists of just Heller and three old buddies named George Mandel, Julius Green and "Speed" Vogel. Green is a successful small-business man, Vogel is a retired textile manufac-turer and a former itinerant herring taster for Zabar's, and Mandel, who grew up with Heller in Coney Island, is a novelist and magazine writer.

Heller's social persona is most manifest in East Hampton, where he spends his summers. His one recent extravagance was the purchase of an expensive house there, not long after he began writing *Good as Gold*. It is a pleasant house, where he and his wife entertain at small, outdoor dinners, and it will soon have a swimming pool. But Heller does not look truly at ease in that setting.

"I've never known anyone so uncomfortable with fame," Puzo says. "We both became successes so late in life, we couldn't normalize ourselves. Writers like being alone. I visit Joe in East Hampton, but after a while I can sense he's dying to get rid of me."

Heller once confessed to his friend George Mandel, "I don't think I deserve all this money. It puts me into a class for which I have very little sympathy."

He has acquired no hobbies, sees few movies, attends the theater only occasionally (although he is devoted to good plays) and takes pleasure trips with misgiving and not much pleasure. What he most enjoys is reading, against a background of classical music. He is a lifelong, insatiable, retentive, analytical reader and it shows in his work. He skims off, here and there, what he needs to fuse with his own contorted attack. His comedy of despair is an unholy mutation, crossbred from Kafka and Dostoyevsky (Heller calls it "the literature of pain") with Lewis Carroll and Evelyn Waugh (the literature of malice and absurd-ity). At times he has tried (wistfully) for a dash of Oscar Wilde's elusive gloss, and (pensively) for a bit of O'Neillian thunder.

Dwelling side by side with the intellectual connoisseur in Heller is the ravenous, undiscriminating gourmand. Food is inordinately important to him and it is difficult to be his friend if you don't enjoy eating. The characters in his novels do a lot of eating, some of it messy. When he

describes a character in *Good as Gold* as being "unable to keep his
hands off food, his own or others'," he is talking about his own voracity
at table. And he is expansive in analyzing the ingredients of a feast,
prepared by members of Bruce Gold's family, that includes stuffed
derma, noodle puddings, cheese blintzes, chopped liver, stuffed cab-
bage, chopped herring and matzoh balls. He has also described "Jewish
corned-beef hash made with almost no potatoes and with hamburger
meat and tomatoes rather than corned beef, which looked, even before
the ketchup [was added] like a monstrous scarlet meat loaf."

Heller himself has to concentrate to control his weight. When he quit
smoking in 1952, his weight shot up to well over 200 pounds. At 5 feet
11½ inches (half an inch is curls), that was too much. Now he diets
strenuously until dinner time. Outside the svelte Joe Heller is a fat
person waiting to get back in.

He has been known to eat two full meals at two separate restaurants
in the course of one empty evening. He might eat three, if someone else
were paying. (He doesn't realize he can afford to pay, or that he would
be welcome practically anywhere, in spite of his unpredictable behavior.)

He was introduced to Craig Claiborne one summer in East Hampton,
where Claiborne lives year round. They hit it off and Claiborne invited
Heller to dinner at his house, a sought-after privilege, fraught with the
sort of social cachet Heller scorns. But he never scorns a free meal,
even if it is *haute cuisine*; that is part of his pose. (Actually, he prefers
large amounts of low cuisine.) The meal was an elaborate, cold buffet
that Claiborne was writing up, and when Heller arrived, it was spread
elegantly, waiting to be photographed. The photographic equipment was
set up, otherwise Heller would have been at the food instantly; as it
was, he kept eyeing it, as he drank his Margaritas, circling ever closer,
like a starved hound. The dining table was laid with pewter *sous
assiettes* that Heller, of course, mistook for the plates on which the
guests would dine.

The instant the photographer removed his equipment, Heller seized
a pewter underplate (the guests had not even been summoned to the
table), piled it with mounds of everything, seated himself, and blissfully
proceeded to empty his plate. Claiborne smiled indulgently. For some
reason, he found Heller enchanting, and they have become friends,
convinced that they share a maturity of outlook, and that they have,
with age, achieved tranquillity. Claiborne will nod sagely as Heller tells

him: "Thank goodness, we don't need love anymore. And without love, all we have left to worry about is passion, bliss and ecstasy."

Shirley Heller will joke about the fact that the one thing she and her husband have in common is their mutual admiration for Joseph Heller. And it is true that Heller is vain, in a quiet way, about his looks. He is delighted with his hair, which he once wore slicked down, and now wears in a casual cascade of speckled curls. Mel Brooks, aware of Heller's vanity, told me, "He has beautiful hair; it was brown when I met him. And he has beautiful eyes. We can say, also, that he has false teeth. At the end of his sentences, I hear a click-clack. But this would be hard to prove."

Women flock to him; it is difficult to judge whether this happens because of his curls, his fame, his hostility or a combination of all three. The only women whom I, personally, know to be really fond of him are his wife, his daughter and his sister. (His mother loved him but she died.)

Heller can be candid about himself—the trustful little boy; it is one of his more disarming traits. In making an appointment with me recently, he said he would see me after he shopped.

"I'm being fitted for some new pants," he said. "I'm hard to fit. My legs are short. Shirley's are much longer, though I'm taller than she. We stood in front of a mirror together in St. Maarten [on a short pleasure trip during the Christmas holidays that turned out to be pleasant]. If my legs were as long as hers, I'd be about six and a half feet tall."

Heller is a great appreciator of his own jokes, but he is also a generous laugher at the jokes of others. "He's the best laugher I know," says Mel Brooks. "He gives a lot back from a little joke. You need outfielders like that."

He has a sardonic laugh, a bitter laugh, a triumphant laugh, an apologetic laugh and a defensive laugh. As for his smile—described once by an unwary interviewer as "diffident"—it is about as diffident as that of the tiger from whose back the young lady from Niger mysteriously vanished. The smile is often pierced by a wooden, orange toothpick plucked from a packet Heller always carries. The toothpick appears immediately after a meal and sometimes lingers on into the night. Heller is no more couth than he is diffident.

One of his most striking characteristics is his accent. It is pure, unreconstructed, streets-of-New-York (Noo Yawk). He also says "awff," "aloive," "toretchurred," "yumor" and "lidderacherr." And he stutters very slightly (a trait he gave to Slocum in *Something Happened*). The stutter is the way you know he is under stress—that, and a glazed look, accompanied by a laugh with a faintly nasty edge.

Heller has his serious moments. Mostly, they depress him. Ambivalent about practically everything, Heller, when he is working on a novel, hastens to the solitude of his studio and lunges at the day's work with a zest that soon wilts. Work never lasts more than two hours. He finds he cannot concentrate on his writing for longer than that.

"It's very hard, but interesting," he says, blandly. "I'm not a natural prose writer. I struggle to shape my sentences. I'm grateful to get any idea that will organize itself into a story. On the other hand, I've been able to use my repressions constructively, to very profitable effect, and to the entertainment and joy of millions."

As he dredges up bits of his life, Heller filters them slowly through his denial process before getting them down on paper, where he can make them belong, not to him, but to one of his protagonists.

"I know so many things I'm afraid to find out," says Slocum-Heller in *Something Happened*.

The line encompasses the essential Heller: his inverted humor, his cerebral playfulness, his psychologically sound intuition, the discernment to formulate a contradiction so true, the involuntary cringing of the man, and the compulsive exhibitionism of the author.

The family Joe was born into on May 1, 1923, was barely Americanized. His mother, Lena, then about 38, spoke little English. He remembers her as an unemotional, self-contained woman. "I was not aware of coldness *or* of warmth," Heller says, stuttering very slightly. His father, Isaac, roughly the same age as Lena, had arrived from Russia 10 years earlier; already on the scene when Joe was born were a boy of 14 named Lee (born in Russia) and a sister named Sylvia, who was 7.

Isaac Heller was an agnostic and a Socialist, who had fled the Czar. He supported his family by driving a delivery truck for a local bakery. Joe Heller has only vague memories of him. The cause of his father's death was a bungled ulcer operation. The elder Heller had been in his early 40's. Joe remembers his mother, much later, telling him that Isaac got his ulcers from eating the bakery cake. Heller rarely eats cake; ulcers are another illness he worries about.

Recently, Heller told me, "I didn't realize then how traumatized I was. As a boy in school I used to say my father was 'deceased.' I was aware without being aware." Then, succumbing to his sense of mischief, he added: "I was fine *then*. *Now* I wet my bed." He chortled at his joke.

If Heller was not a born cutup, he became one at an early age. It seems likely that the repressed horror of his father's death was replaced almost instantly with an outrageous (outraged?) sense of humor. And then, too, there is the fact that he grew up in the carnival atmosphere of Coney Island. To thousands of New York children of that era (even as far away as the Bronx) a day spent at Coney Island, climaxed by a ride on the world's most awesome roller coaster, the Cyclone, was the ultimate holiday treat. But Coney Island was also a neighborhood of poor and hard-working European-Jewish immigrants, many of whom had no common tongue but Yiddish, a language remarkable for its power to convey the bitter humor of displacement and longing.

Heller still has vivid memories of the flavor of the neighborhood and has described it—as it was and as it is—in *Good as Gold*. He remembers also sharing his baby carriage. Marvin (Beansy) Winkler's parents lived in the same building as the Hellers, and Beansy's mother, Marian, was Lena Heller's friend. Heller and Winkler have kept in touch.

"He used to wet my carriage," Winkler says, "and he was 10 months older." Winkler now lives in California, where he manufactures chocolate Easter bunnies (or so he claims; like other of Heller's friends he is apt to abandon accuracy for humor).

"We went to public school together, from first grade," Winkler says. "Joe was a pain in the neck. He was brighter than all of us. He was a needler, a big mouth. He hasn't changed. Well, maybe he's mellowed a little." Heller modeled the fast-talking, self-promoting, thoroughly conscienceless Milo Minderbinder of *Catch-22* on his old pal Beansy.

Heller's sister (now Sylvia Gurian) confirms Joe's exceptional brightness and recalls an episode that occurred shortly after Isaac Heller's death:

"Joe brought home a note from his teacher, asking my mother to come to school and talk to her," Mrs. Gurian says. "We were all terrified. My mother didn't trust her English, so I went. I was only about 12 or 13, and Joe was about 5 or 6. The teacher told me Joe never listened in class and always looked bored. She said she kept trying to catch him, but he always knew the answer. She admitted he was too bright for the class, but he was demoralizing the other kids and frustrating her. All we could do was tell Joe to try to look as though he was paying attention."

Heller appears to have transferred some of his filial love to his considerably elder brother. When Lee Heller was in his early 20's, and Joe about 8 or 9, he gave Lee a Father's Day gift, telling him, "You're like a father to me." (Heller has written about an older brother in both *Something Happened* and *Good as Gold*, and about multiple older sisters as well.) Both Lee and Sylvia gave up their own hopes of college after high school; they went to work, to help support the family. Lena Heller took in sewing.

Heller, himself, worked after school. One job, at 13, was as a Western Union messenger.

"I loved it," Heller says. "I loved the uniform."

Lee Heller, a reserved, courteous, self-effacing man who is now retired and living in Florida—not far from his sister and her husband—remembers his little brother as "a normal, average kid, who read a lot, like me."

"There were always books and magazines in the house. Sometimes he would come to me for help in math. I did not expect him to be the success he became. I was so proud of *Catch-22*. I live in Joe's reflected glory."

Heller's childhood friends from Coney Island also are proud of him, although some had apprehensions at the time.

"Joe was a nervous wreck at 13," Mandel recalls.

Some of his nervousness may have been attributable to a kind of cover-up that had always been practiced within the family. Unlike most of his male friends, he was not bar mitzvahed at 13. Lena Heller was no more religiously inclined than her husband had been. But she was insecure about her nonconformity, and attempted to conceal it.

"My mother used to try to get me to dress neatly on Saturday, even though none of us ever went to a synagogue—except, I guess, once a year on Yom Kippur," Heller says. (As always, when talking of his parents, he stutters very slightly.) "I remember once I embarrassed her terribly, on purpose, by yelling up to her from the street, 'Hey, Ma, throw me down a ham sandwich.'"

At 15, Heller received the second big shock of his life. He attended his brother's wedding, and during the ceremony the rabbi made a

reference to Lena Heller as Lee's—and Sylvia's—"stepmother." Joe
had been unaware, until that moment, that Lee and Sylvia were his half-
brother and half-sister. Isaac Heller's first wife had died shortly after
Sylvia's birth and when Lee was 7. He had married Lena about three
years later.

"Our stepmother raised us as though all three of us were her own
children," Sylvia Gurian recalls. "It never occurred to any of us to
discuss it with Joe. But he thought we had been keeping a big secret
from him."

Enraged and betrayed, Heller brooded about this. In *Good as Gold*
he has covered the wound, characteristically, with abrasive laughter,
portraying a Coney Island Jewish family of the Hellers' generation in a
mocking, often sneering manner, punctuated by grudging splinters of
recalled affection.

Heller entered the Army Air Corps in 1942, when he was 19. To a
poor Jewish boy from Brooklyn, the opportunity to do battle for his
country against Hitler and Mussolini represented upward mobility (a
phrase that had not yet been coined). His mother saw him to the trolley
car on the day he left for training camp and said goodbye, dry-eyed and
collected. Years later, Heller's sister told him his mother had collapsed
into heartbroken sobs as soon as he was out of sight, and had to be
helped home. Heller was astounded when he learned of this outburst of
affection.

He spent three years in the Army, about one year of it in combat on
the island of Corsica with a squadron of the 12th Air Force.

"I enjoyed it," he says, "until my 37th mission." The story of his
subsequent distress is the surrealistic tale of *Catch-22*. Yossarian's
attitudes and war experiences are mostly Heller's, but the meager facts
of his life and background are not—except for the symbolism of Yossarian's having no past at all (i.e., no parents). Heller emerged from the
war as a first lieutenant.

In the Army, he kept a diary of his missions. He had been writing
imitative, superficial short stories since his teens; it had not occurred to
him to draw on his own feelings or experiences. He showed me an early
effort that was published in *Story* magazine in the fall of 1945, when he
was 22 and recently home from the war. It is amusing because of its
hero's quirky refusal to put on clothes in anticipation of company.

"Why won't you?" asks his bemused wife.

"I don't want to. I want to lie here without any clothes on and drink beer." He adds that the company is welcome to join him as he is.

Yossarian also refused to put on his clothes. His friend Snowden had been killed on a mission and had bled all over Yossarian's uniform. Yossarian feared he, too, would be killed if he flew any more missions, and they could not make him fly if he had no clothes on.

Heller's real-life, equivalent nakedness possibly is expressed by his symbolic refusal ever to own or wear a tuxedo.

"I have rented one a couple of times, and I bought one once to wear on a boat, but then I threw it away," he says. "I'll never wear one again. I hate uniforms, I hate uniformity. A tuxedo is worse than a soldier's uniform. A soldier has no choice. Wearing a dinner jacket is *voluntarily* dressing in a uniform, and that is an attempt to dignify a social occasion, to create a sense of pomp."

Heller met and married Shirley Held, also of Brooklyn, in 1945, shortly after his return from the war. She was auburn-haired, slender and vulnerable and has changed very little. A mixture of gaiety and rue, she is as contradictory as her husband. Her loyalty to him is passionate and the names of those who have presumed to write adversely of his work are tucked away in her mind, pickled in venom. Erica, their 27-year-old daughter, is a self-possessed advertising copywriter, saucy and very bright, skipping along in her father's footsteps and, as might be expected, working hard to overtake him.

"I like him more lately," she says. "Right after he finishes a book he gets better; he's serene and sweet." She acknowledges her resemblance to the daughter in *Something Happened*, commenting, "That girl is out to make trouble every minute. As an adolescent, *I* was out to make it every five minutes."

The Hellers' 22-year-old-son, Ted, shares Erica's two-sided view of their father; being Joe Heller's child is clearly an engulfing experience that takes a lot of living down. Ted Heller will graduate this spring from N.Y.U., where he is an English and film major. He has picked up some of his father's ambivalence and is aware of it. To my question "Have you any ambition to write?" he gave me a deadpan Hellerian reply: "No. But that's a lie."

Heller's intellectual and academic background, on which he has drawn for *Good as Gold*, is impressive, and he could hardly wait to remove himself from it. After the war, he attended New York Uni-

versity under the G.I. Bill and later earned his master's degree from
Columbia University. Next came the year at Oxford, followed by two
years of teaching at Pennsylvania State University. He then returned to
New York and began a successful career in the advertising departments
of, progressively, *Time*, *Look* and *McCall's*. In spare moments and
evenings at home he worked on *Catch-22*.

The book was not the instant success many believe it to have been
when it came out in 1961. There were some excellent reviews—and
some terrible ones. Never on a best-seller list, the book picked up
momentum as the war in Vietnam picked up protesters, gradually collecting wider and wider acclaim, until, right after the movie version in
1970, it began selling furiously in paperback. Heller, by then, had
given up his advertising salary, and had taken a teaching job at City
College that demanded less of his time. The job flattered his ego—he
had the title of Distinguished Professor of English—and brought him a
fail-safe annual income of $32,500. Not until early in 1975, after
Something Happened had become a best seller, did Heller feel secure
enough to quit teaching and decide to live entirely on the income from
his writing.

The idea for *Catch-22* came to Heller, as did the ideas for the two
novels that followed, by a process he cannot precisely define, that he
regards as a kind of magic, and that he does not care to question. "I get
an opening line, and a concept of the book as a full, literary entity," he
says. "It's all in my head before I even begin to write. Many of my
ideas for dialogue and plot twists come to me while I'm jogging. And
when I'm close to finishing a book, *nothing* is more important to me. I
might stop to save a life, but nothing less." Heller pauses; the memory
of his most recent period of fanaticism is still fresh.

"When my friend James Jones died, leaving his last novel incomplete, I began to be afraid *I* might die before finishing *Good as Gold*.
Spookily, another friend, Robert Alan Aurthur, died last Nov. 20,
leaving, like Jones, an unfinished project—the movie *All That Jazz* (he
had collaborated on the script and was the producer.) Aurthur admired
Heller and occasionally admitted it; mostly the two needled each other
with affection. Aurthur's wife, Jane, read me at my request a snippet of
a diary entry left by her husband, dated last May: "Am to meet J.H.
Both Joe and I agree book [*Good as Gold*] is a masterpiece. He wants to
hear why I think so."

As Heller, for the third time, awaits publication of a new novel, he suffers from spells of anxiety (though pretending not to).

"I'll never write another book," he moans almost every time I talk to him. His muse is out of town. He broods, and gnaws on his nails.

Will the wrong reviewer like his novel for all the right reasons? Will the right reviewer like it for all the wrong reasons? Will copies be in the stores to coincide with his appearance on the "Today" show? Will he ever get another idea for a novel?

Should he go to Hollywood and write movies? Will anyone give him a job writing movies? Won't he ever get another idea for a novel?

He likes Los Angeles but would miss New York. New York has better hospitals for the care of the heart attack he will soon bring on from trying too hard to get an idea while jogging to stay in trim to avoid a heart attack. He would rather die laughing.

Mel Brooks Meets Joseph Heller

Mel Brooks/1979

From *Washington Post Book World* 11 March 1979, F1, 4. Copyright © 1979 The Washington Post. Reprinted by permission.

Eighteen years, world fame and many millions of dollars fill the time between now and 1961, when Mel Brooks and Joseph Heller first met at Fire Island, New York City's beach playground. Brooks has risen from comic to *auteur*—producer, director, writer and/or star of the films *The Producers, The Twelve Chairs, Blazing Saddles, Young Frankenstein, Silent Movie* and *High Anxiety*. He is currently running the show on a movie entitled *Mel Brooks' History of the World, Part I*. Heller has stuck to the printed word, with one excursion into theater, a play, *We Bombed in New Haven*. The title of his first novel, *Catch-22*, entered the American language; his second, *Something Happened*, topped the best-seller charts for many weeks. His latest novel, *Good as Gold*, now in bookstore windows, is the work referred to below as "this book" or "the book."

Old friends Brooks and Heller have assembled in Brooks' sunny corner office on the third floor of the Executive Office Building at 20th-Century Fox, overlooking the famous *Hello, Dolly* set. The view, which combines turn-of-the-century Yonkers and the Krazy Kat date palms of southern California, is as surrealistic as anything you'll see in Hollywood. Inside, the rays of sunshine dance on the posters in many languages for Brooks' films. The room is dominated by a black-and-white portrait of Leo Tolstoy on one wall, and a hand-printed, almost scrawled, detailed story-board of the French Revolution scenes from *History of the World* on another. Brooks is a small, neat-bodied man with a high metabolism; he is wearing a Lacoste shirt and sneakers. Heller is . . . ah . . . less fit than he once was, but his smile is still a grin and his thick head of white curly hair frames a youthful, cherubic face. Both were raised in Brooklyn, neighborhoods apart. Let's listen:

MB: I rate this somewhere between *The Brothers Karamazov* and those little dirty books we used to read . . . you know, Popeye with an erection.

201

JH: That's a very narrow range.

MB: Right. That's where this book falls, with those little 8-pagers, remember? In all fairness to you, Joe, it's closer to *Karamazov*.

JH: It just shows how an artist's intentions often miscarry in spite of himself.

MB: Let's be semi-serious for a while, because I had to read the book for the interview. It's a big fat book and worth the money. It took me less than a weekend to read such a big fat book. It's very compelling, and yet a very strange book, because it has an utter reality, and yet it has a true madness . . . a little like *Studs Lonigan* and *Alice in Wonderland,* all *mished arein* [mixed together].

JH: There's one point you missed.

MB: Wait a minute and I'll cover it.

JH: That's the point you're missing. Nobody's interested in what *you* think. You're here to interview me!

MB: I've been asked to ask you questions, as a profound West Coast intellectual. There's only three of us. I'm gonna tell you what I think, whether you want or not, so listen. I was amazed how easily the story was pushed along by the characters. There is no story. [Heller begins to rise up menacingly from his chair.] Well, there is and there isn't. It's the story of a family—the meanderings of a family member—and heartbreaking funny reality with the Jewish family, and there is an insanity in Washington. . . .

JH: Is there any way on earth to induce you to ask a question?

MB: Why did Sid have to die? [Sid is Bruce Gold's older brother in *Good as Gold*.] You killed him. You could'a let him live.

JH: Sure. But then I'd have no book.

MB: You could'a killed the father, that sonofabitch bastard.

JH: Everyone expected the father to die.

MB: We hate and love that man.

JH: Ooohh, you felt that little tug at the heart in the end, right?

MB: Yes.

JH: That's not merely art, that's Machiavellian genius.

MB: I'm supposed to say that. You can't say 'Machiavellian genius' about yourself, schmuck. It looks terrible. Ralph Newsome (the presidential aide in *Good as Gold*) is Gracie Allen. It's incredible. You have re-created Burns and Allen, every time he talks. He has a penchant for turning the most simple things into insanity. So a lot of what I loved in

Catch-22 has been shifted to Washington. It's the same examination of the prevailing insanity. So we are not in an airfield in Italy, we are in Washington, and we have a lot of very crazy people. I also loved the character of Andrea's father. He . . .

JH: Since you ask me the question, I'm compelled to answer. Pugh Biddle Conover. He began in my mind as an incarnate villain. All kinds of bigotry and snobbishness and feelings of cold superiority are embodied in him.

And yet, as I wrote him I began to like him more and more because there was a certain purity in his malevolence. He is articulate, he reads Gold's mind thoroughly in all his anti-Semitism, he sees through Gold's head as though it were made of cellophane. Above all, because he proved very easy to like. So when I was writing those two chapters of Biddle Conover, I loved him. Not because he's good, not because he's benevolent, but because he was good in the book.

MB: And he's incredibly free. Because any time he wants to make a crazy rhyme, he rhymes a truism that's not true.

JH: Yes, I went back to my elementary school album for those rhymes. "2 Ys U R, 2 Ys U B, I C U R 2 Ys 4 Me." Or "Learn this, my boy, before you grow old, that learning is better than silver or gold." Pugh Biddle Conover *is* one of my favorite characters in the book, and Ralph Newsome *is* Burns and Allen combined. He always tells the truth, very much like Milo Minderbinder in *Catch-22*.

MB: The writing in this book reminds me of some of the writing in George Bernard Shaw, because he never made bad villains. He always made compassionate villains. Who was the father . . . the munitions maker . . . what play are we talking about?

JH: *Major Barbara*?

MB: *Major Barbara*. The munitions manufacturer who is an ostensible evil turns out to be quite a compelling and understandable character. The bishop, who wants to kill St. Joan. Every time the bishop talked, I said: "F - - k it, kill her. He's right. Burn her; put her to the torch. The man is protecting an institution." And every time Joan spoke, I said: "Kill him." I read your book, and I said: "Aaaahhh, here's the enemy. The anti-Semite, the descendant of money . . ." and he turns out to be a compelling and exciting, lovable crazy character, with his honking.

I look at books in terms of movies and if we had to cut the book down, we would keep every word he has and every movement . . . the honking, the wheelchair.

JH: We'd certainly keep that buffet breakfast.

MB: Fabulous! To have 500 places set, and have one guy sitting there. All he took was a little honeydew. . . .

JH: A trowel of melon from a trencher of something. . . .

MB: Wait a minute. You used another word I liked.

JH: A beaker of orange juice—a trencher of melon from a trowel, or a trowel of mencher.

MB: Either way it works.

JH: And 17 cups of coffee.

MB: And one other little thing. There was—it started with a "C."

JH: Cannikin?

MB: Cannikin. Some of the words are exquisite. In a movie, you eliminate the narrative and you lose, for a good writer. That's why they never made a good version of *War and Peace,* because you just can't give up Tolstoy's description and comments.

JH: Can we talk about me and my novel?

MB: I'm putting you in very good company. Apart from Popeye, I think you're doing very well.

JH: I'm waiting for you to get to your favorite authors. Turgenev, Stendhal, Tolstoy you got already, Gogol.

MB: Gogol is my favorite author. I like Dickens. You like Dickens, too.

JH: I stole from Dickens with a great deal of confidence in this book.

MB: No, you didn't steal from Dickens. Now, about the title, *Good as Gold* . . .

JH: I stole from Dickens more in this book than I would want you to know.

MB: I like details like Andrea's scraping her calluses, the sound of it.

JH: If you've ever been infatuated, even once for a while, with a goddess who made the mistake of scraping a callus off her foot in your presence, you'll know; *you'll know* how quickly love can die. I don't know my place. . . .

MB: In the interview or in life?

JH: In the interview. In life I know my place. If you were a stranger, I'd be afraid of you. I'd be deferential, respectful to you. I would stammer when I spoke to you. I'm taking liberties, I'm exploiting our friendship and I apologize . . .

MB: You bastard. You always, even when we have our eating club, you always take the best pieces. You have no compunction. If there's a lobster claw, it's in your dish. Then you say: everybody now can serve themselves.

JH: You must have noticed in reading this book of mine that I took a number of the best pieces of conversations that we have participated in over the past 15 years.

MB: You even use the words "broke the soup" instead of "broke the bowl."

JH: But you want to know about my title?

MB: I want to know why you picked *Gold*. Gold to me has allegorical implications, but to you?

JH: When I started writing this book the character's name was Weinberg. I knew I was going to change it. One day, after three or four months of pondering, it occurred to me. Silver. Silver is a Jewish name, maybe there's a phrase containing silver. I couldn't think of a single one. Then Gold came to me. Pot of gold, good as gold.

When I got that title I was afraid for two years that somebody was going to come out with a television situation comedy called *Good as Gold*. It seemed like such a naturally good title and I don't know how they missed it.

MB: The fags of Washington, the gentiles on the Potomac, and the vermin of Coney Island—you absolutely mix them. Sid—Sid is a very important character, the brother. My father died when I was very little, so an older brother, *the* older brother, has incredible significance for me.

JH: I have now what's called a body of work. And people are doing what's called retrospective reviews, some from a literary viewpoint and some from a psychological point of view. One thing was pointed out to me which I did not know. In my three novels and one play—in all four—the climactic event is a death. And it's not the death of a major character but it's the death of somebody very close to him, a death that leaves the major character gasping in horror and trembling with relief that he has escaped it.

We know that death in drama is a very powerful thing. We also know that other events can serve as well.

MB: Saul Bellow, Mailer, Malamud—no one could plant two strong feet in two completely different environments and examine them so completely as you did in this book. There is no way for Mailer to examine so Jewish an environment, no way for Malamud to examine so gentile an environment so skillfully.

The other foot of this three-footed animal is in the intellectual community, which is completely different from the poor Jews, and the crazy two-dimensional Washington insane. The only novelist I know who is able to do it successfully is Dickens. You're the only one since Dickens who could handle both sides of that issue with blood.

JH: Maybe that's because that's what I want to do. Bellow can be funny; Malamud can be funny; Philip Roth can be very funny—all three have massive minds and a great degree of education. On the other hand, I shy away from realism. I don't write a realistic book. I mean realism as a technique; I'm not talking about reality.

All my books have some kind of novel idea, some kind of literary conceit that remove them from what we think of as the literature of realism, where the events are to be taken as literally having occurred.

MB: Is it true about $1,000 a day for those Washington people?

JH: I don't know but it might just as well be.

MB: *Catch-22* is based on your adventures as a person in the Air Force in Italy. . . .

JH: And as a survivor during the Cold War.

MB: *Something Happened,* when you talk about the library and the office and the file cabinets . . . you know too much.

JH: My first job after high school was as a file clerk for an automobile casualty insurance company.

MB: But, strangely, I think in this book you tell more about you than in both of them put together. There's more about your feelings and more about your real life. You don't fool around. Would Shirley and your children be upset if they feel Gold is you?

JH: Not after *Something Happened.* [They break up in laughter.]

MB: Very good. If they can live through that, they can live through anything.

JH: *Oy,* what we went through with that!

MB: All these chapter headings, they seem to come out of thoughts in the preceding chapter. A phrase is extruded from the last chapter and leads off the next chapter. How and why did that device appeal to you?

JH: *Oy vey, guttenyu, mamenyu, tatenyu* . . . [A pained invocation of the deity and the ancestors]

MB: *Oy vey* is Jewish for the word Irving.

JH: I thought that one of the unifying structures for the novel would be to have—ideally—every section deal with something Gold was going to write or had written and use that as a title for that section or for the following section.

MB: But do they apply intrinsically?

JH: They don't. I feel the need for a break and I feel the need for a chapter heading. And I will confess something to you. The chapter headings in *Catch-22,* about which many a scholarly piece has been written, were put on when the type was ready to be set and we decided we ought to have some kind of chapter heading, and for many of these chapters, particularly the first 30 or 40, there is nothing significant about the headings.

MB: I think that, for your picture on the jacket here, you should have been in a beautiful suit, professorial, and sitting on a pony. Instead of this handsome, devil-may-care person in an open shirt. You could be William Holden.

JH: William Holden never looked that good.

MB: There is one chapter title that does support the entire book—"The Jewish Experience," the vapor that is coalesced throughout the entire book. This book could be called *The Jewish Experience.*

JH: What you said earlier about this book being my Jewish novel as contrasted with Malamud and Saul Bellow—it's based on the fact that I've had no Jewish experience, other than what's in this novel.

MB: Jewish-American experience.

JH: Exactly. Those of us who were in World War II and came out of the war as very young men grew up aware that we were Jewish, but mine was largely a secular existence. Not much different from, say, somebody from a different part of the country who was not Jewish, but who'd been through the war and was either going to college or developing his talent and going to work.

My sister wrote me a long letter from Florida, about eight handwritten pages, about what it was like to look for a job when she got out of high school. When the ads said: No Jews Need Apply. And I used the letter verbatim in the chapter on the birthday party.

MB: In what specific way have you grown as an artist?

JH: My bank account.

MB: That's the measure of an artist, a bank account? Shame on you.

JH: It's an objective measure. How have you grown?

MB: I am taller than I was as a child. Whose style as a novelist do you admire the most?

JH: I love novelists who write in styles influenced by me.

MB: You care to name any of them?

JH: Aeschylus, Shakespeare, Molière, Proust, Brooks . . . BROOKS!

MB: What about novelists writing today?

JH: Oh, sure. John Erlichman, Spiro Agnew, William Safire is a humdinger. There's a whole new school of fiction writing, and they're full of . . . vitality . . . and inspiration.

Seriously, I think that novels, because they don't cost as much to produce as films, permit a great variety of experimentation. In the last 10 or 20 years, American novelists alone have produced more in the way of innovation and inspiration than ever before in the history of literature. They novelists who interest me are those I call "the crazies." They're crazy, and they suffer. If they don't suffer, they take a great delight in writing about pain.

Using "crazy" in a very flattering way, meaning experimental and grotesque, I'd name Gogol, Kafka, Dostoevski. John Barth. Gilbert Sorrentino, who's completely unpredictable. Pynchon. I don't understand Pynchon, but I'd rather have plowed through Pynchon without understanding him than read a novel that might be superlative, perfect in every way, but in which there's nothing for me to grapple with, and from which there's nothing for me to learn.

MB: I liked *The World According to Garp*.

JH: So did I. John Irving is a very funny writer.

MB: He likes you too, by the way. When I think of you and your writing, a lot of people would compare you with an impressionist painter. Bull-s - - t! Not for me. I know better, because I'm smarter than most people. If I were to liken you to any painter, I would make you Rousseau, the massive French primitive. You more than any other living writer I know are concerned with the honest details of life, the honest details of human thought, human behavior, human exchange.

The picture that we see is a little crazy. It looks like it's real, but if you examine it, there's an insane moon hanging there. In your art, you bridge what there should be and what there is, so that we're not flesh-bound, we're not earth-bound, we're not realism-bound. You root your stuff in utter reality, but the final picture is very big, like Rousseau, and it's haunting. You are crazy, but in a very formal and traditional way.

JH: Also the ethical sense of my books is very conventional. Apart from a certain taste for salacious activities and licentiousness, the ethics in *Good as Gold* are quite conventional. What is being ridiculed, deplored, by me if not by my characters, is a moral corruption, a disavowal of responsibilities, a substitution of vanity, folly where other people's lives are concerned. Without my planning it, I do fall into a conventional narrative form in the last portions of both *Catch-22* and *Good as Gold*. The events proceed chronologically, there are realities which can no longer be avoided, I can't f - - k around any longer, I must make my decision.

MB: The truth wins out. You don't bend it into something you want it to be in the end, that it can never be. You have only one incredible, tremendous fault.

JH: A full head of hair.

MB: No. You will never live unless you have a middle name. And I have the middle name.

JH: Yes?

MB: Makepeace. I know it's been used before by some schmuck, but I think it's a great middle name for you. Joseph Makepeace Heller. You will live forever with that name, and you'd be crazy not to take it.

JH: May I call you Mel?

MB: Of course.

JH: Then please call me Makepeace.

Joseph Heller on America's "Inhuman Callousness"

U.S. News & World Report/1979

From *U.S. News & World Report*, 9 April 1979, 73. Reprinted by permission.

Much that happens in society is of a savage nature. There's a kind of inhuman callousness in the country. On the highest level, the world of finance dominates the world of government, and nobody is trying to solve the problems of this nation as a community. Nobody is trying to deal with unemployment and inflation at the same time.

I deal with disintegration in American society in my books because disintegration appears to be a continuing process. I could list 100 symptoms of decline—from the ethical to the moral to the social: family, love, marriage. That doesn't necessarily mean I'm a pessimist.

But cities *are* decaying. I don't believe there's ever going to be a way to solve our economic problems. I think the era of easy national prosperity is over for this country. The era is past when we could exert military influence in any part of the world.

I'm not sure a civilization ever existed in which there was a built-in correlation between intelligence and power. Those qualities which are important in achieving public power have little to do with creative intelligence or integrity of purpose. I believe that even in its golden age, Athens was nondemocratic: Pericles ran it. Its period as a democracy was relatively short. It may be that history has never been different in this respect.

To run for office now requires an awful lot of money. And we have an electorate that really isn't interested in issues. People give no thought to subjects they're asked about in public-opinion polls—and then feel ashamed not to respond. I'm also not as interested in as many issues as I used to be. I don't understand many of them and could not affect the outcome if I did.

It used to be I could offer a simple answer to every problem. Given a choice between coping with inflation or unemployment, I would say:

"Give to the poor. Redistribute the wealth." But now I realize I know no more about economics than the next expert.

I'm not sure anything can work without major modifications in our economic system, and nobody doing well wants to make those modifications. This resistance to change and the lack of interest in truly fundamental issues make it increasingly difficult for society to come to grips with its problems.

I don't for a second believe that a novel influences behavior in a significant way. However, some people say *Catch-22* did have that effect to a degree. In the mid-'60s, sales of the paperback of that novel began increasing in relation to the Vietnam War and the protest against the war. So possibly it helped shape attitudes.

I know that a lot of people in Vietnam carried around copies, but I don't think it influenced their actions. It just confirmed their opinion that: "This is crazy! I don't know why we're here. And we'd better watch our superior officers because they can be as dangerous to us as the people out there." That turned out to be true.

I don't know where my ideas for novels come from; they come from sources out of my reach. I've written three novels, and none began with a subject or even with a character. I began with a feeling that it was time for me to write a novel. The idea for each book arrived with an opening line that just kind of grew and grew on its own. It just kept germinating, and then I soon had a plan.

Many authors, such as Gore Vidal and S.J. Perelman, speak naturally, almost with the same eloquence they write. They use a literary language in their conversation. By contrast, I—like most people—do not always speak in complete sentences. I have no literary vocabulary that's natural to me. I have a feeling I'm not a natural writer, although I do have a writer's imagination.

If I have to deal with facts and present them seriously, I'm helpless. It may take me weeks to write a serious business letter, and I'm not even talking about an official letter to a lawyer or publisher. I'm no good at all at nonfiction.

An Interview with Joseph Heller

Charlie Reilly/1979

Slightly enlarged version of interview previously published as
"Talking with Joseph Heller," *Inquiry Magazine*, 1 May 1979,
22–26. Reprinted by permission of the author.

Reilly: My congratulations on *Good as Gold*. It's a remarkable book. In fact, I think it has that harmony between humor and profundity that you handle as well as anyone writing today.

Heller: I'm glad you liked it. I'm pleased you enjoyed the humor too because I was just reading a very perceptive review by a professor named John Aldridge who called *Good as Gold* the bleakest of my three books. I think he used the phrase, "an extension of Heller's darkening vision." The more I thought about it the more I could see what he meant.

Reilly: You're kidding. Bleaker than *Something Happened*?

Heller: Bleaker than *Something Happened* and *Catch-22*, the bleakest and most biting despite the—I think he used the word "hilarity." He focused largely upon the Washington episodes and speculated that what Heller is imagining today may well be happening tomorrow. He also commented upon what I have in there, perhaps unconsciously, about the decline of the contemporary family.

Reilly: That's a sensitive response. I guess I was groping in that direction when I talked about the book's profundity.

Heller: Here we go! *Inquiry* is probably hoping for some political views and we seem to be moving again toward an intellectual literary column. I mean that respectfully; *Inquiry* is a good magazine.

Reilly: I'm sure *Inquiry* is hoping for your thoughts about the novel, period. As I collect myself now, I realize that I meant to say the pace and tone of the novel reminded me of what was best about *Catch-22*. There were at least a dozen portions where I put down the book and laughed out loud—and how often does that happen in a book? But as I came to the final passages, as the protagonist's life becomes so frenetic, I got the same eerie feeling I did with both of your other novels. I found

212

what I had dismissed as fun sneaking up on me, and I found myself being absorbed with, well, the moral undercurrents of the book. Still, I wouldn't call it bleak.

Heller: I'm not doing Professor Aldridge justice. If you take a look at the passages he chose to excerpt, you'll get a better idea of what he means. He quoted, for example, from the episode where Gold returns to Coney Island and discovers the extent to which the neighborhood has decayed and declined.

Reilly: That was a powerful passage. It reminded me of Yossarian's walk through Rome in *Catch-22*.

Heller: Both of your comparisons to *Catch-22* are fair, but I should stress I was very conscious of the similarities between *Good as Gold* and *Catch-22*, and I was vigiliant not to repeat the same comic techniques too often—techniques like sudden shifts in time and place. In the final sections I make extravagant use of such techniques, but that was the result of a conscious decision. I wanted those seven days when they're sitting *shivah* to move quickly. But on the whole I tried very hard to avoid the types of aphoristic and verbal humor that I used in *Catch-22*. The temptation to use such things arose often, but I didn't want to make them a part of this book.

Reilly: Although *Catch-22* was set during World War II, you directed a lot of its satire against the then-current excesses and evils of McCarthyism. I wonder if there isn't something complementary in *Good as Gold*. This novel supposedly concerns the "Jewish experience," but at the same time it intensely, ferociously, comments on Kissinger, Vietnam, and post-Vietnam politics.

Heller: The answer to your question is yes. There's a review I've seen which closes with the thought that Gold is Jewish only in his symptoms. The implication, and it's sensible, is that he's representative of the entire country at this time. *Good as Gold* does focus upon the Jewish experience, but ultimately Bruce Gold finds his experience is not particularly more Jewish than, well, mine. I feel that many people my age, people who went to college after the war and became involved in academic or literary activities, have had experiences that are not materially different from those of people who aren't Jewish.

Reilly: It's curious. A couple of people asked me after our first interview whether you're Jewish and I had to say I didn't know because it never occurred to me to ask you. You haven't written about Jewish protagonists or themes before, in other words. But, are you from a Jewish family, similar to Gold's?

Heller: Well, yes, I'm Jewish. But, no, I didn't have a large family like Gold, nor did I become involved in dinners similar to the Gold family's. To tell you the truth, I'm not sure where the idea came from for those dinners in the novel. My wife has a large family and, of course, we all gathered for Thanksgiving and whatever. But there was nothing like the, well, uproar and anger you find in Gold's dinners. What I was trying to do there, at least in part, was to point out incongruities—to suggest that even though Gold was being considered for the position of Secretary of State, inside the home he was still the youngest brother, the kid who didn't know enough to use a handkerchief.

Reilly: So the fact that this novel came well along in your writing career does not reflect that you have been brooding about, perhaps building toward, a novel about the Jewish experience?

Heller: No, emphatically not. I got the idea for this book immediately after giving a reading from *Catch-22* and *Something Happened* in Wilmington, Delaware. Afterwards, in a small question group, a woman asked me why I had never written about the Jewish experience. I answered that I had had only two ideas for a novel in twenty-one years, so I certainly wasn't excluding it. And then I said, I wasn't at all sure I was qualified to write about the topic. I wasn't sure I was that much in touch with the experience as the writers who had already handled it so wonderfully, writers like Bernard Malamud and Philip Roth. But while I was going home on the Metroliner, I began musing about the possibilities and taking notes. By the time I got off the train, I had the idea for the novel: a book about a guy who got an advance for a book about the "Jewish experience" and then realized he hadn't had any such experience.

Reilly: But, by the end of the novel, doesn't the reader at least perceive Gold has a more profound and important "Jewish experience" than Gold himself realizes?

Heller: I suppose, but Gold is correct in perceiving his "Jewish experience" is far removed from, say, Dubin's in Malamud's new book, or from any character in Malamud's work.

Reilly: It's odd. One imagines a writer burning with a lifelong desire to do a *summa* on a single issue. Yet the genesis of *Good as Gold* seems almost casual.

Heller: Each of my novels came about in the same way: I suddenly and unexpectedly got an idea for a book. I didn't know I was going to write about war until I got the idea for *Catch-22*; I didn't know I was going to write about the interior life of a corporation executive until I got the idea for *Something Happened.* The same was true for *Good as Gold.* I have never yet been able to begin with a general subject and then devise a form to fit it.

Reilly: One character in *Good as Gold,* Gold's father, Julius, especially fascinated me. Despite his cantankerous, sarcastic, patriarchal, egocentric nature, I wound up liking Julius Gold enormously.

Heller: Good. If I may immodestly say so, I think that's one of the achievements—I don't have the nerve to say triumphs—of the novel. I had originally decided to depict him as an almost stock character—a nasty, vile-natured, old tyrant—but about halfway through the writing I decided I'd do that but also try to persuade the reader to feel sorry for him at the end. I guess it was in the scene at Manhattan Beach—where Julius kind of "lets go" and abuses all his visitors, revealing their secrets in the most vitriolic way—that I realized this was a man whose nature could be justified by the irritabilities of old age.

Reilly: And the family *is* trying to farm him out. Even Sid, the older brother who quietly supports him, is trying to ship him off to Florida.

Heller: Correct. It's the kind of moral dilemma that I presented often in *Catch-22.* For example, when Yossarian was arguing with Clevinger, I found that although emotionally I was inclined toward Yossarian, morally I couldn't take a side because each of them was right. Yossarian moved the bombline to postpone a mission; Clevinger objected that people would die as a result; Yossarian argued he had a right to decide whether he got killed.

Reilly: I guess a similar dilemma occurs when Dunbar objected to bombing the peasants in the hills and Yossarian figured he had to drop the bombs where they told him so he wouldn't get "disappeared"?

Heller: Sure, and when Colonel Korn asks them whether they'd rather drop bombs in the hills or go back to Ferrara, they all shut up. But, to answer your question, your response is a good one. Julius is right and the children are right, too. When he complains that he took care of his parents and now his children don't want him, he's addressing something that is prevalent throughout the country. We don't want our old people with us. It's similar to a line in *Something Happened* where the text says something to the effect that Slocum's aged mother became a burden to him as soon as he no longer needed her.

Reilly: A couple of other characters whose similarity intrigued me were the social climber Harris Rosenblatt and Gold's youngest sister—Joannie—both of whom seemed to repudiate their Jewish heritage to one degree or another. I didn't at all care for Rosenblatt . . .

Heller: You weren't supposed to.

Reilly: And yet, I found myself quite sympathetic to Joannie, even though when he asks what her Jewish experience is, she responds it's taken the form of her trying not to be Jewish. Do you feel my response is sensible?

Heller: I don't know if it's sensible or not; these are the kinds of things that occur to me and that I put intuitively into the novel. I wasn't aware of a similarity between those characters until you mentioned it, for instance. Now, I *am* aware of a strong similarity, maybe it's analogous, between Gold's father and Pugh Biddle Conover, the arch-bigot.

Reilly: He's another outrageous bigot, and yet I found myself liking him.

Heller: So did I. He's funny and clever and intelligent and articulate, and he reads Gold's mind perfectly. He's quite similar to Julius Gold. But the two characters you mentioned are different to me in subtle ways. Rosenblatt not only wants to stop being Jewish, he also wants to become a Protestant—and for some unexplainable physiological reason, he does manage to get taller, thinner, and paler. Whereas Joannie is simply becoming Americanized and, by disassociating herself from her family as best as she can, she is doing nothing more than acting out Bruce Gold's wishes.

Reilly: You've done something in *Good as Gold* with narrative point of view that is unprecedented, even for you. I must confess that the effect of *Catch-22*'s order out of chaos and the "Beckettean" voice of *Something Happened* had an enormous impact upon me. But, in this one, the unnamed third-person-omniscient narrator actually shows up in the text, concedes he could have served Gold better, and predicts what will happen later in the tale. Then, a couple of pages later, a reference is made to an author named "Joseph Heller." Now, you've never done this before. Had you planned it from the start?

Heller: Yes. From the start I planned injecting the first-person pronoun into the novel fairly regularly, and doing so in a way that would incline the reader to infer that first-person voice belonged to me, Joseph Heller. I wanted very much to have some kind of sustained, perhaps disconcerting, reminder to the reader that this *is* only a story, that it shouldn't be taken too seriously. What happened was, as I wrote the book, I began to worry that the effect might be too precious—I had even conceived at one point of having dialogues between a character and "me"—and I was worried it would prove too jarring upon the reader. What I ultimately decided to do was include a number of lines here and there that would have the same effect but that would not stand out. For example, in addition to the passages you mentioned, there was the occasion when Gold was musing, first, upon the extraordinary situation of awaiting a high government appointment while hustling a book, and then upon the fact that this was exactly what Kissinger was doing. The next sentence says, "in a novel, no one would have believed it." That sort of thing happens often. I don't know if you noticed the way the allusions to Dickens operate. On one occasion the phrase occurs, and it's a borrowed simile, "as solitary as an oyster." In ensuing passages there are a number of criticisms which seem to apply to Charles Dickens but which have also been applied to *Something Happened* and *Catch-22*: too long, too many characters, too many improbable events. But, to answer your question, I finally decided in that one chapter, and only in that one, to introduce formally the "I" narrator. I suppose it was almost an attempt to disarm criticism and, in a humorous way, do something integral to the sense of the novel.

I was aware there were a number of times when Gold was either eating or talking a lot, and I was also aware I couldn't reduce the number without damaging the book. So in an effort to anticipate observations about this, I began a passage by saying:

> Once again Gold found himself preparing to lunch with someone—Spotty Weinrock—and the thought arose that he was spending an awful lot of time in this book eating and talking. There was not much else to be done with him. I *was* putting him into bed a lot with Andrea and keeping his wife and children conveniently in the background. For Acapulco, I contemplated fabricating a hectic mixup. . . .

The point is, I didn't want anyone to interpret or judge this book solely by the standards of realism.

Reilly: In other words, right from the start you wanted to develop a tension between, oh, narrative fact and narrated incident?

Heller: Yes. I knew from the start that, unlike *Catch-22* and *Something Happened,* this novel was going to operate within the context of realistic form. There was going to be a plot. The plot would be narrated, with the exception of a few flashbacks, in chronological order. And the flashbacks would be conspicuous—the reader would have no doubt at those points that he was being presented with antecedent action. Yet at the same time I knew the spirit of the book and most of the events were in the nature of the broadest farce, as exaggerated as those in *Catch-22.*

Reilly: This intrusion of the narrator, this confronting the reader with a tension between narrated event and "realistic" fact, reminded me of Laurence Sterne's eighteenth-century novel, *Tristram Shandy.* Are there Shandean influences upon your novel?

Heller: Oh yes, I had *Tristram Shandy* very much in mind for this book. That's the reason I refer to it so often.

Reilly: And, am I correct in thinking *Good as Gold* Shandean in a very special sense: specifically, in that Sterne's novel, to a significant extent, is a book about the composition of the book *Tristram Shandy?*

Heller: Yes.

Reilly: So, to an extent, *Good as Gold* is a book about the composition of the book *Good as Gold?*

Heller: It is, except that by the time it's over, Gold himself still hasn't started it.

Reilly: Well, what got me going on this question was a line in one of the advance sheets which suggested your novel is the book Gold is working on, or about to begin working on.

Heller: Correct, but he's working on it without realizing it. It's hard to explain, and I am reluctant to predict what would happen to Gold after the book ends. I have a habit of ending my books with at least one question unanswered. I don't know what happens to Yossarian or Slocum, and I have never pretended to know what would happen to them. In *Gold,* I chose that last sentence carefully: "Where could he begin?" I toyed with the word "how" instead of "where" for a time. Finally I decided to suggest, *where* in this sequence of events could he begin a book like that? Does he begin with his own experience? Does he begin with what happens at the end to Sid? *Where* in the world could he begin? Another thing: that line seems to suggest he will do the book. I wouldn't bet he does.

Reilly: At least he seems a lot better off for having gone through all the events and scrapes in the novel.

Heller: He is. He's not necessarily a better man, but he has shaken off those ambitions which are presented in the book as ignoble. He's resolved not to use public service, for instance, as a camouflage for personal and social advancement.

Reilly: And despite his announced contempt for Kissinger, he has finally stopped becoming, in effect, a Kissinger.

Heller: Oh yes. Kissinger was not simply a target of Gold's envy; he was a model for what could be achieved.

Reilly: The book is laced with newspaper clippings, most of them about Kissinger. Are they all the real things?

Heller: Almost every one. Every one mentioning a public figure is authentic. The only changes I made in those cases would have been to reduce—not to change the emphasis, but to make it more manageable. There's one, though, where I mention my own name that's a bit contrived. At that point I was discussing literary agents and had a clipping which rattled off a list of "big names" that a particular agency handled. The list was bracketed by Steve McQueen and Laurence Olivier, and I couldn't resist including "Joseph Heller." Ironically, I realized just a few days ago that I *am* a client of sorts of the agency. The agency that sold *Catch-22* was sold to someone who sold it to someone else who was acquired by the agency I mention. And they process the royalty checks for *Catch-22*.

Reilly: I've studied a lot of satire, and I have to admit that I can recall very few major satirists who deal as directly and vigorously with real figures—people like Kissinger, Helms, Haig, Kleindienst—as you do in *Good as Gold*. Swift, for example, used pseudonyms; Juvenal waited until they were dead; even you hadn't been so specific in your earlier works. I wonder if working with real people makes the writing more difficult, more nerve-wracking, or easier?

Heller: It's not as major a departure as it may seem. *Catch-22* was originally going to deal with some well-known figures, but by the time the book was ready for publication most of them were dying or losing power. In this particular book, I felt it worked well. But, no, it wasn't easier or harder to work with specific public figures. In fact, I suspect that if I were regularly employed as a satiric columnist, I would prob-

ably find it much easier to work with specifically identified figures. And
keep in mind that most of the direct references take the form of verbatim
quotations of newspaper pieces.

Reilly: Another thing that interested me was the effect that writing
about the Vietnam war had upon you. It seemed apparent in *Something
Happened* that you felt a sense of moral outrage over our role in the
war, and in this one Gold seems almost to boil in rage at some aspects
of it. Was it difficult to write about an issue that is so enraging and
draining?

Heller: No, and this is true of *Catch-22* as well. When I'm writing,
I am only interested in writing. Now when I'm not writing, I confess
I can hear something that will make me boil over. A phrase that really
gets to me, for instance, would be one of those neo-conservative
references to Vietnam as a national tragedy, but only because we lost.
That thought fills me with ire. To begin with, the person who says it is
typically untouched by tragedy; like me, he has not lost a son or a job.
In addition, the implication is that if we had won, the war would have
been somehow less tragic. People with that mentality, I have to admit,
impress me as being the scum of the earth.

Reilly: But when writing you don't find yourself consumed with
savage indignation, as Swift put it? When you were creating Gold's
abject fury over what was done and said during the Vietnam era, you
weren't churning inside?

Heller: No, and the same was true of *Catch-22*. One of the most
stirring portions of *Catch-22*, and I know this because I've read it to
audiences, is the passage that describes Snowden's death. When I wrote
that, I recall having finished it and then sitting back and wanting to
smile. It's not that I was dismissive or callous. But I knew it was done
well. I knew it was right. At the moment of composition I felt no sympathy for Snowden, none for Yossarian, none for Gold. It's not that I'm
devoid of such emotions. But many people don't realize the degree of
detachment, the intensity of concentration, required in serious writing.

Reilly: And yet I hope you would agree that all of your works are
intensely moral. In other words, you're not simply playing games with
the issues you're working with.

Heller: Oh yes, definitely.

Reilly: I guess what I'm trying to say is that what Gold says about
Kissinger seems to me to be so right and moral.

Heller: But keep in mind that Gold is not that much of an idealist. If you'll want to talk about a character who can, well, denounce Kissinger, I think the president's unnamed source, Ralph Newsome, might be a better candidate. Ralph uses invective against Kissinger far more effectively. To me, his terms for Kissinger are far more impressive than Gold's since Gold's are largely spoken in anger.

Reilly: Perhaps I'm not prepared to admit Ralph's virtues since I found him so dislikable.

Heller: That's interesting. Most people I've spoken to so far have liked him.

Reilly: Really?

Heller: They like him as a character. There's a candor to him. After the book was finished, he began to remind me of Milo Minderbinder in *Catch-22*. He is willing to say what is actually so. He is genuinely embarrassed when Gold advises him his definition of a friend is someone who would hide him. If you'll recall, after Gold does ask Ralph to hide him, Ralph apologizes and says—and he's genuinely contrite— "Oh God, Bruce, I'm not your friend; I'm sorry if I said anything to give you that impression." Then again, I may be the wrong person to ask. I wound up more or less liking Conover, the bigot, and even the Texas governor—who to a degree resembles John Connally. It's similar to what happened in *Catch-22* with General Dreedle and Milo. Conversely, I have to admit that I have a hero who was intended to be an unsympathetic figure. Morally, Gold is an ignominious person. He wound up the way Bob Slocum of *Something Happened* started out to be.

Reilly: Slocum? Now, surely he came through in the end.

Heller: I sometimes wonder whether I'm the right person to ask about my books. When I was writing that novel, I told people I was writing a book about the most contemptible human being I could imagine. I know I was very surprised when people read portions of *Something Happened* while it was in progress and referred to "poor Slocum." I was just as surprised when people who read drafts of *Catch-22* told me it was going to be a very funny book. I honestly didn't know I had the power to write something that would make people laugh.

Reilly: One final question. Maybe I was forewarned by *Catch-22*, but when I was barely into *Good as Gold* and I realized you were raining characters down upon me, I grabbed a pencil and scribbled a family tree of sorts. At the end, when you again managed to bring all the characters and subplots together, as you did in *Catch-22,* I was filled with admiration. What I wonder is, when you wrote it, did you compose it the way I read it, that is, in an episodic way? Did you have an elaborate master plan from the start?

Heller: I wrote it largely the way you read it. This book required very little in the way of outlining, almost none in fact. In the instance you cited, I decided to make a virtue out of necessity. I knew I wanted to handle a large number of people and I knew it was going to be virtually impossible to linger over each and define each character without killing the pace of the book. So what I did was have Gold react in the book to this swarm of people the way the reader would. If you'll recall, Gold occasionally will forget the names of the people to whom he's talking and will begin improvising names arbitrarily—sometimes it's a name from Dickens, sometimes from Greek mythology. I think this is an unavoidable problem in the modern novel. Perhaps in a Russian novel you could afford the luxury of a couple of hundred pages of character delineation. But modern readers don't have the patience for that sort of thing.

Reilly: I wonder how spontaneous the plotting was. When you were writing the first third of the book, for example, did you have a pretty good idea of where the novel was going? Perhaps not the Acapulco scene but . . .

Heller: Oh yeah, I knew where it was going, and I certainly knew from the early going about *all* the major scenes, including Acapulco. Again, as with the other books, I had folders bulging with notes— quickly typed scenes, character sketches, dialogues—before I started.

Reilly: What about characters who don't show up until late in the novel, characters like Linda Book?

Heller: Same thing. I had thought through all the major characters, and she's a good example, right from the start. At least, I did it as soon as I decided this was going to be a major novel. When I began *Good as Gold,* my intention was to dash off a short, frivolous book. I felt that, after the years and years I spent on *Something Happened,* it would be pleasant to concentrate on something that would be short and quick. At least I finished it in three years.

Reilly: That's true. The others took seven and thirteen years.

Heller: Believe me, I'll settle for three for the next one.

Reilly: Do you have an idea for the next one?

Heller: None at all. Maybe I should go back to Washington and give another reading.

Checking in with Joseph Heller

Chet Flippo/1981

From *Rolling Stone*, 16 April 1981, 50–52, 57, 59–60. Copyright ©
Straight Arrow Publishers, 1981. All rights reserved. Reprinted by
permission of Straight Arrow Publishers, 1992.

He's as reluctant a hero as you're likely to find these days, a graying
World War II bombardier from Coney Island whose shyness is continually at odds with his fierce pride. He has probably written more savage
criticism of the U.S. government than has *Pravda,* although he does not
spurn the rewards of capitalism, even while gleefully predicting apoca-
lypse in these United States. He is unrivaled in his burning, single-
minded hatred of Henry Kissinger.

This is Joseph Heller, author of *Catch-22,* a book that may endure
as the final indictment of bureaucracy and the total chaos brought about
by the System. That the System will soon collapse under its own weight
is a given, according to Heller. Capitalism is a gone goose, he told
me as he let me pick up the dinner check at an elegant Manhattan
restaurant. He can't wait to see what happens when it goes. Unless, that
is, chaos knocks on his own door. Then he might change his mind.
That's what I like about Heller. He is a man of many principles, the first
of which is flexibility.

He is one of the world's most revered writers. Yet his entire published work consists of three novels (*Catch-22, Something Happened*
and *Good as Gold*), one play (*We Bombed in New Haven*), one screenplay (*Sex and the Single Girl*) and writing contributions to two other
movies (*Dirty Dinguis Magee* and *Casino Royale*). If it seems at all
unusual that the author of *Catch-22* would also pen a sex movie,
consider this: he did it for the money. Writers of serious fiction in this
country do not, traditionally, get rich. Joseph Heller's advance for
Catch-22 was $1500: $750 on signing and another $750 on acceptance
of the manuscript. After two decades and more than 8 million copies, its
royalties still can't keep him in Chivas Regal.

Heller was born on May 1st, 1923, to Russian immigrants Lena and

Isaac Heller. He started writing as a child and was publishing short stories while studying at New York University and Columbia. Then, one day, he abruptly quit writing. He had decided his fiction was no good. He was a Fulbright Scholar at Oxford, he did three years in the army air corps, he taught college, he worked in the advertising departments of *Time, Look,* and *McCall's.*

The notion for *Catch-22* came to him in the middle of the night. "It kind of burst into my mind. I was actually pacing the floor at four in the morning. I couldn't wait to get into my office at this small advertising agency and scribble the first chapter." Now, he says, if he had known it was going to take him seven years of work, he would never have written the book. He does not write fast. *Something Happened* came out thirteen years after *Catch-22* and was so unlike his first book that it perplexed critics and fans alike: despair had replaced black humor. A mere four years later, along came *Good as Gold,* a parody of presidential politics laced with vicious attacks on Kissinger. Even though Heller decided not to go to Washington to do research and depended instead on newspaper clippings for his political expertise, the *New York Times Book Review* said Gold's portrayal of Washington was "perhaps more valuable to our understanding of our government than a library of presidential papers." Obviously, people see in Heller just what they want to see.

What I see is a well-read, enigmatic, intensely private, acerbic, witty and opinionated man who contradicts himself with élan. The locale of our talks ranged from his favorite table at Elaine's, where we were flanked by Yankees boss George Steinbrenner and Woody Allen, to the Lone Star Cafe, where Heller danced on a chair while the Sir Douglas Quintet blasted through "96 Tears." He's got, it seemed to me, a pretty good handle on his wheel.

He denied that he was "back on the lecture circuit," even though he'd just spoken at several colleges in the South, had planned some more dates, and was about to leave on a swing through Australia, Hong Kong and Thailand. He said his new novel was going "rapidly," although he declined to say what it was about.

He was also full of fatherly advice. "Never quit a job as a matter of principle," he told me at one point. "You'll always regret it."

Why?

"Do it and you'll find out."

You always seem to incorporate real-life heroes and villains into your books, such as a Nelson Rockefeller or John Connally character. What if you didn't have these people to draw from?

It's not a problem for me. The villains will come along. There were plenty in the Carter administration, and there will be plenty with Reagan. I have a feeling this David Stockman [director of the Office of Management and Budget] is going to become a comic character. It will be like watching Edgar Bergen with two blocks of wood on his knees. Both Alexander Haig and Stockman look like blocks of wood. Haig is definitely made out of wood.

The idea that somone like Stockman, who is thirty-four years old, is a genius! He can't be an economics genius at thirty-four! He can't be a genius in economics at any age, because it's not a field that accommodates the concept of genius.

I read a news story the other day that made me think of you. It said, matter-of-factly, that NATO is absolutely useless, incapable of anything.

Well, I think everyone knows that. That probably came from Haig. You know, I wish the newspapers would tell me why this country is so upset about the possibility of China and Russia going to war. I can't figure it out. It would be ideal for the U.S. The very fact that these two can destroy each other in an atomic war is made to order. Goldwater would be clapping his hands and Patrick Moynihan would be saying, "Hey, look at 'em go!"

Good as Gold almost centers on newspaper articles about Henry Kissinger. Did you begin the book because you were clipping articles on him?

Nope. I didn't. I'm not sure I even thought of using Kissinger at all when I began. But he was in the news, in our lives, so why not in the book—with a good deal of that objective dislike for him that more and more people were coming to feel. I didn't have the idea of using newspaper clippings right away. When I read about David Eisenhower in *McCall's,* about how he wasn't a goody-goody, I thought, "This is just too fuckin' funny and unbelievable to go into oblivion." Then, the idea of using actual clippings came about as a way of characterizing Gold. Gold uses clippings because he hates doing research and is not even really interested in the books and articles he writes.

In Good as Gold, *the president writes a book, after his first year in office, titled* My Year in the White House, *and he spends all his time writing. How did you come by that?*

I dunno. Good comic imagination. But Lyndon Johnson wrote a book, right? Every president since Johnson has written his book. I mean, doesn't it make more sense for them to write once every year, instead of waiting till they're out of office [*laughs*]?

Do you like Gold?

Yeah, in a condescending, disapproving way. I also found myself liking Pugh Biddle Conover, the John Connally character. And I *really* like Conover as a literary figure, and so, it seems, does everyone else. With all his cold snobbishness, he nevertheless sees through Gold thoroughly. Conover is the consummate bigot. I mean, he not only dislikes Jews, but also blacks, Italians, baldies. . . . When Conover says he wouldn't go anywhere to eat with Nelson Rockefeller, I realized, *"There's* a man with taste" [laughs]. Rockefeller was an *atrocious* person. I mean, that man went to Coney Island to eat a hot dog with Henry Cabot Lodge. *That* was invading *my* turf. *There* was vulgarity, and from two such gentlemen.

Have you consciously compared Haig to Kissinger?

Well, Kissinger brought, or helped bring, ruin to hundreds and hundreds of thousands of people, and he escaped with riches and a reputation for competence and knowledge that he does not deserve. He talks gibberish and impresses with jargon. He does not know the meaning of words. He says almost *nothing* with meaning. He doesn't understand anything at all about what is going on in the world, even about what was happening in the world while he was helping make it happen. Before the shah of Iran fell, he said, "We must take immediately whatever remedies are needed. The time to discuss them is in the future."

Oh. Okay. But did he know the remedies? Frankly, he is over his head in the field of foreign affairs and ought to be kept out. Let him stick to directing the North American Soccer Association.

I think Haig will be foolish, but perhaps not quite as foolish as Kissinger was, because Haig doesn't have the education Kissinger had. Haig is a little more dangerous, because I fear he *believes* what he says, whereas I never got that impression from Kissinger. Haig is the guy who tried to keep this man William Watts [of the National Security Council] from resigning after Cambodia. And Haig said, "You can't quit; you've just been given an order by your commander-in-chief." And Watts made the famous remark, "Fuck you, Al. I just did." Haig seems to be simple-minded—along with everybody else who lives by dogmas—when he says there are worse things than war.

Our foreign policy is based on an infantile ignorance of the world. Kissinger was not too understanding of history; he would make historical references because he had a degree in history. Nobody but another historian would ever call him on it. But Reagan and Haig and Howard Baker, on this thing in El Salvador, just seem to be willfully obvious to facts that everybody else in the world knows. It's not a Communist plot; it's not a terrorist plot; it's dissatisfaction with a dictatorial government.

Those political slogans in Good as Gold—*"Nothing succeeds like failure" and "Every change is for the worse"—are just absurd enough to be real. Where did you get them?*

Right out of my mind. Every change *is* for the worse. Nothing *does* succeed as planned and every good intention *does* go awry. That double talk is *true*. Like, this administration will stand behind you—until it has to.

An unsavory part of life in Washington is that the person who blows the whistle on ineptitude or corruption is finished. Like the one who blew the whistle on waste in the Defense Department. Fired and disappeared. John Dean's another one. But Dean was reprehensible. And I think it will be an everlasting stigma on Hubert Humphrey's reputation that he did not speak out against the war. I would love to see a vice-president who breaks openly with the president on an important issue.

Obviously, you care a lot more about politics and its effects than some people might think.

Maybe. Maybe that's why I was able to speak with the clearest conscience in *Good as Gold* against a lot of people in Washington, whom I castigate by name. Now, they were selected carefully. At one time or another, they were all pretty shitty, if on no other issue than Vietnam. Jacob Javits, he was terrible. Christ, Lyndon Johnson would trot him out like a stage prop whenever he wanted support from a New

Yorker with a liberal reputation. Some liberal. He was just ducky on Iran, wasn't he?

If there is a common thread running through your three novels, what do you think it would be?

The *outlooks* are the same. The attitudes and moods of an author remain pretty constant. All three books are very pessimistic, very bleak, very *morbid.* Death is always present as a climactic event that never happens to the protagonist but affects him profoundly. I think I'm drawing unconsciously from experience for inspiration. The child, the dependent child or sacrificed child, is always there. I would think that the death of my father when I was about five years old had much to do with that. There was almost no conversation about it that I can remember, and it may have been by my own choice that I would not let anyone talk about it. Indeed, the traumatized child denies death very successfully, and then sublimates it, which I think is the process that went on in me. But it leaves me very sensitive to the helplessness of children and the ease with which they can be destroyed or betrayed, deliberately or otherwise. In each of my books, when the key death takes place, there's a great deal of pain and tenderness involved.

You were from a poor family. The role of money as a main character in each book could come from that.

Well, you're closer to my books because you've reread them. But that corresponds to my own feelings, which probably derive from having a poor family. We always had food, but it must have permeated my consciousness that there was a struggle for money. There was a period a few years back, before *Something Happened,* when I started worrying about money. I had my savings in bonds—about $50,000, which was all I had in the world. The bonds started plummeting, and I had a few very bad nights, till they leveled out. Part of my most horrible nights was when I felt I might have to give up my apartment, have to take the children out of private school, have to tell my children that we're moving out to Queens or Brooklyn. It was not the poverty, but the *shame,* that worried me.

I would say that most or all serious writers do draw on experience. There are many events I'd never touch and never will. I think in all my books, too, there's a passage on the degeneration of cities, the deterioration of law and order.

Given that deterioration and economic shift in this country, is success—fame, wealth—becoming less the American goal? Is self-fulfillment taking its place?

Yes. I'm not sure young people can be satisfied with success. I think people who want to write would agree with that. For me, the satisfaction was in wanting to be a writer, in trying to be a writer, in writing and in submitting what I did. Even though I wasn't published until I was twenty-two, I began submitting stories when I was about ten or eleven. But the satisfaction came in that there were connections between me and certain wants and needs—needs of the imagination, of the emotions, to express fantasies, and it was private and yet could become public. I know I wanted to be a famous writer when I was ten, but the *want* was its own satisfaction. I felt I *would* be a famous writer, but the feeling was its own daydream. Just having that daydream was a very important reward.

Is there any worth in taking writing courses?

There was for me. None at all, I'd say, for the student who lacks talent. You can't teach talent. And you can't give intelligence. You can't teach a person to be funny. A novel takes two or three years to write. By the time a student is halfway through his book, he'll know much more about writing and about literature, and will have experienced so much more as a person, that there's a good chance he'll lose interest in the book before it's finished.

Have college students changed at all?

Oh, yeah. They've changed tremendously. Also, I've changed. I think the age differences now between me and college students . . . it's so large that I'm not reflexively charmed by the fact that they're in college and they're there to hear me and they're young.

The faculty is another thing that's changed: there's not as much for them to be incensed about as, say, in 1964, when I accepted my first invitation to speak. There was a growing war then, the Vietnam War.

Has anyone in the audiences brought up a connection between El Salvador and Vietnam?

No. I've only been to a few colleges since El Salvador. I don't think

El Salvador has anybody angry outside of New York. This may be
another change in me: I think I'm getting resigned to catastrophe—to
catastrophe built into civilization and particularly our civilization. I'm
reminded of a line from *Good as Gold*: Gold believes that the penultimate stage of a civilization is chaos masquerading as order, and he
knows we are already there. I think this country is in a state of absolute
chaos. And it amuses me, because the people who speak for it are still
as pompous and pretentious as ever.

*They say, "Let's get America moving again," and all that kind of
stuff.*
They don't know what to do. The economists don't know what to do,
the secretary of the treasury doesn't, Reagan doesn't know what the hell
to do, and one reason is because the situation is hopeless. I don't think
anybody wants to face the fact that capitalism has outlived its usefulness
as a system—as a system for *this* country.

Nobody is advocating anything to remedy the situation. If inflation is
part of it, and I've asked this of friends of mine on Wall Street, give me
one proposal that's been made that would encourage an increase in production. Name one product that could be sold at a lower cost. And no
proposal has been made.

What happens if it ever gets to you? Will your opinion change then?
About what? About it being tragic? Of course it will! I think the
situation is tragic; I think that in a grim and unfortunate way, people
have learned to live with tragedies. It's part of the environment, and no
one person, no administration, is going to change it. There is going to
have to be some kind of universal or national cataclysm. Or there's
going to be a great economic collapse, and then it's going to take
somebody with sense and nerve. But people with sense don't have nerve
and people with nerve don't have sense.

So you find it depressing?
If I were your age, I would find it depressing. At my age, it's amusing. It has more of a chance of affecting you than me. I don't expect
anybody of merit to be elected to a high office. I also think anybody of
merit wouldn't want to get into politics. One of the things that did
revive my faith in America, my love for America, was the fact that
Nelson Rockefeller was never able, never *ever* able, to get anywhere in

politics, other than buying the governorship of New York, which is not an important position. I was very proud of the American people.

For rejecting Rockefeller?
For rejecting that particular Rockefeller.

Have you gotten used to the idea that people still think of Catch-22 *as a pivotal event in their lives? For instance, Kris Kristofferson told me that he thought the book had been written for him; it was that personal. It affected a lot of people that way, and the last time we talked, you didn't seem comfortable with that assumption.*
I'm used to the idea that a great many people of all kinds of intellect and in almost all types of occupations look at that book as being something very special.

How much of Catch-22 *is based on your own war experiences and how much is outright fiction?*
The book was the result of a literary imagination at work, not a journalist's, historian's or social reformer's. I would not have had a book if I'd taken a realistic approach. For two reasons: one, I don't think I have the vocabulary, the patience, the eye or the memory to record things as they take place. The second thing is that I had no particularly interesting story of my own to tell. Remove the spirit, the literary personality of *Catch-22,* and put the events in chronological order, and you'll find an uneventful story about a bombardier and a colonel who wants his men to fly more missions than anyone else. My interest was more on the Cold War and the Korean War. The effect they had on the domestic political climate was frightening. And that's the spirit of revolt that went into *Catch-22*. I've been criticized for the ending, for my not being a pacifist and for Yossarian's failures to condemn that war.

But these readers wanted something far beyond anything I was willing to say or feel about World War II—that *any* alternative is preferable to war. That's *not* my attitude, and it's not expressed *anywhere* in the book.

Do you ever think about your influence on your readers?
I doubt novels influence behavior on a large scale. *Catch-22* possibly did, in that it coincided with the Vietnam War. It did not start off as a big success, fated to attract a large audience. People found it a difficult

book to read, and it was by an unknown author. That's why I'm grateful to the hippie generation; they had no trouble with it at all.

I met officers who told me that people in Vietnam were carrying copies of *Catch-22* and telling people, "If you want to know what this war's all about, read *this*." Now, these were people disgusted by a military code that they cherished and saw being defiled. Not by me, not by the antiwar movement, but by pricks like that general who wrote up a citation for himself for an action in which he did not participate.

I have an ingrained modesty that prevents *me* from making too many claims for *Catch-22,* but others have written about its influence on literature and publishing. I was told, for example, that Pynchon's *V.* was given a much more vigorous launching because of the success of *Catch-22.*

Just how bad is the future? What do you foresee?

I've always had faith in the future of this country, for the rest of *my* life, anyway. I put my faith in the fact of native incompetence. I don't think we'll have a Hitler, because we're not efficient enough to have a Hitler. We won't have a military dictatorship, or a military takeover, because the military isn't that efficient.

That's where I see hopelessness, by the way, when I talk about capitalism being on its deathbed. An experienced businessman can't run his business, but the government can't either. So socialism won't work. I mean, we have a history of corrupt government. Corrupt and incompetent and mediocre people are government; that's our tradition. So if we socialize, God knows what's going to happen. It warmed my heart, in the way that watching a Laurel and Hardy comedy might warm my heart, to read about the losses that General Motors and Ford posted. We just assume these companies are infallible and in expert hands, and everything's going to go beautifully. But not only was there incompetence, there was passive acceptance. They, of all people, should be the ones in Washington saying, "Nationalize the oil companies or control their profits."

It's going to be very funny for a while. But the economy is most frightening. It doesn't seem as if there is any possibility for economic growth at present. The Japanese have us on one side and France and Germany have us on the other.

If you were in the same position now as when you were in college, and you started publishing short stories, would you change things? Change your writing?

Given the choice, if Mephistophiles had appeared and said, "What do you want to do?" I probably would have picked being a screenwriter. I wouldn't now, but back then I would have.

I'm not sure that my motivations then for becoming a writer were worthy ones. I wanted to be a writer because I felt I had a gift, and I really wanted to make money and have some kind of status. I never thought it would be in fiction, because I write very slowly. I write dialogue rapidly, so I thought I would be in playwriting or radio. At that time, there were many radio dramas and comedy shows. But now I wouldn't change: now fiction is what I want to do. I still have trouble writing words that are not dialogue, finding words that I like. But if it were too easy, it wouldn't hold my interest. It's the fact that it's very hard for me to write. . . .

If I had known that *Catch-22* was going to take seven years, I wouldn't have done it. If I had known *Something Happened* was going to take twelve, I wouldn't have done it. I always thought it would just take another two years or less than two years, and if you were to ask me when my next book will be finished, I'd say within two years.

When will this one be finished?
Within two years [*laughs*].

Catching up with Joseph Heller

Curt Suplee/1984

From *Washington Post* 8 October 1984, D1, D13. Copyright © 1984
The Washington Post. Reprinted by permission.

The problem with "talking" to Joseph Heller . . .

"So g'wan, start your interview."

*. . . is that at 61, despite the lingering debilities of Guillain-Barré
syndrome, which paralyzed him for months and left him more than
$60,000 in debt . . .*

"Hey, it was over a year before I could get up from the ground to my
feet without help—more than a year and a half before I could get on a
bus in New York."

*. . . despite a slew of reviews so caustic they'd give a warthog
hives . . .*

"Look, I've adjusted to this, that my books are not going to get
unanimously good reviews. Though with this one I had the expectation.
But all of my books deal in a very rough, rude fashion with subjects
about which there are great conflicts of opinion." A breath. "And the
average reader expects to be told in a few pages what the book is about,
expecting the character to be fairly consistent in his personality."

*. . . you can't get. A word. In. Edgewise. The guy is a manic mael-
strom of phrase and gesture, hands waving like he's just walked into a
wall of cobwebs, trademark mane shaking, sentiments tending to the
midbrow demotic, though learned Latinisms bob up at intervals like
stray carrots in the conversational stew.*

All of it served up *molto vivace* in Heller's unreconstructed Coney
Island accent, a high nasal blat like a clarinet full of paper clips. A
cheerfully self-conscious vulgarian, brazenly open-shirted and flicking
an incisor with one of the outsize toothpicks he habitually carries, he's
not exactly à la mode here in the paneled barroom alcove at the Ritz
Carlton, where the author of *Catch-22* ('61), *Something Happened* ('74)
and *Good as Gold* ('79) is billeted on the promo trek for his beleaguered
new novel, *God Knows*.

235

But then Heller has always been a conspicuous anomaly in American letters—a college English teacher and magazine ad man elevated at age 38 directly from oblivion to the rank of Major Novelist on the strength of a single book: the comic-absurdist cosmos of *Catch-22*. Great expectations—which, his critics say, he never subsequently fulfilled. Ditto this time. *Newsweek* called the new book "sometimes funny," but largely "a weariness of the flesh." *The Washington Post* dubbed it "a goof." *Vanity Fair* intoned that Heller "doesn't know when to put a cork on it." And *Time* derided "a disappointing hodgepodge of repetition and irrelevancy." That last, he says, "was like a slap in the face."

But *The New York Times Book Review* found Heller "at the top of his form again," a sentiment he finds "absolutely lovely." Indeed it was, written by author Mordecai Richler, one of the judges at the Book-of-the-Month Club—which, as it happens, is selling Heller's novel.

And besides, he recalls, dropping his cheek to an unturned palm, the first reviews of *Catch-22* were often equally brutal. "Emotional hodgepodge," snorted the *Times Book Review*; "a debris of sour jokes, stage anger, dirty words, synthetic looniness," said *The New Yorker*. But the book proved an immediate success in England, and went on to sell nearly 10 million copies in paperback.

By contrast, *God Knows,* with a 150,000-copy first printing, has a much higher launch momentum. Heller estimates that it will pull in between $400,000 and $500,000 counting foreign sales ("the European publishers' advances are 10 times higher than I ever got before," he says, including more than $30,000 from Finland alone), and the paperback rights have just been sold to Dell, which acquired all four of his books.

"Let me tell you something," he says, as if this were an unlikely eventuality, rocking earnestly forward on his elbows. "It may be immodest, but I believe this book will be my biggest hit, because people love reading it."

God Knows is the protracted deathbed confession of the biblical King David, who lies brooding ("I hate God and I hate life"), recounting his history in anecdotes festooned with flyblown jokes, gobbets of borrowed prose, scores of one-liners ("Show him the door." "I've seen the door") and a hundred dismal memories. His son Absalom has been slain in rebellion against him; an infant son has died in forfeit for his murderous adultery with Bathsheba. Bathsheba herself, now indifferent to his sexual pleadings, connives for the success of her son Solomon, a patent dimwit and one of two unsuitable successors between whom David must choose. He is further tortured, Heller says, by "the longing I give to him—and I don't believe it's there in the Bible—for somebody who would be to him the father that he wants. Saul is inadequate, rejected him. And God as well has let him down." Hence his poignant last line: "I want my God back."

Where did the idea come from? "It had no genesis at all," says Heller agreeably, "other than vain ambition—all *is* vanity and vexation of spirit!—that is, other than the desire to write a novel.

"This one began with the whimsical idea of writing a love story, and what intrigued me was, 'What would a love story for adults be today?' And as I got into it, almost without knowing how it occurred, I was thinking, like David, 'I've got the best story in the Bible. I've got a sex story and a love story with the same woman. Who can compete with me? Job? Genesis? Forget it!'

"I do not have, and never had, any interest in either the Bible or religion. But the more I thought about it, the more promising it seemed." He repaired to scripture and "was astonished in the most ecstatic way at how much material there was—episodes that would lend themselves to a love story, an adventure story, a sex story, a motion picture.

"And I also found those few things that I generally need for my books to give a thread of seriousness and pessimistic philosophy underlying all the comedy." So just as Yossarian in *Catch-22* was estranged from the machinery of authority and law, and Bob Slocum (antihero of *Something Happened*) from the humane promptings of society and kin, so David—bedridden, impotent and guilt-nagged at 70—is estranged from God and man.

His work, Heller says, carries "a tremendous amount of gloom about the immorality of much in life. Most of my books are very moral," attacks on "the presence of pain, the inevitability of age, early death. I try very hard, either as a protest against it or as a complement to it, to deal hugely with laughter of all kinds—including bad jokes and old jokes, particularly if the jokes were Jewish.

"One of the original bold steps of the imagination I took in *God Knows* is in making King David Jewish. In the Old Testament, we don't think of these people as being Jewish. You don't think of Samson as being Jewish, or Josh. But in making this book, it suddenly occurred to me—David is Jewish, and if he's Jewish, then to us he's Yiddish and he should be able to speak with Yiddish inflections and idioms." Including answering a question with a question. "Another discovery I made was that when God speaks to Cain and asks a question, Cain answers with a question! 'Am I my brother's keeper?'—a typical Yiddish answer! Bathsheba is also Jewish, so I have her speaking dialect."

Heller also wanted to examine a failed covenant with "the ideal of a father. David says, 'I've had three fathers in my life—Jesse, Saul and God—and all have disappointed me, all have let me down.'" A major theme—yet the author's own father, a Russian immigrant, died when he was 5, and "I never had a father figure." His notion of paternity is "esthetic, in the same way that I got the family scenes in *Good as Gold*. That's not my family—I only have one brother and one sister." (Step-siblings, actually, as he discovered to his shock at age 15.) "It just comes from listening to people and being able to envision certain situations and combining them."

Veteran Heller watchers will discern an obvious parallel between the effects of Guillain-Barré syndrome—a mysterious, rarely fatal paralysis—and King David's enervated plight. But Heller says no: "That was fortuitous and perhaps prophetic. I was working on the work about a year and a half and had about 300 pages done when I got sick."

While he was in intensive care, so weak that for four months he was fed through a tube in his nose, Heller says he kept his sense of humor—even though when he was hooked to two intravenous bags, "people started making jokes about the Soldier in White." At one point, his old friend Mel Brooks turned up. "He was horrified. Mel Brooks fears death more than anybody in any of my books. I wasn't expecting him. He came in looking glum, and the first remark out of his mouth was, 'Did it begin with numbness in your feet and work its way up?' He'd been reading up on ascending paralysis, and was afraid he had it. And I said, 'I know why you're here—you want me to *immunize* you, don't you?'"

The illness, which stretched between 1981 and 1982, proved costly in a way reminiscent of biblical retribution: The year before, Heller had left his wife of 35 years, and in the ensuing confusion, he says, he misplaced a $90 payment form and "my major medical policy was not renewed." As the rehabilitation costs mounted, he found himself $60,000 in debt and too weak to work for months.

The ordeal "did not affect the content of the book. I don't begin writing a book until I know the ending." He wrote the last paragraphs of *Catch-22* five years before finishing the novel. A prudent practice, since he's no fountain of inspiration. "I've only *had* four ideas for a novel in my life, and I've written all of them.

"What would be terrifying and paralyzing is to start a book and *not* know where I'm going. I once met Philip Roth at a party and at that time he was trying to discipline himself to write every day. He said he would often begin a story and after 60 or 70 pages just *scrap* it because he didn't know where it was going! I said, 'I don't do that because I'm afraid of just that.'"

Besides, "I write very slowly, though if I write a page or two a day five days a week, that's 300 pages a years and it does add up. I can't write on a typewriter. If I do, I do it too fast and it comes out in terrible sentences." Working by hand results in fewer rewrites. And although he has taught English at Penn State and the City College of New York, and spent two decades in the ad biz at *Time, Look* and *McCall's,* "I'm unable to write nonfiction—I would take weeks trying to find an opening sentence for the opening paragraph." As for his recent mini-essay (a promotional coup) in *TV Guide,* "I said, 'Send somebody out with the questions you want me to answer, let me talk into a recorder, give me a typescript and I'll rewrite it.'"

And as for the stage, the author of *We Bombed in New Haven* (1968) will never write a play again: "I like the experience of *writing* a play. I don't like the experience of production. At the first meeting the act of compromise comes in. The thing I like about a novel is it's so *isolated.*" He writes in three or four intense two-hour bursts per day. "I love the work, it's so personal and intimate, I bask in it, I lose myself in it."

By late '82 he was able to dress himself, walk short distances and write in his wheelchair, and *God Knows* was completed at the East Hampton home he has occupied for the past three years. (His divorce arrangement gave his wife the New York apartment.) "When I could begin moving again, I wanted to get familiar with what I'd written, since this is not a chronological story, and there were paragraphs and episodes that appear early in the book that could just as easily appear in the middle, and I'd forgotten where I'd put them." While editing, "I did start adding in some of my physical symptoms, such as the trembling fingers. You won't notice them now because I'm waving." But there is a perceptible quaver as he reaches for his coffee cup. And the left side of his face hangs slack, garbling the last syllables of some words—a grinding frustration to Heller, who envies the fluency of genteel raconteurs like William F. Buckley Jr. or Gore Vidal, not to mention S.J. Perelman, whom he once met: "His whole vocabulary was a literary vocabulary."

Though East Hampton is a traditional summer venue for vacationing literati, Heller mixes primarily with a crony klatch of bachelor businessmen—known ironically as the "Gourmet Club"—with a fondness for *bas cuisine*. He's also close to novelist Mario Puzo, "but we were friends before I was a novelist." Camaraderie among authors, he says, "is not the way it used to be. Possibly in San Francisco and Sante Fe, writers *do* seek each other's company. In New York you tend to avoid each other—there's a sense of self-consciousness, competition, rivalry." (Though during his convalescence he was feted by such local luminaries as Craig Claiborne and Irwin Shaw; and the Russian Tea Room sent out his favorite meal.)

Two companions proved invaluable during his paralysis. One is his long-time friend, retired executive Speed Vogel. "He was decorating my apartment when I got sick—I've never lived alone, I didn't know how—and then he moved in. He's an amateur artist, so he was able to sign checks for me when I no longer could, and he inscribed books for me that would come in the mail." The other is his former nurse, Valerie Humphries. When he was ambulatory, "she naively thought she'd be going back to the city. She's still there. I would call it a love story."

He and Vogel are now cowriting *No Laughing Matter,* the story of Heller's illness with alternating chapters told from each author's point of view ("as my life deteriorated, his improved"); and Heller collaborated with a screenwriter on a script about a fortyish novelist abruptly stricken with GBS. No takers yet: "We did it originally with Dustin Hoffman in mind, but he's busy with *Death of a Salesman.*"

If this seems a somewhat pedestrian agenda for the fabled creator of *Catch-22*—a book whose sense of baffled, helpless outrage perfused

the subsequent decade so thoroughly that its title now ranks a place in
Webster's—well, don't look to Heller for belletristic high-mindedness.

He is unashamedly pragmatic about the origins of his masterpiece.
After an MA in English at Columbia, a year's Fulbright scholarship at
Oxford and two years of teaching at Penn State, he returned to New
York and took up advertising. "The way *Catch-22* began is that I'd just
turned 30 and one day I decided maybe I was ready to write a novel.
Not that I thought there was a *need* for a certain kind of novel. It began
narcissistically: I was reading novels and reviews. And I began to feel
I could do at least as well. Yet even then I proceeded with a great deal
of caution and self-doubt." He wanted to avoid topicality, as he has
in every book except *Good as Gold* (about the seduction of political
power), and "I wasn't really writing about World War II. And the
savage reactions—other than the fear in those few missions—were not
mine. I was a dumb kid in the war and it was like a Hollywood movie
to me."

His agent, Candida Donadio, submitted the first chapter to a literary
quarterly. They took it and "there was enough incentive to go on. It is
widely believed that the book was repeatedly rejected until it finally
reached editor Robert Gottlieb, then at Simon & Schuster and now at
Knopf, who wanted to publish it. Actually, says Heller, it went to
Gottlieb first. "It is conceivable that if my agent had submitted it to 12
publishers—all of whom rejected it—that I, who seem to have so much
self-confidence, would have been practical enough to conclude that it
was not as good as I thought it was" and aborted the project.

Heller received an advance of $1,500—$750 now and $750 later,"
Heller recalls in deadpan. The paperback rights sold for $31,000, which
after the publisher's split and agent's commission netted the author
about $13,000. "It was never a best-seller in hardcover, and it took
about four or five years before the name Joseph Heller would register
with people." Meanwhile, he supported himself by teaching at the City
College of New York until *Something Happened* became a best-seller
and freed him to write full time.

The monstrous acclaim finally accorded *Catch-22*, he says, "was
never an inhibiting factor to me—if anything, it was a source of tremendous encouragement," since he could write the next book "confident
that it would be carefully read and thoughtfully reviewed. If *Something*

Happened had been a first novel by somebody unknown, it might have run into a great, great deal of trouble. Even then, nearly half the reviews expressed disappointment that I had not produced another *Catch-22.*"

Ten years later, he's still dogged by the same dismay. No matter. As he found when *Catch-22* was still a hopeful manuscript, "every person sitting down to write a book feels that it's the best book he's ever written, if not *the* best. That's a natural opinion, if not an objective one."

Humor and the Ability to Create It Cannot Be Taught

U.S. News & World Report/1984

From *U.S. News & World Report*, 12 November 1984, 71. Reprinted by permission.

Humor is one of the ways I cope with the problem of writing novels that generally deal with extremely serious, morbid situations. I don't employ humor as a remedy or tonic. Medicines offer cures, not novels. I try to put a certain amount of comedy into my works because it's in my personality to make wisecracks and think in humorous terms. At the same time, it's in my personality to think of very morbid possibilities and to experience tremendous agony and grief.

The philosopher Nietzsche once said that man laughs because that's the only way he can make his existence tolerable. I'm not saying that at all. I'm funny in my books because I think that will enrich the book and enable me, with my particular outlook and limited talents, to get on with writing.

An appreciation of humor and the ability to create it cannot be taught. Either they are in a person's character or they are not. Many people go through life without ever cracking a smile or making a joke. You can't simply tell a person: "Laugh more, and you'll be happier."

Humor doesn't represent a value in itself, but it helps in determining a set of values. A person who has the ability to laugh will be more tolerant, let's say, of jokes dealing with Biblical subjects. Humor can be very instrumental in helping to keep things in perspective.

My general outlook on life is no different from the average person's—namely, that it's a tough proposition. It has always been. Living can be a very exciting, eventful process that has an inevitable ending. The way we respond to this reality helps account for differences in our character.

I don't have an especially rare insight into human experience. Marriages will be unhappy and happy. People will do things they regret. The innocent will suffer as well as the guilty. I draw on a phrase from

Ecclesiastes that I use in my new book: "The same things come alike to the wicked and the just; to those who sacrifice and those who do not."

In examining the human experience, I find that loneliness is one of the great plagues of mankind. To quote Ecclesiastes: "When two lie together, then they have warmth. But how can one be warm alone?"

Where you have a neighborhood or an extended family, the feeling of loneliness is less likely to erupt than in a highly mobile, transitory society such as our own in which most children leave their families at an early age and where contact between generations is interrupted and broken abruptly. Children do not want to live with their parents when their parents become dependent upon them, while parents are relieved when their children go away to college. In this society, loneliness does come, and very strongly. Many children tell me that their connections with the people who came before them—parents, uncles, grand-fathers—just aren't there.

In my new book, there is an aphorism—"Nothing fails like success"—that is a reversal of the axiom we live by. And I think that the evidence would show that for a great many people the activity of becoming successful is more rewarding than the success itself. It's certainly true of novelists I know. There is a period when you are finished and waiting for the production of the book when you don't know what to do with yourself.

In my own case, it was very exciting to write a novel that would even be published. Then it became very important to get some good reviews and make money, though the reviews for *Catch-22* were not that good, and I didn't make that much money from it. With my second book, I got more-favorable reviews and did make money. Now it's almost something that I can take for granted. It becomes that much less exciting, that much less thrilling in those respects, although the challenge of literary achievement becomes all the greater as a result.

Clive Sinclair Talks to Joseph Heller about the Fall of Kings

Clive Sinclair/1984

From *Jewish Chronicle* 16 November 1984, 12. Reprinted by permission of the *Jewish Chronicle* and the author.

Sinclair: *God Knows* retells the story of King David, but your David is rather different from his biblical original. For example, he's been to New York. Otherwise how could he compare Jerusalem to Coney Island? To put it pompously, he has a contemporary Jewish-American consciousness as well as a Hebrew one, which therefore takes in all of history, from his day to ours. That being so I couldn't help noticing how he keeps his distance from the Holocaust and the rebirth of the state he helped to found. To be sure, he mentions the events in passing, just as he uses the occasional Yiddish word, but he doesn't dwell upon them. Was this unconscious, because you are an American rather than a European Jew, or was it a conscious decision?

Heller: It was a conscious decision to deal with a Jewish consciousness and to set it in two times; he is the David of Jerusalem, but he also seems to be on his death-bed today, talking about today. But my interest was not in making this primarily a political or a pedantic book. It is what I wanted it to be . . .

If you're asking why didn't I say more about Hitler, I think it wouldn't have been possible to do that without saying a great deal more, and then it would have been a different book. My next novel might be one which is centered on Israel or on Hitler or on Jewish persecution.

But I don't really like histories and I don't like biographies and I don't like realism and I could not conceive of having written the story of David in any other voice than the one I used. In fact, I didn't begin with David. I didn't begin with saying, Let me write a novel about David, then ask myself, What's the best way to do it? They came together: David and the voice and the deliberately anachronistic approach.

Actually, I began just by thinking about the lines. I've got the best book in the Bible. That's the way all my novels begin—they've never begun with a subject, they begin with the ambition to write a novel without knowing what the novel should be about. In 1953 I didn't decide to write a novel about World War Two, the only decision I made was to write a novel and the only idea that came to me was *Catch-22*.

Good as Gold came to me exactly the way it's described in the first paragraph, which states that Bruce Gold had often been asked why he had never written about the Jewish experience, most recently by a woman in Wilmington, Delaware. I'd gone to Wilmington, Delaware, and was asked that question by a woman. Coming back on the train I began thinking about it, and by the time I got off I had the notion for *Good as Gold*—the character, subject and approach to it.

Sinclair: Despite the Jewish themes that link *God Knows* and *Good as Gold* I felt that your new novel was closer in spirit to *Something Happened*. Both are told in the first person, both mix family and public relations, both culminate in the death of a beloved son. In short, both books seem to be suggesting that family life is not only the be all but also the end all. Am I right?

Heller: Definitely. In writing this book I was aware of a similarity in tone or outlook to *Something Happened*. In that novel the family was a counterpart of the company, indeed the company was more comfortable for Slocum because his status was defined and relationships were defined, whereas family relationships—unpredictable and painful—were more oppressive to him.

David has strong family sentiments, but I don't really depict family situations because I don't know what they were in biblical times. I don't know how often the king saw his sons or even his women. I think what does exist in *God Knows* is David's inner voice, solipsistic and self-centred, which is not to deny the things that matter most to him throughout the book are family relationships.

When young the desire to have a father in Saul or in God, as a parent an ultimate feeling of responsibility for having irresponsible children. The two tragedies in his life—I make them the important tragedies— are the death of the infant he conceives with Bathsheba and the death of Absalom. When Joab, having killed his favourite son, says, "This was a war not a family quarrel," David says, "To me it was a family quarrel," and Joab says, "Let's keep that our secret."

Sinclair: There seems to be a definite coda in *God Knows*, a development of the unbearable conclusion of *Something Happened* when

Slocum, out of love, accidentally smothers his child. If I may quote, "What is it with these fathers who want to destroy their children? Whence comes this royal and noble willingness to spill the blood of their own offspring? . . . I never hated Absalom. I know if I were God and possessed his powers. I would sooner obliterate the world I had created than allow any child of mine to be killed in it, for any reason whatsoever. I would have given my own life to save my baby's, and even to spare Absalom's. But that may be because I am Jewish, and God is not."

I know it's in the Bible, but there's something particularly American—Jewish-American—about this harping upon fathers and sons. Roth and Singer always seem to be on the side of the son, Malamud on that of the father.

However, you seem to be writing from the point of view of a son who is abandoned by his father, young David, but also from the point of view of a father who blames himself for the iconoclasm of his children, David on his death-bed.

Heller: You're right. I did try to do both here. Somewhere in the book David says, I've had three fathers in my life—Jesse, Saul and God—all have let me down.

Finally David is not a father figure, if anything he's the dependant child, wanting very much the warmth of Bathsheba, who can be a mother or a wife to him, and missing very much his God. That's why at the end old David gets the vision of himself as a youth.

First he rejoices in it, but then he gets so angry at what life is that he looks for a javelin to hurl at this head, understanding at last why Saul threw one at him. There's a feeling that something was wrong, that his children have not turned out the way he wanted, just the way being king is not the rewarding experience he thought it would be.

Sinclair: So David's double-vision is essentially tragic, despite his wisecracks. Not only do circumstances make him the unwilling assassin of his sons, they also turn him into the would-be murderer of his younger self. What had David done to deserve such a fate?

Heller: God knows.

Joe and Speed Spend a Summer Day Laughing about *No Laughing Matter*

William Goldstein/1985

From *Publishers Weekly*, 1 November 1985, 32–33. Reprinted by permission of Publishers Weekly, published by R.R. Bowker Company, a Xerox Company. Copyright © 1985 by Xerox Corporation.

> *"They read the chart at the foot of the bed and asked impatiently about the pain. They seemed irritated when he told them it was exactly the same.*
> *" 'Still no movement?' the full colonel demanded.*
> *"The doctors exchanged a look when he shook his head.*
> *" 'Give him another pill.' "*
> Yossarian. *Catch-22.*

> *"There are four beds in the Intensive Care unit—and usually the other three people were in comas. About every other day one would die. And those alive are being kept alive by ventilating machines, pumps are going all the time. I thought, I've got to get out of here."*
> Joseph Heller. *No Laughing Matter.*

No Laughing Matter is Joseph Heller's first nonfiction book, the story of his bout with Guillain-Barré syndrome, a mysterious disease that "short-circuited" his nerves and left him completely paralyzed in December 1981. In summer 1985, long since completely recovered, Heller suns by his pool in East Hampton, eating heartily and laughing. He is describing the terror of his first weeks at Mt. Sinai Hospital.

He was able to move his hands, his feet and his head—a little. But not his arms or legs, his hips or shoulders. He could talk, which saved him, he says. He kept his friends, a sense of humor and, therefore, his sanity. "Intensive Care," he jokes, "that's an environment where only a crazy person would be content to stay. If you wanna get out, it means you're sane." *That's some catch, that Catch-22.*

No Laughing Matter could not have happened if *Catch-22* didn't exist. Because if Joseph Heller hadn't written *Catch-22*, he wouldn't have met Speed Vogel, whom he saw reading *Catch-22* on the beach in the summer of 1961. Without Speed (Irving) Vogel, Heller wouldn't have co-written *No Laughing Matter,* because there would have been no friendship to describe. Not only is this Heller's first nonfiction book, it's his first collaboration. It's also Speed Vogel's first book.

One thing that might have been the same without *Catch-22* is that Joe Heller probably would have contracted Guillain-Barré syndrome anyway. But if he hadn't written *Catch-22* (and *Something Happened, Good as Gold* and *God Knows*), who would want to read about it? Heller might have been like a guy he knows, a fellow G-B patient who has written an account of his bout with the debilitating affliction. "He could only move his eyes. He was some case. The irony," Heller explains, "is that he was a writer for an oil company, and he's getting rejection slips! He sent me one that said, 'We like it very much, but Joseph Heller's coming out with a book on this.'"

With Speed, his East Hampton housemate. (Joe lives in the big house with his former nurse Valerie Humphries; Speed lives in a smaller house on the property with Lou Ann Walters, of the *New York Times.*) Speed wrote his parts of *No Laughing Matter,* and Heller his. It is not a true collaboration.

"I don't think of having written with a collaborator at all," Heller cautions, pointing across a table crowded with food prepared by Speed, retired from the textile business and a self-described artist, cook, plumber, sculptor, hairdresser and playboy. "He wrote his pieces and gave them to me, and I wrote mine and dropped them off. . . . I was never sure if he read mine, and sometimes I would ask him a question about it—'Did you see . . . ?'—and then I'd get another chapter of his, and it might indicate to me that he *hadn't* read something in mine.

"He never has liked my work," Heller exclaims. "He loves my illness!"

At first, *No Laughing Matter* was to have been Speed's book, a collection of pieces he intended to call *Poor Speed, His Friend Joe Is Sick.* Joe, recovered, was finishing *God Knows* and doing his book tour while Speed "was writing down anecdotes." By late 1984, with nothing pressing to work on, Heller got involved.

"We talked a little bit about something we could do together," he says, laughing. "To make it worthwhile, in the sense that there could be money for it." Speed's book, he knew, "was not an idea [as suggested by Lu Ann Walther of Bantam] that would command much of an advance." (The best that agent Candida Donadio could get Speed for his own book was $20,000.)

"We had decided to do it," Heller remembers, "and I told him my idea for an opening chapter. And I said, 'Why don't you write about the afternoon when we were together and I began to get the symptoms?' Then I began thinking about what I'd put down in the next chapter—my getting the symptoms, what I did that day, and then getting to the hospital and his hearing about it. It's not really the same thing from different points of view; it's the same thing, as he knew it, and as I knew it. Often, I said something like, 'Why don't you do that so I can go into the details of being in Intensive Care?'"

For Speed, what was funny "in the beginning was that I really was very obnoxious with a lot of my friends who are writers, by saying, 'Hey, you know, Jesus, it's easy, I mean it's really easy! What are you talking about? This writing stuff is really easy.' I teased my friend Julie Green, who's in the diamond business: 'Hey Julie, you're crazy to be in the diamond business. Pitch in with us. Writing's easy! Come!' Like the Rover Boys." (Speed's attitude changed, though. "Everything I wrote I had to rewrite," he laughs.)

Novelist Heller, who doesn't think "of writing as easy or hard. It's the easiest kind of work for me to do. . . . I make it hard for myself, I get bored with it so fast," admits nonfiction "is much harder than fiction. There's a precision needed when dealing with information," he says, "and at the same time you need personality." He was frustrated "each time I wanted to find a way to change a word. I felt so trapped, wanting to say afternoon for day, but realizing that then I would have to talk about hours."

But the major difference for Heller is, "none of my books are realistic books, and this is, by necessity. So I try as infrequently as possible to relate things in chronological order."

Heller says he and Speed "had to figure out how much to tell about Guillain-Barré because we didn't want it to be a medical book." But he has done research on the syndrome that is included in *No Laughing Matter*. Statistics show that Guillain-Barré strikes 1.9 per million people each year. No one knows what causes it, though it often follows a viral

infection of an ordinary kind. It is "what we now consider an auto-
immunological disease—the immunological system probably begins
producing antibodies of a kind that attacks the tissues, the coverings of
the nerves in the peripheral nervous system, and by inflaming them, in
effect short-circuits the nerve impulses."

Contracting Guillain-Barré, Heller learned, meant "a gradual loss of
motor ability. It is progressive, but then after about 12–20 days, it
stops. It reaches what they call a plateau—there'll be no further damage
to the nerves." In some people this is total paralysis. Others, like Heller,
retain some ability of movement.

Recovery, "which nobody can affect or determine," is very slow.
Many people do not become fully functional again, but others do. "Just
the way the extent of damages is arbitrary," Heller says, "the extent of
recovery is also. The nerves begin regenerating, and then they don't
regenerate any further." Physical therapy, to overcome muscle atrophy,
can begin almost immediately.

Heller spent four months at Rusk Institute, where he underwent daily
therapy. "But there's nothing on the weekends," he remembers, "and
those are the worst days because it is hard to keep your mind occupied."
Valerie, who "never had so much fun taking care of a sick person,"
Heller jokes, came with him from Mt. Sinai to be his private nurse
during rehabilitation.

All the while that Joe was in the hospital, Speed was "acting sort
of like his *major domo,* going to his apartment, picking up his mail,
delivering it to him, getting his messages, delivering them to him. Then
I found it was easier to live there, since I had decorated it anyway."
Speed took care of all Joe's checks as well. "Rather than get a power of
attorney, Speed's something of an artist," Heller says, "so he could do
my signature better than I did. People would send me books to sign and
Speed would do it."

There was a funny episode from that, Heller relates. "When I was out
of the hospital, I went into a divorce trial"; Heller had separated from
his wife, Shirley, before he became ill. In an examination before trial,
"I was asked if I had ever written any checks to a woman my wife
suspected me of having an affair with over the past years. I said no,
which is the truth. And I thought it was the truth at the time I said it."

But before the actual trial began, "I went through my check stubs and
I saw a check for $50 to her." Before Guillain-Barré, when beginning

work on *God Knows*, Heller had taken an apartment in Santa Fe,
intending to write there for a few months a year. "When I realized I
wasn't going to go back there, I asked Speed to call the landlady and
give up the apartment, get my stuff sent back and send her 50 bucks to
cover the postage. So he had written out a check to this woman.

"When I said I had never written out a check, then, I had been telling
the truth. A year goes by—in the courtroom the lawyer tries to attack
my credibility, and he's allowed to read this question about the check
from the deposition. He said, 'This is the ledger in which the check is
noted,' and I said 'Let me see that. That's not my handwriting.' Then
my lawyer took over, 'Do you know who wrote that?' I said 'Yes'; he
said, 'Who?'; I pointed across the courtroom and said, 'Speed Vogel,
Irving Speed Vogel, he took over everything and wrote all my checks.'
The judge said, 'He's answered your question.'"

About 85% of G-B patients achieve what is considered 100% recovery—and Heller himself is considered 100% recovered despite a few
residual effects. He has not regained the full use of the rotator muscle of
his left shoulder, though he has learned to compensate unnoticeably for
its loss, and he has trouble saying words that require one to pucker and
close the mouth; his cheek muscles are still weak, which sometimes
creates problems for him while eating. The rest of his muscles, he says,
"don't work as well as they did before. The difficulties are in the very
fine muscles," he demonstrates, "in the fingers, the hand; it's very hard
for me to stick my left hand out with the elbow tucked in. It's hard
reading the *New York Times*."

Sixty when stricken, Heller, a runner and swimmer, was in peak
physical condition for his age. Now, though he walks, swims and jogs
regularly, Heller says, "I sometimes get cramps in the calves of my legs
just by moving. It doesn't happen often, but I get it a lot at night—any
sudden stretching, moving your arm when you're sleeping, turning your
leg one way or another. And this angers me because if I take a deep
breath to sigh, or occasionally sneeze or yawn, I will get cramps up my
whole torso into my neck. I know they'll go away in half a minute, but
it always takes me by surprise."

Throughout the entire ordeal, Heller never felt actual pain, "though
I wasn't all that comfortable and nights were intolerable." A lack of
"sensations we associate with being sick, a headache, nausea," made

it hard for him to identify himself as ill. Hence, the sense of humor throughout *No Laughing Matter*.

"Actually," Speed says, identifying how illness changed Heller, "what I found remarkable, and so did close friends, was that Joe suddenly got sweeter in many ways—and it was pretty hard, because he wasn't the old Joe and we started to worry! We wanted the old Joe back, but we were kind of touched all at once that he was a very different human being: he was patient, he was kind, he was all the things he never was before. So in some ways, of course, Guillain-Barré was beneficial."

"I think my sense of values has improved tremendously," Heller says. "Certain things that would upset me very much in the past—particular relationships—my ex-wife, Valerie, they don't bother me at all." Except Speed, in print, in their own book, he laughs. "There are a number of things that he writes about me which I don't like or I think are inaccurate, but of course, I felt it was important that he write his pieces and I write mine.

"He has me snarling," Heller says, "he has me a difficult, impolite person"—"Impolite? I use that as a euphemism for what you really are," interjects Speed—"And," Heller continues, unruffled, "I said to him I don't think I'm this way, but if this is the way you see me. . . . He said, 'Go ask Valerie.' So I asked Valerie, and she said he's right." Adds Speed, "He changed, but only for a while. Now he thinks he's okay again."

"I tell you," Heller laughs, "I'll never write another book with him."

Speed tries for the last word. "Before he never writes another book with me, I'll never write another book with him!"

"He's retired and I'm a writer," Heller explains. "In a sort of laid-back way, I'm a workaholic—I'm busy for two hours at a session and then I like to stop. . . . So Speed and I have a lot of time to hang around together."

Usually I Don't Want to Be Too Funny

David L. Middleton/1986

Previously unpublished. Printed by permission of the author.

Having recovered from Guillain-Barré syndrome and literally gotten
his feet back under him, the wheelchair period of his life now receding comfortably into the past, Joseph Heller is on the move again.
Catch-22, which announced the arrival of a prodigious talent and simultaneously blazed the trail for a new direction in the development of
fiction, was his only novel in the 1960s, but it was followed by two
books in the '70s and, at the time of this interview, Heller was working
on his third book of the '80s, the novel then called "Poetics" but
published in 1988 as *Picture This.*

The consensus opinion still holds *Catch-22* to be Heller's outstanding
work. The book continues to rack up impressive annual sales figures,
and Simon and Schuster recently reissued it in a reprint edition on the
occasion of its 25th anniversary. The *New York Times Book Review,*
which did not review the novel favorably a quarter of a century ago, ap-
plauded Heller's formative contribution to American letters with a lead
article by John W. Aldridge on October 26, 1986. The Air Force Academy had Heller on campus to participate in discussions of *Catch-22*
in particular and war fiction—especially including that based upon the
Vietnam experience—in general.

In early November, 1986, Heller was invited by the Department of
English of Trinity University, San Antonio, Texas, to give a public
lecture and to meet in small discussion groups with students as part of
the Stieren Arts Enrichment Series. I have compiled the following
interview-essay from the responses which the novelist gave on various
occasions during the four days of his visit. Like the answers, the queries
are collated, and I've also summarized them to give readers a clear
sense of the point of departure for Heller's answers. All of his words
are direct quotations.

Because of its being the anniversary of Catch-22, *a great deal of public attention has been focused again on the content and the form of that book. Mr. Heller was asked whether, as he looks back on it, this novel is his favorite, and, if such a thing were possible, would he rewrite it in any way.*

Well, yes, I'm very pleased with it, and it may be a "favorite" insofar as I have one. There is nothing in it I would want to change. I'm still very happy with the narrative construction, with the overall structure, with the ending—and the rightness of that ending has certainly been debated. It's impossible for me to think of *Catch-22* being told within a different structure, or of the characters being presented realistically. I really don't take the time, when I'm at work on a book, to make a decision about whether character or structure comes first. I get an idea for a book, and then I get a lot of sentences down on notecards, and as that grows, I begin to organize them. I certainly do not advocate my method to anyone else. It's extremely wasteful, getting a version in longhand and then going over it in typescript, and so on. But I know by now that it's the only way I *can* write.

I had very early success as a writer. I hadn't started undergraduate college work until I was 22, but as an undergraduate taking a short story writing course, I began having those stories published in very good magazines. As a result, I got quite overconfident. When I left college, I began to realize the stories were really not much good, and I took a "vacation" for several years. My stories were secondary. I would be reading other short story writers and writing about the experiences their characters were having. Not until I was 30 years old did I feel I should try writing a novel. That novel was *Catch-22.*

The book has been incredibly durable. Even now when I'm out speaking on campuses, I'll be standing in line in a college bookstore and there will be two people there, one a student, the other a middle-aged parent, and both will tell me that the book has changed their lives. That is very satisfying.

Nor did the success which it ultimately achieved inhibit me later. It never has. If anything, when I was writing the second book, and I worked on it twice as long as *Catch-22,* I was *encouraged* by the growing success of the first book, which was not all that big a hit when it was first produced. It encouraged me because I knew that as *Catch-22* became better known, it would attract a more serious, careful reading of the current book I was doing. I'm not competing with that first work at all. In fact each of my four works is quite distinctive in terms of what we might call "style," for want of a better word.

Young writers are always curious about the process of submitting manuscripts. Catch-22 *is a fascinating case because it turned out to be such a big book for Heller and so important for American fiction writing generally, an experiment in handling such serious material as World War II. What procedure was followed in trying to place the novel?*

Since I wasn't thoroughly convinced the experiment would be a success, rather than spend time wastefully, when I had the first chapter, I had it submitted for publication, and it appeared in *New World Writing*. Then I received a few letters from editors of publishing companies expressing interest in seeing more. So when I had 200–250 pages, I had that submitted to those editors who had shown interest. The fact that the response was good was important. Had there been *no* interest in that section of the novel, I am not at all sure I would have continued. Everybody I've met who is writing has a substantial mixture of emotions about it. There is a great deal of apprehension, mixed with an almost egotistical amount of confidence—which is really not very stable.

Hadn't Mr. Heller's sense of "stability" been affirmed over and over by the sustained success of that first book?

Oh, yes, indeed. In other countries where I've been, in Europe, the book does very well. In Czechoslovakia the only time it was out of print was in 1968 when the Russians came in for about two years. Then there were no editions, but now there are. I've been a failure in France until *God Knows*. None of my books sold well there at all, even though gradually everybody knew about *Catch-22*. There were no editions. It's now in print because *God Knows* was a big hit, and then the first book was brought out in a new translation. *Catch-22* is in Sweden. They use the phrase there in English, and from someone who had recently been in Russia, I learned it's there, too—some Russian word that means "catch." So it exists *all over.*

To show you how relevant the material of that novel is, I would say that just going to lunch today [November 5, 1986] and reading a newspaper, I was absolutely befuddled to see that Pepsi Cola, which owns the Pizza Huts, is concluding a deal with Russia to establish a thousand Pizza Huts in Russia. At the same time, we have Americans being shot

down in Nicaragua for delivering arms to rebels to continue fighting
against a Russian-influenced country! Now, does that make any sense?

*Understanding the early history of the drafting of that novel may be
useful to a student or scholar struggling to make a claim about its
uniqueness. At the time he began work on it at the age of 30, other examples of war fiction which might have been at hand as models were so
very different in both conception and execution that one must wonder
to what extent he was aware of being influenced by literary antecedents.
What were these influences, and was the novelist conscious of being in
virgin territory and thus at risk with his work?*

Yes, I certainly was influenced by Céline's novel, *Journey to the
End of the Night*. Also, I suppose I knew that the method of presenta-
tion of information, which is very indirect, was influenced by William
Faulkner's *Absalom, Absalom!,* and to a lesser degree by *The Sound
and the Fury*. As regards tone, I was well aware of the comic novels of
Evelyn Waugh.

But I want to make a distinction here between an "influence" and a
"model." There is nothing that functioned like a "model" for what I
wanted to do, and I knew in that sense that I was doing something very
original. I was dealing with a familiar period, World War II, but in a
different setting. I didn't begin the book until the war was over for eight
or nine years. So I was aware that I was dealing with that subject in an
unusual *way*.

Earlier you asked about Kafka. I like Kafka's use of anxiety and
mystification, but there are very few written works of his that I like. I'm
very much aware that all my books, even the comic sections, have that
type of mystification or exaggeration, or make use of anxiety in them in
a way that I might not have come to on my own had I not been aware of
Kafka. But I don't like his novels, and most of his short stories I don't
care for either. It's just that—attitude.

At the same time that I was writing *Catch-22*, other American writers,
with no contact with one another, were writing books different from
each other, but also moving away from the conventional form of the
novel. Ken Kesey was writing *One Flew Over the Cuckoo's Nest*,
Thomas Pynchon was writing *V.*, Kurt Vonnegut was writing *Cat's
Cradle,* and Jack Kerouac had published *On the Road* about a year or
two before. J. P. Donleavy was working on *The Ginger Man,* too. All

of us were doing those things pretty much simultaneously. A mistake
many people make is to pick the date of publication as the time of the
writing of the piece. So they call *Catch-22* a "novel of the '60's." But
most of that work was done in the period between 1953 and 1960.

*Indeed, our current sense of literary history demonstrates that Heller
and others were producing a new kind of American fiction in the '60's,
as though they had anticipated and were as a group rising to take up the
gauntlet Philip Roth would fling down in his seminal essay, "Writing
American Fiction," in 1961. Yet* Good as Gold *adapts a traditional
narrative structure, and* God Knows *draws heavily upon traditional
Biblical subject matter as well as on the device of the internal monologue.*

Good as Gold does come the closest to following a conventional form
of narration. It has a chronological order, the protagonist does have a
"goal" (whereas in my other books they don't), and he is moving toward
that goal. But even there, the degree of extravagant exaggeration into
the improbable indicates to the reader that he's not supposed to treat
the work as anything but a book. In one paragraph, in fact, I made
reference to the book *as a book.* And one chapter [a subsection of
Chapter VII] begins with Gold noting that he's spending a lot of time
"in his book" (that is, in the book the reader has at hand) having meals
with people.

But no, I don't think there is a return to the traditional generally
in my later works. In *God Knows,* one of the aspects away from the
conventional is the mixing of the Biblical language, verbatim, with
literary language and contemporary vernacular, as though it were the
author's or the narrator's own. I suggest by that that the narrator, King
David, is still alive, still telling his story. In fact, at the end of the book,
he *is* still alive and is still telling his story. I also took the anachronistic
approach there, having David talk about the state of Maine and making
him feel competitive toward Shakespeare as a writer. He does manifest
what I actually perceive to be an extraordinary amount of competitive
feeling among contemporary American novelists. At the same time,
we're very generous to each other, very helpful. Some have been to me,
and I've tried to be to others, but there is that feeling of where each of
us stands in relation to everybody else at a given time. That bothers

David a great deal. It shows up in relation to Shakespeare, and in his being patronizing to John Milton.

Also, my David—who is presumably a Jewish king, although he's not particularly Jewish in the Bible—he is Jewish in my book. David in the Bible is not at all what anybody would associate with Jewishness. But he's also written Bach's "B Minor Mass" and Mozart's "Requiem," and either Bach's or somebody else's "Ave Maria." I like very much the idea of his writing religious, Christian music. And I tried very hard in the book not to make any reference to anything in the New Testament. Only twice did I use a phrase that's in there. One is an obscure phrase that I finally tracked down as coming from Matthew: the birds of the air have their nest, the beasts of the field have their lair, but the son of man has nowhere to lay his head. And the second is when David in one of his tirades against women—almost all of which, I think in fact every phrase, is taken from one part of the Bible or another—says it's better to marry than to burn. That's most directly from Paul.

In *Something Happened,* you do have an interior monologue and a confessional novel, and you also have an unreliable narrator. He knows things which he doesn't tell. And the action is progressing. In the conventional first-person novel, though, the action is complete when the narrator starts discussing it. In *Something Happened,* that isn't so.

All of my books except *Good as Gold* are retrospective. That is, the person in the book who is "writing" the story has already been through most of what has happened. The question for me, then, is how to present that so it is engrossing to the reader and will create a certain amount of suspense. The writing becomes a task of "proportion" . . . I don't have the word I want . . . of discovering the proper formula, the chemical mixture, how much of what to introduce how quickly— in what proportion.

The short story, "Love, Dad," stands alone so well that some critics may find it difficult to accept the explanation that it was made from material excised from Catch-22. *Does Mr. Heller customarily try to cut publishable stories from work in progress?*

That story was from the book. All my books are close to 200 typewritten pages longer when I finish them than either I or the editor wants

them to be. So I'm very happy to be cutting. They are all cut at least
100 pages, maybe 200. Usually there are no episodes taken out. What
I cut are repetitions. But that story was about eight or ten or twelve
pages of a chapter in the novel, and the whole incident was deleted.

I was at the Air Force Academy a week or two ago, and the English
Department faculty are doing a lot of scholarship on that book. They
reminded me about another chapter I had forgotten entirely. They had
been into the archives and by looking at one of the early manuscripts,
they knew about material which subsequently disappeared from the
published book. As they were talking about it and telling me, I couldn't
remember, but it came back to me. I'm going to find that section, and
perhaps publish it. If I did, I would offer it to *Playboy* first because I'm
boycotting the 7-Eleven stores.

*This new computer age has forced many of us to play catch-up as we
set about to adapt our lives to the ubiquitous machine. Heller has noted
several times in the past (and did so again during the Trinity visit) that
he tends to work in longhand. The novelist was asked whether the computer had any impact on his composing strategies.*

Oh, yes, almost certainly. One thing it's done is it has slowed me
down. People tell me it takes four to six months with the machine to
memorize the commands. I've memorized most of it now and the way
I'm using it is as an intermediate step between the longhand version and
the first typewritten version. In the pre-word-processing past, when I
had a fairly long section in longhand, 200–300 pages, I would then go
to the typewriter and begin rewriting. The rewriting involves a great
deal of cutting, because often I put the same thing in different places
knowing I've done it before. But I'm not sure just where to look. I've
gone over the longhand version with a pen first, and then in the course
of typing, and typing slowly, there will be new thoughts, improvements
in dialogue, amplifications, and then I would have a typewritten version
which I went over with a pencil, making changes, which I'd then give
to a typist.

Now, from the handwritten version, I go to the word processor,
repeating that same process. There it's a tremendous help in making
changes. You don't have to start a new page. And then I found—with
this new novel, which will be called "Poetics"—when it was printed, I
could read it again, make changes, and then go to a typewriter and type

a new copy. The computer is also very handy for storing research information or notes.

Did Mr. Heller approve of the changes that were made in Catch-22 *when it was adapted for film by Mike Nichols, particularly the presentation of the cinematic Yossarian as more subdued and melancholy than his fictional equivalent?*

I neither approve nor disapprove. They make movies, and I sold the motion picture rights to them. When I did, I knew that was going to happen, and I really haven't much sympathy for those authors you occasionally see on television who complain about what was done to their work. If they really cared that much, they wouldn't sell the motion picture rights. I *didn't* care when I sold the rights.

You have very different objectives in writing fiction and nonfiction. The fiction I write involves a great deal of confusion. It's very slow in giving the reader answers, whereas the main obligation in writing nonfiction would be to give information clearly, usually in chronological order. I've had a crack at nearly every form of writing that we know about, with a good deal of success, and then I decided I wanted to write fiction rather than anything else. I prefer it over working for movies or television, for one reason, because you're working by yourself. In the other forms, there's always some degree of collaboration. You're a salaried employee. It's not even real writing. You write something that somebody else wants written a certain way, and then they have it rewritten to specifications.

When I'm working on a book, all my spare thinking time and writing time is devoted to that book. Not even to the *whole* book either, but to the next paragraph, the next page, the next transition. I like writing fiction because I'm in intimate contact with myself. It's thoroughly engrossing for me, and one reason is that it's difficult. In the past, I have left a book—my second novel—to work on something else, but that was out of economic need. Now I can't conceive of doing anything else until a book is finished.

For a long while after its appearance, certain aspects of Catch-22 *seem to have been misunderstood. Has that happened with his other books, and if so, has Heller now lost respect for an audience—popular or academic—which misreads? When engaged in the fiction writing*

*process, does he have a particular kind of reader in mind, and does he
then aim at generating any certain response in that person?*

No, they haven't been misunderstood. Occasionally I'll read a review which I feel is inaccurate, but I seldom disagree with even the
unfavorable reviews of my books, because the points of disagreement
are usually matters of taste. I would have been a fool not to expect a
lot of hostility, particularly from Jewish reviewers, to *Good as Gold*.
Politically I was taking dead aim at neo-conservatives, and it was very
uncomfortable for a good many Jewish people who were leaning toward
a conservative viewpoint and who want to be assimilated more than I
want to be. I would have been a fool not to expect to offend many
people who have sensitive feelings towards the Bible and who were
angered by *God Knows*. Those who say it's sacrilegious and disre-
spectful are not being inaccurate. It *is* sacrilegious in the loosest sense
of the word. When a reviewer says there is obscenity or blasphemy or
sacrilege in a book, or says that *Good as Gold* is distasteful, I would
have to say the reviewer is expressing his reaction, and it is justifiable.

If they say my books are long and repetitious, with the exception of
Good as Gold, they're right. But some others are designed deliberately
to be repetitious. In *Something Happened,* there is a psychological
justification for it. It's very close to human nature to think repeatedly
about things, to go back to certain episodes. In *Catch-22,* a number of
the large actions have occurred before the book begins, and they are
referred to as the author gets close to revealing them in their fullness to
the reader. *God Knows* is similar to *Something Happened.* David can't
get over the loss of those two children. Most parents can't, and their
minds will just keep returning to that. My books are simply long as
contemporary novels go. The average novel is about 300 pages or less,
and mine are 400 and over. But I've been very fortunate. I've never had
a disagreement with a publisher over a manuscript.

In writing a book, one has a distant hope that upon publication, trum-
pets are going to sound. If, however, the response is negative, that does
not affect me. I would rather get good reviews than bad ones, but it
doesn't matter to me now as much as it did with *Catch-22,* when those
first two or three poor reviews kept it from selling successfully the first
year. Had those been better, particularly that one in the *New York Times
Book Review,* it might have become a best-selling book, which it never
was.

I do write for a particular audience, but it's not that specific. I don't think about it, but I'd like my audience to be at least as well educated as I am, and to know something about politics and literature. I like to think I'm writing a novel that I would love reading if somebody else had written it. That's a way of saying I'm writing to my own taste, and I'm fortunate that my own taste is the taste of a good many people in this country and overseas.

If I didn't think people would want to read my work, I wouldn't begin it. That's why when I have a section completed, I generally submit it. I think like everybody else, I want to be widely read.

There's a wonderful biography of James Joyce by Richard Ellmann, and in it you find that the amount of self-promoting he did with *Ulysses* is phenomenal. The story is hilarious. You would not know, but from the time he wrote his first book of *Ulysses,* Joyce was recruiting people to write papers about it, to read it, to buy it.

Certainly I'll never have an audience as large as Sidney Sheldon or Judith Krantz or Jackie Collins. That won't happen. But it's not unrealistic for me now, after *Catch-22,* to reach a sizable audience in hardcover and another sizable audience in the paperback edition. I don't choose easy books to write—well, maybe I do. But they're the only kind of books I *could* write. I could not write a book like those of Stephen King. But *Catch-22* is twenty-five years old, and it still sells in very large numbers each year, and that is very rewarding for me.

Does an awareness of audience extend to Mr. Heller's literally giving work in progress to a colleague or friend to read and criticize?

I do *not* read pages to my friends, and I will never let anybody read an unpublished story to me. I won't even let them tell me a long joke. What I will do is begin showing sections of a book to people when I get to a certain point in the writing of it. I am not looking for a detailed analysis. What I want is a general reaction. If they're confused about something, I'd like to pick that up from their remarks. Or—and here's something I have to watch carefully—if they're excessively pleased about something, I feel that's dangerous. The easiest way for me to get a pleased response from readers is to be funny, and I can do that. But usually I don't want to be too funny. So if there's too much of that, I feel I have to go back and tone things down.

The effect of the opening sections of *Catch-22* was really much more confusing than I wanted it to be. I gave it to two friends, one of whom was a very careful reader, and he could not keep track of those first 80–100 pages *at all*. I knew if he couldn't do it, it was more tangled and obscure than I wished, so I began redoing those early sections.

Since he had just indicated an effort to guard against selling out to a glib humor, it seemed fitting to discuss what Heller believes is affirmed in his fiction. Primo Levi's Survival in Auschwitz *speaks of the ways a person can be "decomposed" and made to lose characteristic, human properties. Heller has not used the Holocaust as a context for his fiction, but his characters do face extremely serious kinds of political and social and personal chaos. As they do so, what is it that keeps them "whole" or "human"?*

I believe my characters have a fairly accurate view of themselves in relation to their surroundings. All of them are susceptible to a feeling of self-pity and a feeling of being menaced, circumscribed, that amounts to social injustice. Now, with David, he's fairly proud of that, of the way he manufactures occasions to get rid of his enemies, all of which come from the Bible. Also, in my books, I don't believe I ever create situations in which there is very real, unremitting horror that is inescapable. Yossarian's moral agony or torment, for example, doesn't begin until the war against Germany is just about over. Then he senses, and eventually verifies, rumors that other people in other units are being returned home after completing a certain number of missions. So it dawns on him that the Fascist enemy is receding as a threat and the new enemy are people wearing his own uniform and speaking his own language, serving the same country. That is not nearly the same as being in prison, or being tortured. It's not the same as being in a concentration camp. All of my people do live in the free society that America is.

One can find a great deal of fault in this country, and you and I do, with certain individuals or the insensitivity of bureaucracies or the obsession with money that has grown so large in this vast generation. Senator Goldwater said he's glad to be out of Washington because the obsession with money there and in our business life has become disgusting to him. All of us can object to that, and we may find that our deadliest enemies are not overseas in Russia—which is an abstraction—but here, with people who are opposed to abortion, with people who don't want fairness in the schools. Nevertheless, it is still a free society that my characters live in. I would not *ever* make a comparison between a writer living in Russia and a writer living here. And somebody in Auschwitz or being interrogated is in a much different position—there are interrogation techniques which can demoralize a person completely and get confessions without torture. But my characters are not in that horrible a situation.

I also think there is an area of choice my characters have. Of course choice in crucial issues never involves a satisfactory solution. If it did, there would not be a dilemma. Yossarian, before he takes off with a feeling of exuberance—see, here is something I would change in *Catch-22*. It is stated that he does not expect to get to Sweden. But there are people who have missed that. It was certainly missed in the movie. So I would emphasize the fact that he has no *realistic expectation* of getting to Sweden from where he is. The chaplain says to him, "You'll never get there," and he says, "I know that. But at least I'll be trying." There is no happy solution.

Yossarian's got everything he wants and he's still unhappy. For David there's no solution because he's old. He's old and he's going to die. Yet *that's* not a dilemma. We face that, we face it because we have no choice. Our ancestors faced it and our contemporaries are facing it.

Isn't King David in God Knows *choosing of his own free will to reject God at the end of his life? He appears to be motivated largely by aggressive anger toward God for what he takes to be colossal injustices done him.*

Well, no, I think he would like to have a relationship with his God, but he can't. He's lost like Slocum, who says, "I wish I could believe in God." Sure, David wants his God back, but he's experienced too much, or his experiences are such that he *can't* get him back. So in that sense, David's predicament can't be called a dilemma. He's a man suffering what many of us do suffer. I wish I could believe in God, and I wish he could be the idealized God of the Old Testament and the New Testament. I have to say "idealized," because in fact in the Old Testament, he's not such a pleasant being, and in the New Testament, I don't think he's that pleasant either. God doesn't appear much in the New Testament, but the extent to which he is present, he's not somebody I could approve of. A being who sends his son here to be crucified in order to redeem sin—I mean, one would not have to be a god to erase the blackboard. The whole idea of justifying that original sin thousands of years later is not an approach that I or David or many reasonable people could approve of.

I didn't say this in the book, but I think that the feeling many religious people have for God today would indicate that God is for them more of a woman than a man. I think the Catholic attraction for Mary illustrates the embodiment of those features of a Jehovah who has *none* of them. Not even forgiveness. Jesus is something else. I'm talking about God.

King David is pretty clearly the victim of a shift in values that grows out of his advanced age and impending death. Combined, those devastating influences leave him totally disinterested in a variety of satisfactions, including the lovely Abishag. In the sense that David's problem is a function of age, would Mr. Heller compare David's frustration with that of the younger Yossarian or Bruce Gold?

Yes, certainly. King David doesn't care about Abishag, but that's not to disparage the girl. He's just at the point in his life when he wants something else. There was a time earlier, with Bathsheba, when he was willing to give up his God for that woman.

I don't say this in the book, but I would guess that when he says he wants his God back, he also wants his youth back, he wants that hope back he had as a young man. That's why the vision comes to him of himself as a young man playing for Saul and he reaches for a javelin to throw at him. He hates his situation, that has moved him from a hopeful young man to an old man who's got no power left. The only power he still has is to decide whether Solomon or Adonijah will reign, and he really doesn't care. That's why he says in the first chapter that it might make a difference to him if he cared about his children or the future of his country, but he doesn't care about either of them anymore.

I'm trying to suggest there too that to him, as to many people who take a historical approach, it really doesn't matter who one names as a successor. There are very few periods in the life of this country when it made a difference which man won the election for president—in terms of that man's character or ability.

As one of today's supremely skilled satirists, though, whose tempera-

ment tends toward the cynical, Mr. Heller was pressed as to whether he
finds himself giving in to the temptation to denigrate everything? *Does*
individual effort, personal decision-making, not induce a difference in
the evolution of our daily lives as we now lead them? Is it characteristic
of his fiction to be without hope as regards human life in the aggregate
and optimistic as regards any particular life?

I would say as far as the course of history or the fate of nations goes,
I don't think it matters. If we look back, in *God Knows* it really doesn't
matter what happens to whole nations. The fact that Spain declined,
or Jerusalem declined, or the Roman Empire declined, when we look
back upon it now, it has not had that much effect upon us. Incidentally,
I'm not much on philosophy. What I'm saying now is not something
that I would advocate for other people to subscribe to.

What I'm saying is that the individual life is indeed very meaningful.
In fact, what happens to an individual, from the individual's point of
view, might be *all* that matters. It's in the collective sense that David
does not care what happens to his realm after he dies or what children
he has left. The two he cared about, the infant and his favorite, are both
dead.

Heller mentions in No Laughing Matter *that he had about one third of*
the manuscript of God Knows *in hand before being struck down by the*
paralysis which brought his work to a total, if temporary, halt. Life-
threatening illnesses usually have the effect of getting one's attention,
and occasionally they provide the motivation for radical changes in
one's life. Even though he was well into the fictionalizing of the Biblical
David, was the Guillain-Barré syndrome so arresting as to affect the
shape of the novel substantially or to alter the way Heller-the-survivor
now lives and writes?

Actually I feel great since I had this disease. I think I'm better medi-
cally than I was before. Oh, it's left me with muscular weaknesses,
which you'll see when I go up stairs, but I'm in very good condition
now. And, no, it had no effect on the design or even the details of the
book.

Go back to the fact that I had that book very well begun, and I had
the ending. I had the last two or three pages on paper. I *knew* where
I was going. The same thing was true of *Catch-22*. I'm often asked

how I was able to sustain interest in it over that seven-year period. The answer is I was already an adult. It dealt with events of the past, and my approach was to show how that affected events in the present. My political attitudes were shaped, my attitude toward integration, my attitude toward the national nightmare of McCarthy and the House Un-American Activities Committee. I had already an attitude of skepticism about the veracity and the ability of people in high office. And my *income level* was fairly good by that time. The only thing that could perhaps have affected me would have been some traumatic event— another Pearl Harbor. Even an assassination couldn't change me that much, because within two to three weeks, the government would be operating again. So not only was the plan for the book on paper, and notes for working it out, but also my attitudes were pretty much set.

The same thing is true with *God Knows*. The idea for doing something on the story of David came to me while I was daydreaming. It came to me in the form of . . . of a daydream! The daydreams I had pretty much dictated the character of the book. Only after thinking of it for days did I go to the Bible and read the story of David, and then I found so much there that I had not suspected existed. And some of it, I saw, would fit right in with that tone, almost of flippancy, that makes it possible for David to have a kind of timeless resiliency so that he can be reflecting on his life as though he's still in bed and still dying. Even now.

I did not begin writing it—again, I did set down the first paragraph, and then I began organizing it, collecting material, figuring out where I was going to end. The idea for the ending, even the actual language, comes to me two or three years before I get there. That's one of the private thrills I get from writing a book, to write something which I know is going to be a good beginning or a climax, and then reach it two or three years after I first put it down on paper. A particular instance that comes to mind from *God Knows* is the chapter which begins with Joab coming to David and using the biblical quote about the trees putting forth green leaves [Chapter 10, "Naked We Were"] and David says "So what?" and Joab tells him they've got to invade Europe. Another one is when David is looking over at Bathsheba and he hears a voice saying, "Go ahead, take her. Fuck her, fuck her" [also Chapter 10]. And he says, "Is that you, God?" When it turns out to be Mephistopheles, David says, "Oh, shit." I had that on an index card maybe two years before I got to it, knowing I would treasure it, and when I got to it, I said, "Hallelujah!" It's like a journey that takes three or four years, but the arrival at the destination is still deeply satisfying.

Now, when I got out of the hospital and started writing, I found myself putting in certain physical symptoms. When Bathsheba gives him a bowl of food to eat, I had his fingers trembling, maybe two or three things of that nature. Those were coming from my own experience. My hands were trembling then and they probably still do when I hold a fork. But I took those kinds of details out again, realizing they were not adding anything new. If I were going to do things like that, I would have to go back to the beginning and have his hands tremble. I do have him feel cold from the beginning, and that's pretty much what I stuck to. I confined myself to what was part of the original plan.

The illness had no effect on the book other than to interrupt it, and then it actually accelerated its completion. While I was in the hospital, I believed I had three years more work to do on the book. When I submitted what I had to the publisher and he wanted to publish it, a contract was prepared that provided for those three years. I would get income for that time. But then I finished it in a year and a half, or less than a year and a half, and began outlining and collecting material for *No Laughing Matter*. So the illness—I couldn't go any place without somebody helping me, so I was home a great deal. Since I was home in a wheelchair, I was able to write. I'm out of the wheelchair now, but that work pattern, that living pattern has remained. I still spend much of each day, sometimes three parts of each day, writing. I try to work from 10 until noon, or until I get done what I know I want to get done, that small segment, three handwritten pages or occasionally five. Or perhaps only two and a half. Then I can read it in the afternoon, and I can repeat that work pattern in the afternoon. And sometimes I'll get up in the evening just to finish a paragraph or do a transition, and before I know it, I've got another three pages in less than two hours.

That's my life now. I'm past 63 years old. I've moved out of the city. I enjoy writing more than anything else, and those things that are related to writing like organizing material, doing research, taking notes, and reading books that will sort of give me information.

I've got Thucydides with me here in San Antonio because I'm going to use certain sections of it in "Poetics." I've not read it before, but in books I have read about the Greek period, there are many quotations from Thucydides which I've written down on my note cards. Now I'm going to read the full chapters that enclose those quotations. That kind of reading done in relation to writing I enjoy doing. I actually think I'm working when I'm doing reading of that kind.

As an author, he must have made an early decision to stick closely to the Biblical sources of the King David story for narrative incidents. In addition, whole sections of dialogue are often lifted from the King James version of the Bible. Was there ever a time when the original material took over and seemed effectively to control the author, like the "facts" of a nonfiction novel? Was Mr. Heller aware of being "constrained" by his sources?

I was never constrained. There was so much there that I could use. I took the basic episodes in the life of David, which really begins before David appears in the Bible, and I have some of Moses, a little bit of Abraham, and what I did was include them accurately, the way they are in the Bible, and begin to embellish them.

The concern I had was really how far to go with the use of anachronism, including language as well as references. I realized there's always a danger in going too far. If I had wanted just to write a comic book, I could have taken out the serious elements, but that would have become a commonplace form of humor.

The very necessary events concerning David and Goliath and Bathsheba and Jonathan—those all work to my advantage. I invent dialogue for him and Bathsheba. As the novel took shape in my imagination, it encompassed *almost all* of those episodes from David's life. It turned out that many others there was no room for. There is one in which he has Saul's grandchildren hung on some pretext, but that would have presented him in such an unsympathetic light as to change the book, so I simply omitted them. Of course you could not tell the story of David without Goliath. Conceivably it could be told without much of the antecedent episodes from the life of Saul. And it could be told without making much of Samuel. As David says, Samuel doesn't even appear in and is not mentioned in the second book of Samuel. But as the novel occurred to me and I began to see it imaginatively, it incorporated those episodes. And it did incorporate a good many references which eventually I decided to leave out.

Also, I've tried to make use of certain ambiguities. In the Bible there are two accounts of Saul's death, one in First Samuel, the other at the beginning of Second Samuel. In one, he falls on his sword; he asks his servant to kill him, which is right out of *Antony and Cleopatra*. In the other one, a wandering individual from one of the out-tribes he's eliminated passes a room where Saul is and Saul asks him to kill him, which he does. The killer then comes to David with Saul's bracelets and tells him what he's done, and David has him killed for stretching out his hand to kill the Lord's Anointed. And what I do is have David mention both versions and say the way you feel about Saul's death depends on which you believe.

The Bible we get from King James has four hypothetical sources that were used to compile the Pentateuch. A "J" source, an "E," a "P," and something else—a "D," I think. Much of the work of that King James group was to consolidate earlier versions of the Bible, as well as to translate them into English. I may be wrong there. They may have been consolidated before, but there are definitely four versions of the early section of the Bible, dating perhaps 1,000 years apart. There are two accounts for how Adam was created. One is that the Lord says, "Let there be man," and the other is he makes a statue out of dust and breathes into it, but there are two different creation accounts.

At any rate, I was not "confined" by the given account. I did invent that conversation with Joab about wanting to go up through Europe and conquer Germany and England and Scotland by building on what seems to be the martial nature of Joab. It was natural to turn him into that kind of person. The essential brutality of the man is there in the two or three times when he ruthlessly, *ruthlessly* kills people. The point is that there were enough episodes there for me to feel "liberated" by the material. I think there are other Biblical stories in which I would not be able to do that. The story of Joseph is very narrow. It's good at the beginning, but then he suddenly drops out. Jacob's and David's are, I think, the two longest stories in the Old Testament. And if somebody wants to— I won't—they could see parallels between Jacob and David in their feeling toward children, for instance.

John Gardner was an advocate of what could be called "supply-side aesthetics." He proclaims (in On Moral Fiction) *that it is time novelists began to resist this century's tendency toward trendy cynicism and instead set about writing the kinds of stories that provide society with*

myths to live by, *not to die by. Fictionalizing scripture, to what extent
was Mr. Heller, either consciously or unconsciously, also engaging in
"sacramentalizing" fiction.*

I would say to no extent. What I'm doing has been done before.
Other novelists have written about David. And there are countless examples of historical fiction. We may be in danger of thinking *God
Knows* is a work of accomplishment in areas where it isn't. It may be
better than the others, but that has been done before.

I am not particularly interested in the Bible nor in David. The first
part of his story is awfully silly, actually, and very familiar. I'm not
particularly interested in religion beyond the level at which it appears in
God Knows and in almost all my books. There are a couple of dialogues
in *Catch-22*, and Slocum in *Something Happened* thinks about God
occasionally. But there is no effort on my part to delve deeply into it.

I suppose in that sense I'm kind of unscrupulous. Henry Kissinger in
Good as Gold is only interesting to me as a subject to insult.

*In a frequently anthologized essay, Joan Didion writes about the
sense in which the act of reading is "intrusive," a kind of forcible
invasion of an audience's most private space. Isn't the reverse also
true? Doesn't a reader have the potential to intrude upon a story in a
potentially creative way, and perhaps more importantly, doesn't the
writing of a story have such an impact on an author that it threatens to
take its creator over completely and change him or her in the process?*

I'm not sure I understand the question. But what I do feel is this.
Writing fiction, and probably nonfiction, is basically a manipulative
experience that is rather cold and detached. Manipulative in the sense
that one is aware of a "wish" and an obligation—if that wish is to be
fulfilled—of being intriguing. Of being appealing and of manipulating
the responses of the reader. Or at least gaining his attention, engineering
a response, creating enough interest. The "detached" part comes in
when I am writing about an experience that tended in actuality to be
pathetic. In writing it I am not experiencing pathos. I may have experienced it before, and I will recognize the intrinsic possibilities of
that scene. The death of Snowden in *Catch-22* as I described it is still
vivid in my mind. I knew what impact I wanted that to have. And each
time I've read from that, no matter how many people are in the audi-
torium, there will be a total silence until I'm finished. But when I came

to write that, that was written in perhaps one evening. I wrote perhaps six or eight handwritten pages and I knew it was right. I rewrote them, but in writing it, I'm organizing details in the best way to make them effective, forgetting that I was affected by the subject of those details. A person who's in a mood of deep compassion, or anger, or depression, is not going to feel like writing. Northrop Frye says this about Shakespeare. It was conjectured that Shakespeare wrote his tragedies after the death of his son. But Frye says a man in a state of grief is not going to be able to write *King Lear* or *Hamlet*. It's the same way for me in writing that scene. When writing that death scene, when I had it on paper, my mood was one of exaltation. I was the writer, not the reader, the man who created that event and put it at a certain point in the book where it was going to be profoundly affecting to the reader. I felt triumphant when I finished it, not compassionate, not horrified. Triumphant.

What I'm saying is that the writer is made to be manipulative, he's cold, he's detached. A man writing a tragedy, Arthur Miller, with *Death of a Salesman,* which has such a pathetic ending, when he attended the previews and heard the weeping in the audience, he didn't want to weep with them. He wanted to walk outside and say, "By George, we've done it!"

I don't know what Joan Didion said, but I can say that I write and I want my books to be read. The reader is not intruding on me if he's reading my book. If someone says to me, "I'm reading your book and I love it," I welcome that kind of intrusion. Her proposition does not sound significant. In justification, I'll say I'm either misunderstanding what you're saying, or you're not giving me the full argument. I can't imagine that immersing oneself in an author's story would be an intrusion. It reminds me of one of Aristotle's silly propositions in which he wonders whether the dead are affected by what we do. The book is published, and once it's out there, thousands of people read it without our even knowing about it. Let me just say I don't understand it. There are many things about writing and reading literature that I'm *eager* to admit I don't understand.

She may be saying this: Will the reader understand it if I say this way? Must I say more? Must I say less? Am I being as confusing as I want to be, or am I being too confusing? In my case, am I being too repetitious, am I moving too quickly? Am I too turgid or too obscure? Those are questions I ask myself in doing *Catch-22* and everything else.

She may mean that the reader intrudes that way, interfering with something that is total self-expression. The adolescent view of writing, that one writes whatever one feels like writing, spontaneously, at the moment it comes to one, is more nearly a form of therapeutic expression than it is carefully arranged literary art. Essays, poems, novels are all planned and rewritten. One reason they are is to satisfy oneself. I've never written anything that I didn't feel I would enjoy reading. If she means that, that there is an implied communication between the author and reader, and the author's awareness of it, then I would agree.

Each of Heller's first four novels represents a distinctive departure from the others. Does the novel in progress also take a new direction in either content or style? With what technical problems of fiction writing is he preoccupied at present?

In terms of prose, yes, it's quite different. I'm trying to write a book that is going to read, without my emphasizing it, more like a lecture than a written work, a lecture given by someone who is slightly pedantic and a little condescending to his readers. There is almost no literary language in it so far, and I don't think there's a single adverb in it that ends in -*ly*. And I've used very few adjectives. In that sense, there is a completely different tone than what I've written before, and it is more of an intellectual book. It has very little in the way of emotion in it.

I think I'll be finished by next February. I got the idea a year ago last October, so I've really moved along on it. I may read the opening paragraph tonight, and I may read the last lines of the ending paragraph, and my joke will be, "Now if I could just get what comes between."

As to "technical" problems, I am always interested only in those that I'm encountering in the book at hand. I've never had a "writer's block" as we understand it, and I've never been able to work quickly either, until I get to about the last one-fifth of the book. Then I can write all day long and the language comes out the way I want it.

The major technical issue for me is how to organize the fictional information I want to present. I've thought the book out in draft before I begin writing, and I have on paper and in my memory a whole storehouse of information about that book, maybe too much for my own good. I will work from a series of notecards which I compile during the period of thinking about the book. There is no sequence to them, but once I have enough, I begin putting them into order. By the time I begin writing, I usually have the last few pages or the last paragraphs written. So the biggest problem I face is how to present that information. Where, when, what words to use on certain things, what the sequence should be. I can't conceive of an author writing a book in which he does not know pretty much all that's going to happen in the middle, what will happen to the characters. So much of the effectiveness of the ending is determined by what has come before, that I think it's necessary to do a great deal of preparation.

In only one of my novels is there a chronological sequence. In the others, the situation is retrospective, so the question becomes how to present that so it is engrossing to the reader and will create a certain amount of suspense. I usually have too much in the way of ideas, and too much in the way of imagination. The problem is with the sentence-by-sentence business of writing. But this one shouldn't be more than 300 typewritten pages. I've just written a handwritten version of a long chapter, although I want mostly to have short chapters. This one is 70 pages, which means it will type to about 70 pages. I will cut it a great deal, because I know there are things in there I want to use later on. It's a life of Rembrandt told in terms of the history of the Dutch Republic at the time he lived. They're handled almost synonymously. In 1669 Rembrandt died, and Cromwell admitted the Jews into England. There is no causal relation there, but the book is a history of that period and a biography of Rembrandt. When he was six years old, he entered grammar school, and the Dutch took possession of the Dutch East Indies.

But although I am doing another historical novel, it is actually about America and Russia today.

Of course I've been speaking all along now from the viewpoint of a successful novelist. Luckily I have my original editor, so he won't be intimidated by me. The book I'm doing now, if I said, "Publish it the way it is or I'll take it somewhere else," they would publish it. And there would be people who would buy it even though it was a bad book. I now work from an author's position of strength. I don't need the recognition. I'm economically secure again, thank God, after the illness.

I'm a very happy man who writes books about unhappy people.

Joseph Heller, Novelist
Bill Moyers/1988

From *Bill Moyers: A World of Ideas*, ed. Betty Sue Flowers. New York: Doubleday, 1989, 28–37. Based on *Bill Moyers' World of Ideas*, Season One, Public Affairs Television, 26 September 1988. Copyright © 1989 by Public Affairs Television, Inc. Used by permission of Public Affairs Television, Inc., and Doubleday, a Division of Doubleday Bantam Dell Publishing Group, Inc.

Moyers: When I read *Good as Gold* for a second time the other night, it made me laugh out loud at three o'clock in the morning—the White House assistant who runs around saying, "We're going to tell the truth, even if we have to lie to do it"; a President who spends his first year in office doing nothing but writing a book; or the assistant who says, "We don't want yes-men in this Administration, we want men of independent integrity who will then agree with everything we decide to do." Why is politics so funny to you?

Heller: Politics is funny to me because it *is* funny. We're talking about American politics now. You gave three illustrations from the book. I think almost everything in *Good as Gold* about politics that makes a reader laugh is drawn from things that are actually happening on almost a daily basis. American politics is funny. There are many, many things that one could say in criticism of it and a few things one could say in praise. But one of the things you could say in both praise and criticism is that it is ludicrously funny.

Moyers: We look to politics for so much entertainment. Entertainment now dominates the staging of politics.

Heller: Politics for me is a spectator sport. But it has become less and less entertaining for me over the years, so I'm less and less interested in it than I have been. I have not voted for the last twenty to twenty-five years. I've come to a rather cynical belief that there are many illusions incorporated in democratic philosophy. They tend to be very pleasing and satisfying, but they are misleading, and they are fantasies. One of them is that the democratic ideal is even possible, that there can be such a thing as participatory democracy. One of our illusions—and it's a very comforting illusion—is that by voting, we are participating in government. Voting is a ritualistic routine. The right to vote is indispensable to our contentment, but in application it's absolutely useless.

Moyers: Isn't the ritual important to the notion of democracy? Isn't the very act of voting an affirmation of consensus toward the society in which you live?

Heller: No, that's where the delusion is—that one's vote matters at all. It doesn't. That the election matters. It doesn't. That the victorious party will be responsive to the wishes of those electing it. That is not true.

Moyers: Did it matter to you that Robert Bork was defeated when he was nominated for the Supreme Court?

Heller: Of course. But that was not done by election.

Moyers: But Walter Mondale would probably never have submitted Robert Bork's name to the Senate.

Heller: I'm not saying that there are not differences between Administrations. There are. Occasionally, there is an election in which there is an issue of tremendous importance, an issue that divides the two parties. That happens very seldom, by the way. Most of the voting and party membership is pretty much based on something that might be called parochial loyalties. That's the reason someone like John Connally could switch from the Democratic Party to the Republican Party so easily.

Part of our fantasy is this: We think that we elect the President and choose the people who will represent us. In actuality, that doesn't happen. What happens is that we are presented with two candidates, and we are confined to picking one or the other to win. It makes no difference how strongly we feel about them. Normally, the candidates are supported by people who are from the same financial and social status. Whether they come from Democrats or Republicans, they are backed by money. Finance is extremely important in American politics. H. L. Mencken says that this is the only society in which virtue has become synonymous with money and that the United States is the only large state ever founded solely on the philosophy of business.

In the course of a campaign, the candidates for both parties will make promises they know they can't keep to the people they think are foolish enough to believe them. What's most important is getting elected. The best qualification for a candidate in American politics is the ability to get elected. Apart from that, everything else becomes secondary.

Moyers: But, like taxes, isn't politics the price we pay for civilization?

Heller: We can't eliminate politics. And no one who has enjoyed democracy has knowingly voted for a different system of government. It is congenial, it is entertaining. For you and me, who are among those in this country who are well fed and well housed and who can be reasonably sure that our income will continue and enable us to live as we are living, there's no substitute for democracy. Consider how few the alternatives are.

Moyers: That's true. But there's a paradox in what you're saying. You talk about our enjoying the system that we live under and yet it's a little bit like a man who says, "I'm enjoying this train ride, but I'm not going to pay for my ticket." In John Kennedy's election, for example, a change of one vote in every precinct in America would have elected Richard Nixon.

Heller: That change of one vote in every precinct for the same candidate was unlikely to happen. I'm more cynical than you. You seem to feel that if Richard Nixon had been elected, things would have been much worse.

Moyers: They would have been different. Who knows what would have happened if JFK had not been assassinated, for example?

Heller: We can't guess, but I'm inclined to feel that it's something of a sentimental daydream to believe that things would have been significantly different if John Kennedy had not been assassinated.

Moyers: That's not cynical, it's fatalistic. It's as if our fate is sealed.

Heller: After studying history for my recent novel *Picture This,* I've come to the conclusion that men don't make history; history makes personalities.

Moyers: But by refusing to vote you are assaulting a fundamental premise that's been drilled into us in this country—that the individual matters, that the individual counts, that the accumulated effect of our joint expression is to be heard.

Heller: I do believe the individual is important. But the individual does not count to governments. Governments are not normally concerned with the welfare of the people they govern. Even history is not concerned with them. During Rembrandt's life, the potato was brought over from South America and cultivated successfully in Europe during the Thirty Years' War. The cultivation of the potato was more important to more people than was Rembrandt's painting of Aristotle or William Harvey's discovery of the circulation of blood. The potato gave tens of thousands of people life. You will not read about it.

Moyers: Good government is that government which not only assures the survival of the republic, but also honors the individual, even when it refuses to flatter him.

Heller: That would be fine, but then what would its objective be? Would it be to improve the living conditions of the population—or would it be simply to improve the gross national product? We tend to measure progress by profit. That's one way of looking at progress, but it's not the only way. We have more millionaires now than any nation ever had in its history. At the same time, we have more homeless. We have very real problems here, and we don't even seem to agree on what they are.

Moyers: Why did you go back to ancient Greece for your recent novel?

Heller: I went back to ancient Greece because I was interested in writing about American life and Western civilization. In ancient Greece I found striking—and grim—parallels.

Moyers: Grim?

Heller: Extremely grim. In the war between Sparta and Athens, the Peloponnesian War, I could see a prototype for the Cold War between this country and Russia.

Moyers: Our popular notion of Greece is of a wise, humane, intelligent, moderate society. Is that what you found?

Heller: No, I didn't find that at all. In fact, I found that as democracy was instituted, Athens became more chaotic, more corrupt, more warlike. Democracy came to Athens with the rise of Pericles, who favored democracy because he could control it. But commerce was important to Athens, so business leaders then obtained control of the political machinery, and Athens became more and more warlike. No historian blames anyone but Athens for the Peloponnesian War. The government of Athens was completely chaotic from the time businessmen took over with the death of Pericles. I have part of a chapter in *Picture This* that I like very much, in which I draw on quotations from the plays of Aristophanes. In one play, Aristophanes blames Pericles for starting the war, and blamed Athens and Cleon for continuing it. Cleon tried to have Aristophanes jailed for sedition, but he failed. Aristophanes in succeeding years wrote two more antiwar plays. Each one was voted first prize by the population, and each time the population voted to continue the war.

Moyers: My favorite passage in *Picture This* is a very short one: "The motion in the Athenian assembly to invade Syracuse was deceitful, corrupt, stupid, chauvinistic, irrational and suicidal. It passed by a huge majority." What are you trying to say to us?

Heller: I'm trying to say that the emotions of people in a democratic society are no more rational than they are in any other type of society. They are manipulated. It is the function of a leader in a democracy, if he wishes to be a leader, to manipulate the emotions and the ideas of the population.

Moyers: You remind me of the Gulf of Tonkin Resolution passed by Congress in 1964, which in effect gave Lyndon Johnson a blank check to go to war in Vietnam. Congress didn't intend it to be a blank check, but that's how LBJ interpreted it.

Heller: That's exactly what I'm talking about when I speak of the manipulation of emotions and the engineering of consent. Lyndon Johnson told Congress what had happened at the Gulf of Tonkin. And what he said had happened had not happened. I remember Senator Fulbright saying afterward, "I never believed that the President of the United States would lie to me."

Moyers: In *Picture This* you say, "There were always factions enraged with each other in Athens, and in all the factions there were men who were just and evil; selfish and generous; vicious and peaceful." What's new?

Heller: I would not say anything to that. You're getting now to the central theme of *Picture This*. I'm not good at talking about my novels until I've read the reviews, but that's very much what I'm trying to say in it. Things have normally been this bad, and they've never been much better. In what I hope is an amusing way, it's really an extremely pessimistic book. Of course, everybody agrees that the quality of our government is not what it should be. But it's never been much better than it is now, and that could be said of just about every Administration in our history.

Moyers: Somewhere you say that the history of our country is replete with scandalous government, corrupt government, inefficient government.

Heller: Yes, I've done some reading on the Constitutional Convention. The bitterness and factionalism there before the Constitution was adopted, the various devices and tricks employed to get Massachusetts to accept the Constitution—that was amusing to me. Within ten years of the adoption of the Constitution, the Alien and Sedition Acts were passed; within less than ten years, the Federalist Party split into the Republican Party of Jefferson and Madison, and the Conservative Party of Alexander Hamilton. Those Virginians and other populists who did not want the Constitution and the Federalists were almost always at each other's throats, and adopted various tricks to win their points. What interested me was that when Alexander Hamilton and others made reference to the democracies of Athens and the popular republics of Italy, it was always in a derogatory way. The word "democracy" does not appear in the Constitution at all. Democracy was always a threat that they wished very much to avoid.

Moyers: They feared the passions of the mob.

Heller: They felt that the mob—and that's a word they used—would not know how to vote, would not know where their interests lay. The other fear was that the mob indeed would know where their interests lay, and they would vote for their interests.

One of Plato's severe criticisms of Athenian democracy was that the people would set up a popular leader to champion a popular cause. Now, we would assume this to be the function of a political leader—to give the people what they want. For Plato, that meant a chaotic government. He felt that a government run by the people, responsive to the wishes of the people, would be a government administered by officials who then had no control over public affairs. Give the people what they want, and the leaders will not be controlling government. I think if he were living today, he would see that those fears have been realized. As I said, candidates make promises they know they can't keep to people they feel are gullible enough to believe them, and for the sole purpose of getting elected.

I don't know if things have ever been better, but I do feel that with the advent of television, the nature of politics has changed tremendously. I was young when FDR was running. I had no idea that he was as severely crippled as he was because we never saw him. It probably would have made a difference.

Moyers: I think the primaries have changed politics more than television. Television is superfluous at the conventions because the primaries have already made the choice.

Heller: In ancient Athens, every male citizen could attend every meeting of the assembly and did have a direct vote on almost every measure. That was not representative democracy; it was true democracy. It didn't function any more effectively than our own, which has been called representative democracy, but which I don't feel is representative at all. I don't even know who my congressman is, and he doesn't know who I am, and certainly he doesn't care.

One of the themes I had in mind in *Picture This* was that instead of a major person as a character, I would use an idea. The idea was of money and conquest and commerce as being the constants in human history. In *Picture This*, they are always present. When the Dutch were losing to England, they sent their capital and their businessmen to England to organize the Bank of England, Lloyd's of London, the Stock Exchange—demonstrating once again that money follows different laws from the rest of nature. Money goes where it will increase fastest rather than where it's needed, and it has no national loyalties. We've seen that since the end of World War II. It may be that we no longer have to go to war to take possession of a country's resources.

Moyers: I'm struck by the fact that two men I admire very much as writers—you and I. F. Stone—have both written recently about Socrates.

Heller: Of course, Stone's picture of Socrates is antithetical to mine.

Moyers: He pictures Socrates as detesting democracy so much that he refused to defend himself because he would have to appeal to the freedom of speech, which he thought would be vindicating democracy.

Heller: But Stone goes a little farther in suggesting that Socrates was involved in a plot to overthrow democracy—for which there is no evidence that I could find. The classical scholars who reviewed Stone's book pointed that out as well.

For me, Socrates is appealing in part because he has no reality other than the idealization given him by Plato. Socrates, I was amused to learn, never wrote a word. He was too smart to be a philosopher. He was one of these men that I believe exist in every advanced culture, about whom we never hear, and who are truly the wisest men in the society because they have transcended the human vanity and ambition to be noted for their wisdom. Socrates never wrote a word. Plato's four books dealing with the death of Socrates are famous, particularly the death scene of Socrates and his last words, with which I begin the novel, and with which I end it. I took the portrait of Socrates as presented by Plato, and as he was gossiped about by other writers. Stone took the same material and came up with a different figure. Socrates, like Hamlet, is fascinating because he's so vague, you can see in him whatever you want.

Moyers: I found what you wrote appealing, that "Socrates would not violate the law to save his life. He did not know if the law was good, but he knew what it was. And he would not flee Athens to avoid his trial or execution."

Heller: That's why I, too, idealize him, and that's why Plato's *Apology* is one of the imperishable works of Western literature.

Moyers: When you discover that kind of reverence for the law, it clashes with Richard Nixon and Watergate and Colonel North and John Poindexter and the ethics of Ed Meese.

Heller: What I say in *Good as Gold* is that politics is important to someone like Bruce Gold, not because of the power so much, but because of the social acceptance, the social prestige of moving with a better class of people. You meet pretty women, you get invited to big parties.

Moyers: Did you learn anything about our society by looking back at Socrates' time?

Heller: No, my opinion of this society did not change. But it's not a wholly negative opinion.

Moyers: It's a paradoxical opinion.

Heller: Well, if you expect the democratic system of government to provide efficient government, you're going to be disappointed. Again, Hamilton and Jefferson and Carlyle and others assumed that in an industrial society the captains of industry would and should be the political leaders. They assumed that they would be men of intelligence, men of integrity, men of vision, and men who, having achieved wealth, would no longer have the accumulation of wealth as their goal and would be interested in the public good. That has not happened, as we know.

Now if we're going to talk about good government, I will confess that I don't know what good government is or what good government should be, and I don't believe anyone else knows, or that we can reach agreement on it. In a general way, we could say we would prefer a President who does not lie We would prefer an Administration whose members do not use their position to accumulate more wealth for themselves or their family or friends, and who are not cheats in one way or another. We would like men who are competent, who, having agreed on an objective, are intelligent enough to find new ways to achieve that objective. But beyond that, when we come to what is good government, we have a severe division of opinion that is present in both political parties. One, which we might call the traditional or conservative opinion, believes that the government should do no more than preserve order and defend against foreign attacks and provide every member of our society, now including blacks and women, with an equal opportunity to advance as far as they can, and if they don't succeed, to suffer whatever miseries are inflicted upon them, as happens when we have a recession.

The second view is that the government has an obligation to promote the general welfare and provide for the economic needs of the people to the extent that it can. Those are two different positions, two different philosophies of government. Depending on what the needs are or who's in office, attempts are made to promote the general welfare, but there is always broad disagreement on where the general welfare lies. Now, for example, we are the only Western country that does not have a national health program. At the present time, a large faction of people in the country find it more important to send money to the Contras in Nicaragua than to provide low-cost housing. Concerning New York, I can understand that attitude. Prejudice. The homeless in New York tend to be black and Spanish. But when I was in California a few months ago, the homeless were shown on television. And there they are white, blue-eyed, blond. So homelessness is not just the product of New York City with its masses of people on welfare.

Moyers: The founders were aware that the highest role of government at times would be to correct excesses and to prevent bad things from happening.

Heller: Yes, but what would be a bad thing? Forget earthquakes and droughts—what would be a bad thing?

Moyers: Wars that are fought not in the national interest, but because of some abstraction.

Heller: What wars have we fought that you and I would agree weren't in the national interest?

Moyers: I would say that Vietnam was a war that was fought for a marginal—

Heller: —the only exception that comes to my mind is World War II, and I'm not even sure that the War of Independence was in the national interest. During the Revolutionary War, one third of the people were in favor of the war; one third were against it; and one third didn't care either way.

Moyers: There's a wonderful passage in *Good as Gold* where Bruce Gold, the professor who's called to Washington, knew that the penultimate stage of a civilization was attained when chaos masqueraded as order. And he knew we were already there. Our political system projects the appearance of order. What do you see behind that mask?

Heller: I don't see that it projects a system of order.

Moyers: When you looked at the two conventions this summer, they were organized—

Heller: Oh, the conventions are organized. Of course. It's like the pregame entertainment to the Super Bowl. The conventions were good. But governing well is an impossible job. Somewhere in *Picture This* I say that Aristotle never conceived that cities would merge into provinces, provinces merge into states, states merge into countries so large as to be ungovernable. New York City is ungovernable by any standard, and I believe the federal government is ungovernable. There are too many factions to please, and self-interest is still, as it almost always has been in history, the most powerful motivation for people.

Moyers: Do you see no system behind the bureaucratic structures? No governing principle behind government? No organization behind the appearance of things?

Heller: No.

Moyers: Is it just chaos?

Heller: It's not chaos. Thank God for the Bill of Rights, and thank God for the Supreme Court, and thank God for the free press. We are a free people. Most of us are prosperous people. I say most of us, although perhaps close to half the population lives near the poverty level. But that may be better than the situation in most other countries. We do have some wonderful traditions. We don't have a tradition of revolution, and I don't believe we'll ever have another revolution, mainly because revolutions are middle-class phenomena. Revolutions are not conducted by the most underprivileged in a society. They're usually conducted by educated people. When Patrick Henry said, "Give me liberty or give me death," he was living in a part of the world that had more liberty than any other place.

Moyers: In once sense politics is a substitute for the church. Watch Jesse Jackson's speech at the Democratic Convention or Jerry Falwell's prayer at the Republican Convention. And politics also competes with theater. Politics now provides us with the drama.

Heller: Isn't it disgusting to realize that there are organizations and specialists who exist in grooming candidates for election to office? They tell candidates what to wear, how to stand, where to sit, what to say. But isn't it equally disgusting that we know about it, and that we're not revolted?

Moyers: Politics is our national soap opera. We know that we're watching a soap opera, but we watch it and respond to it.

Heller: Well, you can exclude me. I didn't watch this convention, I didn't watch the last one, and I don't vote because I don't see any point in voting.

Moyers: Do you give money?

Heller: Yes, I give money because money may help determine the outcome of the election. But I would never cast a vote. It's useless. It does not accomplish anything. There was a recent editorial in the *New York Times* that talks about the progress of the blacks. It's been almost twenty-five years since the Civil Rights Act was passed, and it quotes figures on how many blacks hold government positions. My response to that: Walk through any big city, or walk through the poorest part of any small town, and then see if the conditions of the blacks have been improved by the fact that they have the right to vote. The exceptional can now get ahead. That's one of the things I love about this country, and I love about democracy. There really are very few official prohibitions on any individual advancing if he's able to do it without violating certain laws. But as a group—maybe close to fifty percent in this country still live near the poverty level.

Moyers: In *Catch-22* Yossarian decides that the system really is insane, and he becomes a hero by escaping it. He leaves in a rowboat and at the end of the book, is heading for Scandinavia, pulling himself away from the shore. But in *Picture This*, your new book, nobody escapes.

Heller: In *Catch-22*, Yossarian doesn't escape, he's trying to escape. His choices are: Accept the corruption and benefit by it, join us, become one of the boys, and we'll give you a promotion, we'll send you home a hero; or else, go to prison for refusing to fly more missions; or fly more missions until you're eventually killed. The only way he can assert himself without accepting any of these obnoxious alternatives is through saying no. Now he knows he's not going to get to Sweden. The novel ends with him going out the door.

In *Picture This* the subject is not war so much, although wars are continual in American history and in all Western history. In *Picture This* I say that peace on earth would mean the end of civilization as we know it. There is an element of hope in *Catch-22*, and it ends in a very positive way. *Picture This* doesn't.

Moyers: Both you and I. F. Stone went back to ancient Greece seeming to look for a simpler golden age, and both of you, after writing your books, appear disillusioned with what you found.

Heller: Give me more credit. I didn't go back to ancient Athens looking for something better than now. I went back looking for a subject for a good novel. I will say this: To someone who wants to be any kind of artist, but particularly a novelist, there's no better environment in which to work than a democracy. A novel by nature is an adversarial form of expression. It is very critical. It is wonderful to be able to write with complete freedom in this country, to talk to you with absolute freedom and know that each of us could be as insulting to any public official as we wanted to without suffering any official type of punishment.

Moyers: So the fact that democracy is absurd doesn't make it undesirable.

Heller: There's no other form of government that we can envision that we would prefer to democracy. We would prefer that we had a better class of public officials than we have, that they were more committed to the responsibilities of their office than to the people who financed their coming to office. Instead, it's as Bruce Gold said in *Good as Gold:* The only responsibility of office is to stay in office.

You know, the ideology of democracy is a perfect ideology. The faults come from the human application. There are parochial loyalties in people—ambition, greed, self-interest. People find loopholes to fight for their own ambitions. We all know that a lie is a vice. We know that greed is a vice. We know that patriotism is a virtue, provided we can define what patriotism is, and provided there's a popular national cause which calls upon it. Let me give you a sentence: "All societies we know of are governed by the selfish interests of the ruling class or classes." Can you think of many countries or societies today to whom that would not apply?

Moyers: No.

Heller: That statement was made by Plato in about 380 B.C. in *The Republic*. Can you think of many societies in the interval to whom it would not apply? No to that one also, right? We are living in more dangerous times than the past because our techniques of annihilation have improved. But the nature of society, I'm sorry to say, doesn't seem to have changed much for the better.

Moyers: In dangerous times many people pray for miracles. And that brings me back to the novel you published in 1979, *God Knows,* the story about David from the Bible. As you yourself have indicated, it's really about the silence of God, the discovery that just when one needs God most, there is no answer. You don't believe in miracles, do you?

Heller: I don't believe in miracles because it's been a long time since we've had any. I forget who I'm quoting now, maybe Mark Twain, who said, "The longer I live, the longer I begin to doubt the wisdom of God."

Moyers: But perhaps there's something else behind that silence. Perhaps God is silent because the best way to bring us to our senses, to bring us to accountability and self-deliverance, is to make us see that we have to perform our own miracles. Maybe that's the key to democracy.

Heller: If that's the best way, by destroying thousands and thousands of human lives, of American, Vietnamese, Nicaraguan—masses, masses, masses of lives—if that's the best way God can find, then I think he'd better resign from office and turn it over to George Bush or Pat Robertson.

No, I can't believe that God would operate like that. I don't think anybody would say that. I think you and I and even professional politicians would agree that an efficient level of government is preferable to an inefficient level. An unselfish Administration is preferable to a selfish Administration. All right-thinking persons would agree on those objectives. The problem we face is how to achieve them.

Moyers: That's the old dilemma.

Heller: Well, there's no known way.

Moyers: You didn't find one in Athens, did you?

Heller: No, I didn't find one in Athens. At the same time that we are always complaining about the quality of government—and these complaints have existed since government was founded—we delude ourselves and create a kind of pantheon of past presidents. In my own experience, I think that with the exception of FDR in the first four years, we haven't had an exceptional president. Thomas Jefferson and Madison had exceptional minds. Jimmy Carter was outstanding for his good character. But I don't know if the presidential decisions have been that important. I think you would find the same thing if you looked at the history of the monarchies. There is no system I can envision that would elevate to public office the kind of people that we would like to see elevated.

Moyers: Therefore?

Heller: Therefore, we go on and keep our fingers crossed and hope that things will not get worse than they are. There's almost something contradictory in what I say. I'm one of these people who profit from the profit motive. I deal with money as a phenomenon and an inducement and portray this directly in my books as well. Yet, I'm very conscious of money. I don't sell my books to publishers for a small amount of money. Negotiations are very intense. I know the value. I also know when I have enough. But I also know I'd rather write the books I want to than leave writing and go speculate and double or triple my money.

Moyers: The theme of *Catch-22* was the perverse nature of human intentions, that the regulations designed to save us wound up strangling us in the end. Yossarian stood up against those. He said his no, as you indicated, and rode out to sea. If he came rowing up out here on the south shore of Long Island this afternoon, what do you think would be the theme of the novel you would now cast about him?

Heller: If he came rowing up, I would say to him, "Get out of here. Don't destroy a good ending." Probably you would be talking to him now and not to me, wouldn't you?

Contemplating Joseph Heller

Kevin Haynes/1988

From *W*, 19–26 September 1988, 33. Reprinted by permission of Fairchild Publications.

EAST HAMPTON, N.Y.—On a day when Paul McCartney was spotted on the beach and Bianca Jagger ate breakfast at a Main Street cafe, Joseph Heller was home boiling water for coffee.

He prefers the serenity of his modest two-story home here on eastern Long Island, with its blondwood floors and airy rooms full of sunlight, to the prospect of venturing onto nearby Main Street, choked with summer visitors and bumper-to-bumper traffic.

Heller will be making the trip into town shortly, since he and his second wife, Valerie, are meeting friends for lunch. But for now, Heller wants to enjoy a cup of coffee and contemplate his contemplation of Rembrandt's "Aristotle Contemplating the Bust of Homer."

The painting, created in 1653, was the inspiration for Heller's fifth novel, *Picture This,* an art and history lesson that draws very political parallels between way back then and right this very minute.

No one can change history, says Heller, but it keeps on repeating.

"I believe this may be the most damning, critical and pessimistic of my books, and I think it's the one that's the least biased," says Heller, 65, who saw similar descriptives attached to reviews of his first and most famous book, *Catch-22,* the hilarious antiwar novel that has sold more than 25 million copies since its publication in 1961.

In *Picture This,* Heller chronicles the evolution of democracy and Western civilization by tracing Aristotle's life in ancient Greece, his rendering in Rembrandt's studio in Amsterdam and the long journey that brought the painting to New York's Metropolitan Museum of Art in 1961 for a then-record $2,300,000.

"What made me go in that direction was discrete and naked ambition," he says over the kettle's shrill whistle. "The painting didn't fascinate me so much as the opportunity it evoked. It was almost like a Rorschach test.

"As I contemplated it and began doing research, I saw something that was both inspiring and dismaying: Apart from technical improvements, not much has changed in the nature of human beings and societies and the quality of government, the nature of civilization and the values we have."

As Heller tips the kettle, his hand trembles slightly, a side effect of his bout with Guillain-Barré syndrome, a mysterious virus that virtually paralyzed him for several weeks in 1982. With his friend, Speed Vogel, he wrote a book about his illness. He also married Valerie Humphries, the nurse who helped with his lengthy rehabilitation.

"My health is very good now, except for some muscular weaknesses, which you would not notice unless I was walking up stairs or eating," says Heller, who used to run three miles a day. "I probably could not run normally, so I no longer try."

Coffee mug in hand, Heller leads the way out of the kitchen, through the sparsely furnished living room and his small, neatly organized writing room and pulls open the sliding glass door that leads to the poolside patio.

"This is the most political of my books," he continues, sitting at a table in the shade. "I do feel that good government is something which no one has ever been good at for very long. No individual, no dynasty, no political party. It's almost a matter of dumb luck.

"The conclusion I came to was dismaying," he adds, "and it is that the Democratic Party, in general, is no better than the Republican Party and no different. It's not a notion I held before."

Needless to say, this insight has done nothing to spur Heller's interest in the upcoming presidential election.

"My thoughts about the election are very much like my thoughts on the Olympics: I wish they would take place very eight or 10 years instead of every four years. I wish newspapers wouldn't give so much space to them. I'm not interested in either one."

Especially the race between Dukakis and Bush.

"I haven't voted in 20 or 30 years and I don't ever intend to vote again," Heller vows. "Bill Moyers was here about two weeks ago, and I said to him the right to vote is a precious right to have, but it's useless in application.

"The individual doesn't affect the election, doesn't participate in the selection of candidates and, having voted, has no control over what the government will do. The candidates are most responsive to those people and institutions that contribute the most to their being elected and remaining in office."

Heller's next project, long anticipated, will be a sequel to *Catch-22,* his biggest bestseller and a standard in contemporary American fiction.

"The reason it's popular, I'm gonna tell you now, is it's an exceptionally good novel that remains exciting, titillating and humorous and relevant to every country. I believe that *Catch-22,* through some lucky instinct on my part, dealt with matters in a way that are perennial sources of discontent in any advanced society. It was dumb luck with exactly the right attitude of spirited and emotional and very sad irreverence and comedy."

Heller offers several reasons for tackling the difficult prospect of following up on his greatest success—"not to make it better, to make it different"—including its commercial potential.

"I'm in the twilight of my career," he says. "I'll be 70 years old before my next book is published . . . But I may not do it if I can't get the idea. It has to be a book that exists independently of the first book."

By the way, the man who wrote *Catch-22* recently got around to reading it again.

"I finished it about three weeks ago because I'm making notes for the sequel, taking out extracts," says Heller, suddenly breaking into a wide smile. "It's a very good book."

Catching Heller

David Nathan/1991

From *Jewish Chronicle* 22 February 1991, 20. Reprinted by permission of the *Jewish Chronicle* and the author.

> He would be crazy to fly more missions and sane if he didn't; but if he
> was sane he had to fly them. If he flew them he was crazy and didn't
> have to; but if he didn't want to he was sane and had to.—*Catch-22*.

Today, some 35 years after he wrote those lines, Joseph Heller looks
out on the world from the temporary haven of an Oxford College on the
banks of the Cherwell and marvels at how much and how little the
world has changed.

He looks at the Gulf War and wonders why it was ever started. "I
don't know why Bush insisted on fighting it," he says, "and I don't
think he knows why. I don't think he knows why he invaded Panama
either. Somebody tells him to do something and he does it."

Those who know their *Catch-22* will remember that in the war that
Captain Yossarian fought with equal ferocity against the Germans and
his own superiors, there was a General Scheisskopf, whereas today we
have a General Schwartzkopf. Today, we have a John Major whereas
Heller, with satirist's licence, invented a Major Major who so lacked
distinction that people who met him were impressed by how unim-
pressive he was.

There was a Milo Minderbinder who believed that war should be
conducted according to the strictest principles of private enterprise and,
as the price was right, bombed his own airfield. Today our troops are to
be bombarded by weapons supplied by our own contractors because the
price was right.

"There is," says Heller, "a character called Colonel Korn who was
only concerned with his public image. Today, we have a Bush.

"Since Roosevelt's second term, every president we have had has
been inferior to his predecessor," continues Heller, who surveys the
scene with a kind of sad relish. "It's hard to believe that someone can be

inferior to Ford and Reagan, but we have it in Bush and, waiting in the wings, is Quayle or somebody equally incompetent."

You know, that might be the answer—to act boastfully about something we ought to be ashamed of. That's a trick that never seems to fail.—Colonel Korn.

But, what do we do about people like Saddam Hussein?

"Hussein," says Heller, "was not a villain or a problem two or three days before he went into Kuwait. I don't know that it was incumbent upon the US—and Britain—to do anything about it. I can see a reason for continuing it now that it has started, but I can see no good reason for starting it in the first place.

"I think everybody approved the initial reaction of taking measures to forestall an invasion of Saudi Arabia, but Bush went beyond that. Then he made that ridiculous statement that it was not going to be like Vietnam. It is exactly like Vietnam—a country four or five thousand miles away which poses no discernible threat to the US."

Yossarian, the arch-survivor of *Catch-22*, is described as an Assyrian and given—by accident, Heller says—an Armenian name. How Jewish can you get?

"Yes," says Heller. "It was intentional that he had no past, and that he was somewhat of an exile. Yes, Yossarian was very Jewish, but I didn't know that until years later.

"But I didn't plot that. That comes from the unconscious."

Yossarian will emerge in Heller's next book, still two years away. The principal characters are two Jews from Coney Island, where Heller was born.

It is, he says, a kind of biography with him and his friends reviewing their lives. Yossarian, at 68, will play a small role in it.

Heller is nearly 68.

Colonel Moodus believed that the young men who took orders from him should be willing to give up their lives for the ideals, aspirations and idiosyncracies of the old men he took orders from.—*Catch-22*.

Index